THE GREATEST POWER IN THE UNIVERSE

The Ascended Masters Akasha & Asun
and the Ascended Host

Love's embrace is often thought as
being meek, without power, without will.
However when Love is fully embraced in the
Totality of Its Divine Activity, It has a Conquering
Presence that is an undoing of what is not real.

The Akasha Mystery School
Vancouver, Canada
Publisher, Angelic Encounters

Publisher Angelic Encounters
Royal Adams
1825 Shiloh Valley Drive
Wildwood, Missouri 63005
Telephone: 636-458-7823
Email: RAdams1825@aol.com

Akasha Mystery School
Vancouver, British Columbia, Canada
Web Site: www.akashaonline.com
Email: angels@akashaonline.com

First edition 2007
Printed and bound in the United States of America

Library of Congress catalog number in progress
ISBN 1-929996-98-5

Cover and interior design: Louise Emma Gallant
Portrait of Akasha & Asun: Gayliaa Berzins
Editor: Yvo Swart
Editor's note: The Canadian dictionary is used for this book.

Akasha Mystery School

Web Site: www.akashaonline.com
Email: angels@akashaonline.com

The Ascended Masters Akasha & Asun

Their Life Changing Messages
for Awakening Humanity

Their Messenger, Shaddai Usa Akasha
commonly known as Usa
('U' is pronouced like 'ou' as in soup)

Editor's Note

The material for this book has come forth from the Great Ascended Masters. In our desire to remain loyal to Their original transmission revealing *The Greatest Power in the Universe*, we have used creative licence regarding the respected rules of good grammar and punctuation.

TABLE OF CONTENTS

19 **DEDICATION**

21 **ACKNOWLEDGEMENTS**

23 **AKASHA & ASUN**

25 **QUOTES FROM AKASHA & ASUN**

27 **PREFACE**

27 Beloved Sanat Kumara

27 The responsibility of cleaning up a portion of discord that exists in this World

29 My Sacred Fire Love is the Violet Consuming Flame that has within It the Spiraling Blue Flame with Gold at Its centre

30 Just hold a picture of a flash, a tiny golden Flame, just flashing into this condition

31 The Ascended Hearts Flame of the Ascended Masters will keep a condition from ever taking on a duality

31 When the Light vibratory action of the physical body, the emotional body, and the mental body responds

33 We want the perfection we have on Venus to come into your Worlds

35 Ah, how the Heart sings! Ah, how the Soul sings!

36 Your Field of Dreams may grow beyond your fondest imagination

37 Sanat Kumara's Sacred Bloom—the Rose...

38 Ask the Ascended Master's Consciousness to come into the human form

40 Give yourselves permission for your Beloved Presence, the Ascended and Angelic Host

41 Prepare yourselves for Grace

43 Go beyond what you have dared to dream

45 Such is my Oath; such is my Way of Life!

53	**CHAPTER ONE**
54	The renewal of the power of attention and intentions
55	The journey from the Great Central Sun
56	You can evolve a Heavenly Body of Light around yourself that literally becomes a Sun's Presence
57	In order to experience Life in the physical Universe you require a physical body
58	The Mid-Self, known by many names...
59	Time and space is an educated matter, it is an educated matter of intention
60	Planet Earth delayed Her Ascension into a Fifth Dimensional Vehicle
60	Angels and Cosmic Beings are coming to the Earth now
61	Archangel Michael is the Archangel of the First Ray, not only to your Earth, but to your entire Universe
62	The Purpose of Jesus' Ministry was to walk through everything that would happen at this time
63	The Ascended Masters will yet remain invisible
64	Desire to see your own Beloved Presence first
65	It is impossible for discord to connect with you without your attention
66	You have to re-train the mind—what is my Vision...my Field of Dreams...my Spiritual road map?
68	Start training your mind to visualize the Higher Self of those that you interact with each day
70	What is your Presence doing?
71	It is impossible for anyone to battle you if you are visualizing the Higher Self
74	Oftentimes human beings are trying to impose the Light on a human concept
76	The Higher Self will project sufficient Sacred Fire Love to correct a condition
78	The correction of old erroneous belief systems
79	Human beings created a very conscious experiment—to learn all that you are...and to learn all that you are not
81	Will you be Olympian?

83   CHAPTER TWO

83   A Message of the Divine Mother

84   Divine Desires! To live your Higher Purpose—Your passion! Your calling!

85   If we have the will of human beings, there is not one humanly created evil that we cannot silence

86   If I am called forth with enough desire, I can walk into the atmosphere of any city and my own Light would forbid any evil taking place

87   We cannot, under Cosmic Law, give more than is the present energy accumulation of those who desire us

87   Invite Us to correct the cause of conditions with Our Sacred Fire Purity and Power

88   My Angels gather the constructive and the dynamic calls, prayers, and decrees of students of the world

89   When you call upon Our Sacred Fire Love

91   I, Michael, Am in your memories

92   We want you to telephone God more often...

93   How will those numbers of humanity, who are helping, grow?

94   You might say, 'What am I going to do without my human desires?'

95   It is a gentle journey that embodies the Holy Spirit

96   The Great Book of Names in Archangel Michael's Cathedral of Light

97   My Angels of the First Ray place that Cosmic Blue Flame around all constructive manifestation

100   Call upon the total accumulation of all your good to now come forth into expression through you

101   There is no Cosmic evil, there is no such thing

102   The door to the Fifth Dimension, the door to the Realms of Light, is open

104   Divine Desires bring forth the creativity of your inner genius

105   Great assets of your Soul will come forth that give you new talents, new abilities that you did not have before

107   To live your Higher Purpose—Your passion! Your calling!

109   And so, I Michael, say, O Humanity, reach up, try us.

111   We come to you and we evaluate the energy around your bodies

111   Call for more Light from your own Higher Light Body Christ Self and the Ascended Host for safe increase

113   Go to your Christ Self and Us and call forth the Cosmic Light directly down your Life Stream

114   We project Our Sacred Fire Love from Our Octave according to the will of humanity

116   Struggle—ask its cause, effect, record, and all memory of it to be removed

117   The human feeling body...Majestic! A spectacle of Light

118   There is not any healing that takes place without the Sacred Fire Love of the Higher Self and of the Angels

119   Angels of the Cosmic Christ Blue Lightning of Indestructible Purity and Power

121   The worded expressions of Ancient Prophets can resonate with you

124   There is a means to have all the money and supply...

126   Invoking the magic of former legends through stories...

127   There is not anything that the human mind is capable of conceiving that cannot be manifest somewhere

127   The diversity of the next seven years of your Planet—the Light has spoken!

128   You are in the years in which the prophecy of Jesus the Christ will come into manifestation

129   It is out there in the streets of everyday life that your Light be a Blazing, Flaming Presence of the Light

130   'I AM Come', 'I AM' that Light that cometh into the world that Lighteth up every man, woman and child

131   I came to the Earth in the Name 'I AM' and I came to pour the Light of the Spirit 'I AM' into a physical body

132   Archangel Michael's Blessing

135   CHAPTER FOUR

135   The Power that you have to qualify each day

137   Illumination

137   Gold and the Ascension Thrones

140   Problems with refraining from eating red meat without the use of the Sacred Fire

142   Liquor and drugs create tears in the emotional body

143   Any condition in your life has its root cause within your mind and your feelings

146   My Beloved God Presence...speak to me concerning all the matters of my life. I am here, I am listening...

147   It is possible to live without mistakes

148   Your physical body desires to evolve...to grow equal to the expansion of your consciousness

148   What is in your atmosphere is much worse than the density that has collected in your bodies

149   The attention is the window in which you connect with what is in your World

151   The Electrons in your body are waiting to receive the points of Light at the centre of each cell

152   Your atoms can be qualified with human thoughts and beliefs, but your electrons cannot.

153   CHAPTER FIVE

153   Hold within yourself a Desire to love your Life free

155   Light, Love, Self, are but different worded expressions for the One Great Activity 'I AM' or God

156   The idea of imaging, visualizing, is a tremendous activity

157   A state of being in which there is an 'Isness' that finds a deep restful and peaceful place within yourself

158   Words are vehicles of energy; your words are the vehicles of your thoughts and feelings

159   You have to be specific as to what financial freedom feels and looks like to you

161   If you are going to be the artist of your life, you are going to start paying attention to the details

162   The energy of discount stores

164   Ask Saint Germain—Shakespeare—to give you the inner meaning of Life hidden in cipher code within His Plays

165   You can move around what is manifesting on your stage of life

167   The real 'estate' of the Planet must increase

169   Those who are of greed and selfishness and have hidden plans against humanity will be exposed

170   The shadow of darkness seeks those who do not have a vision for humanity

171   Washington's Vision

172   Call for the release of whole new Legions of the Angelic Host, to stop the planned destruction of humankind.

174   The Light will prevail through new great councils and leaders

175   "...Do through this outer self..." that's the key! That is the key covenant! That is the key desire!

176   One lovely temperature of comfort in the Earth's lower atmosphere

177   The true Law of giving and receiving

179   CHAPTER SIX

179   The thoughts and words that you place behind the words 'I AM', become more important

180   A new Unity between Master Jesus, the Archangel Michael, and the Ascended Master Victory from Venus

180   Another Threefold Activity...Beloved Nada, Beloved Charity, Beloved Mary...

182   Ask yourself, "What is the perfect application for me today?"

183   Are there Ascended Beings that I feel an extraordinary amount of closeness to?

184   Feeling trapped in a situation?—the Goddess of Light can help...She has experienced it.

186   What does the Mighty Violet Flame and the Cosmic Blue Flame do?

187   The Fourth Dimension was collapsed—it doesn't exist anymore

189   The Planes of Bliss...where you go to after you leave your body

191   Angels building the great Cosmic Wall of Light

193   Karmic conditions are being consumed by Beloved Mary

195   Ascended Beings who created and own this System of Worlds also have the right to protect this World

197   CHAPTER SEVEN

197   A Seraphim Angel Blessing

198   Anchoring the new paradigm—the Diamond Heart, the Indigo, the Violet Soul

199   The Soul initiates levels of attainment

200   The understanding of the Twelve plus one

200   As developing Beings of the Diamond Heart you begin to realize and remember that you are a Spiritual being

202   The Indigo Soul—the Life Stream between your physical body and your Higher Self begins to expand

203   Initiations of the Indigo Soul

207   The Way-Shower frequency...

208   The Violet Soul brings the Authority of the Violet Flame and the Violet Ray into your life

209   Levels of the Violet Soul—the Rainbow Man, the Rainbow Woman

211   Grooming yourself beyond Violet Soul into Radiant Rose Soul

211   You have come to invent the future

213   You are building a new Etheric Light Grid onto the Earth

214   Service to Godself 'I AM', Service to Humanity and the Earth, and Service to the Spiritual Hierarchy of Light

215   Qualify your every day, and then your Life experience can show you that there is an easier way of doing things

216   Give yourselves the time to be in touch with the dream inside you

219   Do not feel there is any limiting condition in your body that you have to accept

221   CHAPTER EIGHT

221   Warrior Angels and the Angels of the Cosmic Blue Flame Sword

222   Angels of Immortal Love and Power

224   Beyond 'coincidence' is usually an Angel

225   A Meditation and Invocation

225   A call to the Angels of Archangel Michael for the disconnection from any discordant energy...

227   A call for the Planet and Her atmosphere...

227   A call for your city, your country...wherever you live...

228   A call for the Angels to assist you

231   CHAPTER NINE

231   The civilizing of humanity, the evolution of Divine Man and Divine Woman

233   Summer and autumn—the attending of your garden of manifestation and the harvest

234   If you could see what the Ascended Masters are doing at this moment for the Earth!

235   There is a new kid on the block

237   Perhaps the visions of Nostradamus and the prophets, can be those dreams that begin a new cycle for humanity

238   Invocation to The Greatest Power in the Universe

239   The Golden Healing Hands of the Ascended Jesus Christ

239   The Buddha and His Emerald Green Ray

240   Mary, the Mother of the World, and the Angels of the Rose Pink Ray of Divine Love, Mercy, and Forgiveness...

241   Archangel Michael and His Angels of the Cosmic Blue Flame of Immortal Love and Immortal Power

241   The God and Goddess of Purity and Their Angels of Eternal Purity

242   The Queen of Light, and Her Angels from the Great Heavens

242   Saint Germain, Chohan of the Seventh Ray, the Violet Ray, The Seventh Seal

247   CHAPTER TEN

247   The Authority of Sanat Kumara came forth four million years before the first of the 'I AM' Starseed arrived

248   The Authority and the Will of the Mighty Sanat Kumara is Evolution Itself

249   A Logos will take on a physical embodiment in order to become the Authority over a physical planet

249   Sanat Kumara took up His first embodiment on the Planet Venus and became the Cosmic Christ to Venus

250   The Son of Brahma

250   Sanat Kumara has been the Authority over all Divine Plans that your Earth has been progressing through

251   The Divine necessity for change

252   Mozart, Chopin, Alice Bailey, Madame Blavatsky, Edgar Cayce...all over-lighted by Sanat Kumara

253   A challenge for your Christed Selves and the Ascended Masters—how will your physical bodies sustain the Vibration of the Violet Soul?

255   The Goddess of Venus, offers Her Cosmic Love Supreme to assist the physical body to assimilate the Violet Soul

256   Balance in rest, good foods, and fresh air for the Violet Soul body

257   The Violet Soul compels wonderful activity in the physical body

258   Sanat Kumara from Venus speaks...

259   Venus—the Guardians of the Earth and those who would embody on the Earth

260   I have opened a Dispensation to all the Children of Light

263   I, Sanat Kumara, offer you a Miracle Mantle of My own Heart's Flame Sacred Fire Mastery of Love Divine

264   Akasha, the Great Cosmic Angel of the Eleventh Dimension

265   Cosmic permission of the Great Divine Director who is responsible for all Souls in this Solar System

266   There is just the one Mighty Flame that each of you are in physical embodiment

267   In former civilizations there were manifestations of the Sacred Fire in the Sacred Temples on this Earth

267   Every individual must learn to draw the Unfed Flame, the Mighty Flame of God Life, into their own life

268   The return of the Mighty Flame of Life over the atmosphere above Earth

269   Some of you journeyed for a time to Venus...you know how to build the Flame of 'God, Goddess, All That Is'

270   I, Sanat Kumara, Am here on your Earth with the Seven Lords of the Flame of Venus, and the Mighty Victory

271   Do not ask Me—Command Me!

272   The world delights in itself

274   Be a blessing to the World, the Planet, and Her Kingdoms by sending your own Light Ray forth

277   **CHAPTER ELEVEN**

278   It is just wonderful what is coming to Earth!

279   Many of great Cosmic Authority are presently tending to World events

280   Projecting the likenesses of Ascended Masters into World events

282   Calling your Presence to come forth into action

283   It is not a good idea to do your prayer decrees for a couple of hours to the point you become tired

285   Slam-dunk!

287   Mount Rushmore

287   Stonehenge

288   The Ark of the Covenant, an Oath, a Promise, will again be revealed

288   The Threefold Flames...and old ideas of wars...

291   The degree to which Akasha can continue to assist you...

291   You are here to make an impact

294   If you are going to do nothing, do it well!

296   All things considered, the future for me is a holiday

298   The intellect only knows the past. The Heart knows the future you want

299   A 'runner' is an experience or a person that brings you into a situation

300   Do not restrict your Life. Let it.

301   The experience of wanting

302   Anything good and constructive that I could possibly desire—this is God in me, desiring

304   Asun's Benediction

305   **CHAPTER TWELVE**

305   Resurrection Day

306   The first three years of every decade of this last century a sinister force has always tried to control humanity

307   This Resurrection Day was intended to take place forty years before 2003! What happened at that time?

308   In the middle of two wars, two Armageddons, a way was found to release the Light back to humankind

310   Master Jesus' role and Plan for the Resurrection cycle

310   It is your destiny to become Sovereign Creator Beings of Divine Love

311   You are Souls who have prepared centuries of time for this cycle of Resurrection—and now it is to find your unique expression of who you are

313   A Global Village Community is growing amongst humanity, there are many who have come and served

315   All you have ever had to do to create reality and experience is think it, see it in your mind, feel it, and hold it in your heart and be ready to take action

316   A Message from a Tall Master from Venus—the Mighty Victory

317   The Sacred Fire purification of the people of Earth and the structure of the Earth, the Planet

318   Saint Germain—the Violet Ray from the Great Central Sun

318   The Sacred Fire of Venus is anchored in the Earth

320   If you want your freedom and your ultimate Ascension only through your own Great God Presence

322   Without the mystical Sacred Fire there is no Light, there is no Earth, there are no Elements, and there are no Kingdoms...there is nothing!

323   If you let your nations take you into a Third World War, your own Kingdoms will rise up

324   Young people demonstrate and try to stop World Organizations and World Trade, because behind all of this is some of the last of the old archetype energies

325   You can help to stop an impending disaster if you will call to us on Venus

326   The Consciousness of Pan will rise

327   Rise up! You have a voice!

328   If you could see the energy in your atmosphere...you would climb inside yourselves, look up to your God Presence quicker than anything else you would do

331   CHAPTER THIRTEEN

331   One day your eyes shall be opened—and you shall see that Mighty Presence!

332   God loves you so much that even your own great Ascended Self will respect any feeling you are having

333   Free will is a vibration, the will, the quality that you hold within your Feeling Side of Life

334   Your Presence wants you to come in joy, not just when you are in trouble

335   You are more than a physical structure, an atomic body...

336   Eternality and immortality is your Gift of Life

337   Many places on your Earth are going through a significant increasing of Light

338   The activation of the Threefold Flame—Peace to the people of the Middle East

338   All races in the World are of the Golden Race

339   God is always greater than its individualizations. This is the Miracle of Life.

340   Speak to the Elements of your physical body; they have placed themselves under your command

341   Your own God Presence can produce its Perfection in you, when you maintain harmony in your Life...and in the face of all appearances!

343   CHAPTER FOURTEEN

343   The Light of the Resurrection Cycle

344   You cannot manifest in a physical Universe without the Feminine aspect of God

345   Energy is being amped up on Earth at this time

346   The Resurrection is the lifting back up into your Whole Divine Mind and Being, your Christed Self

347   If you keep talking about the chaos that you seem to be in sometimes, you are just furthering it

348   The three Phases on the Path of Mastery

349   The mind is vast beyond anything that science dares to speculate

350   It is the Light of the awakening Heart that frees and raises the mind into a higher frequency of consciousness

350   All manifestation is a vibration of energy

353   Where are you in your consciousness? What do you believe?

354   The future Christ Beings will fulfill Their Higher Purpose in all walks of life

355   You do not have to learn anything, rather discover everything!

356   It is very interesting your ideas about being born into a masculine body or a feminine body

357   Let God do the detailing

358   I believe...

360   The way people act towards you, is a good indicator of a limiting perception you are secretly holding about God

361   The Seven Sacred Weeks

362   2003, the last Christmas under the Cosmic Dispensation, the Christian Dispensation

363   From the Electrical Age, through the Wireless technology, and into the new Crystal Age

364   Beloved Mary has been raised within the Spiritual Hierarchy, as the Sacred Mother, Goddess of Earth

365   You have an expression on your Earth...You ain't seen nothin' yet!

369   **PRODUCTS FROM THE AKASHA MYSTERY SCHOOL**

369   Other Books Available from Akasha & Asun

369   Meditations

369   A Sacred Alchemy of Meditations, Prayers and Contemplations

370   Audio Books from Akasha & Asun

$\mathscr{D}$EDICATION

We dedicate this book to you, the reader. May your own Inner Light be enriched by the Great Light Rays of Knowledge that is offered in this book from the Ascended Masters. May the material in this book assist you in your Great Walk of Life, help you to live your Higher Purpose and reveal to you the Divine Plan for you and Humanity.

We dedicate this book to the Ascended Masters Akasha & Asun, the Archangel Michael, the Great Being Sanat Kumara and the Master Victory from Venus and to the entire Ascended and Angelic Host and Their Divine Plan to assist Humanity and the Earth at this time.

We dedicate this book to *The Greatest Power in the Universe*, the Mighty 'I AM' Presence that is within and above every Human Being and to the Living Flame of God within the Hearts of Humanity. We dedicate this book to the Light of God that never fails. God bless you.

$\mathcal{A}$CKNOWLEDGEMENTS

I wish to offer my love and gratitude to Yvo Swart, our primary Editor who offered her love, passion, time and energy in transforming the recorded audio transmissions of the Ascended Masters Akasha & Asun into the written word. Yvo's dedication to her own Spiritual Path and her Heart wide open to the blessings and Messages from the Ascended Masters has invoked within her a loving, and caring attention and perfection in editing the live transmissions from Akasha & Asun and others of the Ascended Host into a book format for all of us to read and enjoy. God bless you Yvo and may your own Inner Light continue to expand and be a blessing to this world.

I wish to thank Josie McGuire, Ashaya Carter and Ophellia Ben Emanuel who offered their time and energy into the secondary editing of this book. I extend my gratitude to Louise Emma Gallant who offered her incredible talent in formatting this book for production and in the creation of the Cover Art Design.

To those who have dedicated hours of their time, the transcribers, who transcribe the live transmissions of Akasha & Asun and others of the Ascended Host and produce the manuscripts that are readied for editing, thank you so much for your great contribution and service you are providing. Our transcribers are Barbara Summers, Isabelle Faith and Katherine Kanius. And a special thank you to Diana Howell who has edited a wealth of Akasha & Asun's messages that are forthcoming. I thank each of you in the great task and service each of you have provided in transforming the live transmissions of our Beloved Akasha & Asun into the written word for all of us to read and enjoy.

I wish to express my gratitude to the thousands of folks around the world who have opened their hearts to the love, blessings and living messages of our Ascended Akasha & Asun and the Ascended Host.

$\mathscr{A}$KASHA & ASUN

Beloved Akasha & Asun...centuries of time past, Beloved Akasha & Asun began Their ministry as Seraphim Angels in Divine Service to this system of worlds. Then after Their Service as Angels, thirty-seven thousand years ago They came to the Earth embodied as human beings and gained Their ascension and freedom twelve thousand years later. They are amongst those who are ascended and free offering Their love and wisdom. In 1987 They made contact with Usa and chose him as Their Messenger.

Akasha & Asun reveal the nature of our mental and emotional bodies and how to master our thoughts and emotions to produce a much happier and fulfilled life, how to make a deep personal contact with a hidden spiritual centre that dwells within each of us. They offer a journey of Self Realization, one of Deep Inner Transformation and Personal Triumph in all areas of our lives. They show us how to develop loving relationships with our self and all life around us, how to transform our physical bodies and attain vibrant health. Are you looking for a sense of True Power in your Life? Are you ready to receive Golden Keys to creating all that you desire and manifesting your 'Field of Dreams' now? Are you ready to make a real and lasting difference in this world? Discover what makes you the person you want to be. Discover the source of your Inner and Higher Power and what drives your passion for life. Discover the Greatest Power in the Universe!

Akasha & Asun offer us a Spiritual Awakening, not an organization that you join, rather a path that you can live from your heart, that reveals to you a source of inner guidance, fulfillment and the means to live a passion filled life. Akasha & Asun are here to help us experience Spiritual Fulfillment in every area of our lives, to help us to live an extraordinary life of greater love, peace, happiness and abundance. They are speaking through Usa, Their Messenger. Akasha Mystery School organizes and makes available the knowledge Akasha & Asun are offering Humanity at this time.

Have you ever thought...What is my Higher Purpose on Earth? What have I come to do? Are you seeking greater peace and a meaningful life? Are you looking for answers and solutions to the daily challenges that affect our lives? Do you know there is a Higher Power that you can connect with now? Would you like to transform challenges into opportunities? Do you live life to the fullest each day? Have you heard of Ascended Beings? This book may very well be the greatest gift you have come across...come now and embrace, embody, experience, and express the Greatest Power in the Universe.

❋

QUOTES FROM AKASHA & ASUN

Your thoughts, feelings and desires, your spoken words, your actions, your deeds, your lack of actions, and your choices and decisions are always setting into motion the energy that offers you a world of experience and human relationships—a field of manifestation—that will either free you or limit you.

There is something that is greater than the judgment of negative or positive—it is Life Itself without the polarizing duality. Life Itself without this polarity invites the totality and presence of Divine Love in which there is no absence of Love.

Life always has a discovering and raising activity within it, a raising and expanding sense to it…and it is this raising…this expansion of a light filled consciousness… where one does gather higher knowledge of the Tree of Life. And when that knowledge is integrated and applied, it becomes wisdom that is comprehended by you, and it is never lost.

When you realize the inner 'I' is your True Source and is Infinite in measure—whether your resources come to you or through you, it makes no difference, for there is only one Source.

If there is imperfection in my world, there is an imperfect thought and feeling in me. Take ownership of everything in your world. Choose and choose and never stop choosing the very best and finest you can be.

Say Yes to Life! If you don't go within, you will go without. You have the ability to affect everything in your world, for there is nothing there that is fixed. Be willing to succeed and give yourself permission to succeed. Be open to your divinity expressing through you now.

It is not a good time to be climbing some mountain in the Far East in search of truth. The mountain is within you. You will never find anything but total love and wisdom, joy and acceptance waiting for you when you turn within.

Whatever your attention is upon, that you become. Wherever your attention goes, there you are.

Try to maintain harmony at all times.

Stay in your heart. Allow yourself sometime each day to be an empty cup to be filled with God Source. The lover's path to enlightenment is one of ease, effortlessness and grace.

It is within your Divine Nature to embrace, embody, experience, and express the fullness of your Godself in the whole activity of Divine Love.

The Seven Pillars of the Diamond Heart include an authentic heart, a courageous will, a discerning mind, a strong spine, a healthy body, a Herculean life force and a conviction of purpose.

26

$\mathcal{P}$REFACE

Beloved Akasha, Ascended Master of the Rose Pink Ray, delivers a message from Venus, from the Glorious Son of Venus, Sanat Kumara

Beloved Sanat Kumara

All of you are Individualizations of Godsource in this world. All you precious Humanity are of the Light and are all one equal cell in the great family of the 'I AM Starseed' that live on the Earth today. As each of you is an equal cell in the great family of life on the Earth, each of you is responsible for a portion of everything that exists in this world, including the discord.

The responsibility of cleaning up a portion of discord that exists in this World

In bringing this to your attention, I, Sanat Kumara, will say to you that, whether it be the Ascended Master Beloved Lady Leto or whether it be the Great Master from Arabia, Beloved Serapis Bey, whether it be the Ascended Chananda who oversees India or any of the Ascended Host who have gained their Ascension—they too have called for the purification of the world.

I assure you, Children of the Light, that before these Ascended Master Beings gained the ascension in their lifetimes they took the responsibility, and used their authority, to reach up to their Great God Presence; they used their authority to make the call for the release of that which purified a portion of the discord that is in this world, along with the purifying of their *own* human creation.

Just as those out of your own history have also contributed to a cleansing of a portion of this world—that the Divine Plan for humanity and the Earth might move forward—must each of you, before the hour of ascension is at hand, be the responsibility and the authority for the call that releases Our Sacred Fire Love from our Octaves into your world, for the cleansing, the purification of your own human creation. But also, there must be the rising up, the willingness on your part to use the authority the Great God Presence gives each of you to be the release—by your call—of *Our* Sacred Fire Love from our Octave, from your *own* Great God Presence, from the physical sun that loves your world so great, or the Great Central Sun that loves the universe into manifestation.

And I say to you, Dear Hearts, if you will hear my words and if you will accept them, I will mentor with your own Higher Christ Selves. You will see what I and others can do for you, because it is *our* authority to release the Sacred Fire Love, Purity and Power and direct the Great Cosmic Rays of Light and Sound into this World. It is our authority and it is our responsibility to release into this world what it most requires to throw off that which is destructive—that is *our* responsibility; and I assure you that we have never shirked this responsibility. Wherever there has been a call that has reached up to us—for us to release that Sacred Fire that removes a portion of humankind's unfortunate creation—we have responded. So that is *our* authority, which is *our* responsibility!

My Sacred Fire Love is the Violet Consuming Flame that has within It the Spiraling Blue Flame with Gold at Its centre

In the unascended state, *your* authority, Children of the Light, is to make the call. That is your authority and that is your responsibility. Our authority and responsibility is to answer the call, and to release that Sacred Fire Love. In my case, my Sacred Fire Love is the Violet Consuming Flame that has within it the Spiraling Blue Flame which is gold at its centre. And so with this, I, Sanat Kumara, offer to you another gift, if you will accept that you are responsible, because you are one of the many life streams destined to this world, and you take your responsibility for a portion of discord that has wreaked havoc in your world, then any time you see discord, call my Cosmic Violet Consuming Flame into action!

I know what is in your world. I know that which is an offence to life, what is an offence to love and to God, that which exists in your world. I know all that you have to do is to walk out in your cities and you will see destruction and discord. So when you see what is in your world which is an offence to life—if you see destruction, discord—form that habit of training yourself to command your Presence to release the Violet Consuming Flame that has the Spiraling Blue Flame in it. Release it right where you see discord, where you see destruction and problems; or where you, Dear Hearts, have those who turn to you for assistance. If there is one who requires assistance in your world, if there is that one who has things that are out of place, things that are out of balance, call my Great God Flame to them and into the condition they are facing.

Just hold a picture of a flash, a tiny golden Flame, just flashing into this condition

Your planet, the Third-Dimensional reality, is a reality that is attempting to be loved by the Ascended Host and the love that is within your own Heart Flames to bring back into order, to bring back into Divine Design, that which I, as the Ancient of Days, knew—and what you knew when you lived on the Earth in the beginning—was an experience called 'the Garden of Eden.'

Just form the habit of sending forth the Violet Flame that holds the Spiraling Blue Flame within it wherever you see discordant individuals or conditions, wherever there is destruction. Do this quietly. Whether you see it or whether you hear it—when you hear it on your modern means of communication, your satellites that bring you these moving pictures on your television sets—you can send that Violet Flame that carries the Spiraling Blue Flame within it, and send it there as a Consuming and Healing Flame, to do its perfect work.

Then, once you have done this, call upon me, or any of the Ascended Host, to place our Golden Heart Flame, or our Individualized God Flame, where the problems seem to be. See it just as a flash of light and try to hold that picture for a moment. So, picture a flash of gold, a Golden Flame, just flashing into the condition; and this means to you that this is the Mighty God Flame of an Ascended Master.

Now you have the Violet Flame and its Spiraling Blue Action, which will correct the condition, *and the* Golden Flame of an Ascended Master that will bring about the correction and the transformation of any wrong condition into the pure Electronic Energy of Source and its Divine Plan!

The Ascended Hearts Flame of the Ascended Masters will keep a condition from ever taking on a duality

And as you get polished in the use of this power, as you accept the authority; if you will give us the responsibility and the authority to answer your call, we will do our part. And if you will do your part, you will find that you have given yourself and you have given this world what it requires for healing and correction. But not only *correction;* for when you only leave the condition as corrected, then, Dear Heart, that correction could become re-qualified through a misdirection of someone's thoughts and feelings sometime in the future.

But if you call forth the Heart Flame of an Ascended Master Being into that thing that you have called forth the Sacred Fire to correct, then you see, because that one has gained its liberation through all physical substance, the condition cannot take on duality again. As the Ascended Being's Heart Flame is flashed into that condition, to liberate its Divine Design, to liberate its Divine Intention, that it might go forth into glorious manifestations in your lives, then, Dear Heart, it is the Heart Flame of the Ascended Masters that you call forth into that condition *after* the use of the Sacred Fire, that will keep that condition from ever taking on a duality natured consciousness again.

When the Light vibratory action of the physical body, the emotional body, and the mental body responds

I bring to you *another* understanding, Dear Hearts. We have seen time after time that the Students of Life become frustrated because they do not yet experience the manifestations, the expressions, or the perfection, of their Mighty 'I AM' Presence in physical reality. "Why do I not have more *perfection* of my Great God Presence, and

31

why do I not have greater *expressions?*" We have studied the notes and the discourses that our Beloved Akasha has shared with you, and we find nothing is missing for you to understand and apply the knowledge given. However, I shall simply give you another worded understanding, another worded expression, that I feel will assist you. Until the 'light vibratory action' of the physical body, the emotional body, and the mental body, responds only to the light vibration of your inner self, the light of the Sacred Heart Flame, there is yet obstruction to your own mighty Great God Self, the Master Self, from expressing its perfection, in you, through you, as you, and out into your world.

With this understanding, I sense that you could remember what our beloved son, Asun, has given you, and that is, the moment you are aware of what is required in your lives, that you would then follow up on that with desire. Each of you could hold within you the desire that the vibratory action—the vibration of your minds, your physical bodies, and your emotional bodies—be raised as quickly as possible, through your willing use of the Sacred Fire to purify and harmonize; so that your human self responds more to the vibration of the inner light within your Golden Heart Flame, that is, the Master Flame of your 'I AM' Presence in you; and what your beloved Akasha has given you the understanding—your Great God Presence I AM, in you and above you.

Hold that desire. Remember that desire and decree once a day.

"I desire the vibration of my mind, my body, and my feelings, the vibration of my brain—the vibration of my outer self—respond only to the inner light of my Heart Flame, my Master God Self. And I call my Great God Presence and the Angels of the Sacred Fire Love into action; holding a sustained action of that Violet Consuming Flame and its Spiraling Blue Flame as Love's Purifying and Harmonizing Presence that will certainly bring the resurrection of my outer self to that place where my self responds only to the vibration of light within my Master Heart Flame. This is my desire and command.

"Mighty Presence of Life let us move forward on this. Beloved Sanat Kumara, would you respond to my call? Great Host of Light, Great Violet Flame, hold the action of this Sacred Fire Love within this outer self—and its commanding presence, its compelling presence, its expanding presence—so that the vibration of my outer self responds only to my inner light; so that there is nothing that can further impede or obstruct the expressions, the love and the perfection that my Mighty 'I AM' Presence wishes to do through me, in me, for me, or express in my world."

Dear Hearts, the Mighty 'I AM' Presence of the Ascended Host loves to perform all activity and loves to produce all manifestations. And your own Beloved Great God Presence has waited centuries of time to produce its own expressions, its own manifestations, and its own perfection in your outer lives. It is now time to let your Great God Presence have every opportunity to provide for you, to create for you healthy and youthful physical bodies, enlightened minds, pure feelings—and all the perfect manifestations you desire—direct from the Universal. Do you agree?

We want the perfection we have on Venus to come into your Worlds

Venus is a very happy place. It is a place of such beauty that it almost takes the breath away of one who visits our worlds. Your Planet is our sister. You are the future guardians of your world, and future guardians of a new Planet that is formed in another system.

All evolution takes a guardianship role, and there is a wonderful destiny that waits for the people of Earth. We want the perfection we have on Venus to come into your world. We want you to experience such lovely happy moments throughout your life. We desire you to experience the true act of creation. We desire you to experience the inner joy and inner ecstasy that can only come from having the experience of being a Creator Being, in which there is no discordant creation, there is no lost will, fragmentation of self, or core perceptions that limit reality. We desire that you inhale, my Dear Hearts, the victory over everything that has ever limited you in this world.

Your own soul's desire for the greater freedom that is coming for each of you—the feeling and the joy and the happiness of manifesting directly, through the command of life, the Sacred Fire manifestation of all that you could ever desire and require in your life, is part of your higher purpose. When you see these happy manifestations take place in your life—because you understand the power of the Sacred Fire and the necessity to make that command for your own Inner Flame to take its toll within your outer self; for your Presence to enfold you in a mighty Golden Flame of its Ascended Heart, and then reach up to any of us and ask us to enfold your human experience, including the experience of thought, feeling and physical interaction with our Heart's Flame of Our Sacred Fire Love's Miracle Mantle Control to Life—then you have set into action the correct Command to Life, that sets life free.

Begin with a call to your own Golden Heart's Flame in your physical bodies, then to the Great God Flame in the Mighty Presence that stands above you to surround you, and the Unfed Flame from our Ascended Hearts and our Temples of Light, to come into the mental, physical, feeling, and the entire energetic environments of your life, for the absolute undoing of the discord that has ever registered in your life. Follow that with a call to the Cosmic Light to raise and seal the energy of those areas, so those areas never again take on a shadow that could ever disturb you.

Ah, how the Heart sings! Ah, how the Soul sings!

This is what life offers you. This is what we offer you. The great journey has begun; the journey towards establishing patterns that allow the perfection of your God Presence into action in your life, the journey of the letting go of the little 'I' and the opening of the way for the Mighty Mystical 'I' that is found in the inner splendor of your Heart Flame and the Ascended Heart Flame of your Higher Self Presence. Remember, your Presence is the Greatest Power in the Universe.

You are entering moments of your resurrection journey, the beginning of that journey up and out of all chaos and limitation. It is your destiny to walk upon the Earth as great beings of joy, great beings that have conscious and constructive manipulation over all the elements of this world: great beings that have come to create a fellowship through the discipleship of your own Christed Selves on Earth; great beings of light that form such a network of light that the hordes of discordant creation run when your Presence walks upon this Earth.

Great will be your future happy moments of fulfillment. Ah, how the heart sings. Ah, how the soul sings as it registers within a physical embodiment the feeling of accomplishment, the feeling of ability, the feeling of true capacity and capability; the feeling to maneuver successfully through an outer world experience and to have mastery over that world. No more failure! Oh, the wonderful deep feelings of joy that will well up within you, the wonderful qualities that the soul has waited for centuries to express into your outer countenance.

Anticipate these moments. These are true joyous feelings that capture the whole inner atmosphere of the outer self, allowing the final moments for the preparation of the great 'I' to come forth within you. All separation, all duality will be set aside. The true knowingness of your being in Christ, your ability to be untouched by that which is not the light, your abilities to create, to protect and your abilities to go out into the world and free the world and life that is yet under such tyranny—all these happy moments of joy and feelings stand only moments away for you, Dear Hearts, as that which is not the light leaves the Earth forever.

And so, be of good cheer and be of good heart. You have taken your stand in the light that knows no limit. You have taken your stand in 'the light that prevails' at the end of each day. You have taken your stand where the eternal sunshine of an Ascended Master's Heart Flame can come in, through, and around you!

Your Field of Dreams may grow beyond your fondest imagination

It is for this reason that I wish to focus now on your outer lives. Close, but not yet close enough, are you shifting into an inner recognition of your love to life—your unique gift that you have to offer to life, and the unique way that each of you can be an instrument in which the divine expresses through you. Each of you can uniquely be an instrument for the Ascended Master's Divine Plan for the freedom of all on Earth.

36

To this vital point do I draw your attention to allow that which is your Field of Dreams—the things you dream to have and accomplish, to experience, your outer field of activities—to so receive the Eternal Flame of Life that it may go beyond the horizons of what you have yet established—that your Field of Dreams be all that you could ever desire. Hold a place within your heart for us and within your own God Presence, a desire for us to assist you in your outer life. We will not let go of the people of Earth. We cannot help those who engage in the destructive side of life, but we can help every human being who turns their attention to their Presence first and then to us in the Ascended and Angelic Realms of Light.

It is not for me to say; it is for your own discerning intelligence to decide as to how much time and how much effort seems to be yet required in which you stay the course and endure what seems to be going on in your life. Only the mighty 'I AM' higher discerning intelligence decides when assistance can be given according to your efforts in your affairs. But I assure you, when you say to your Presence, "I am absolutely through with all limitation in my experience, and I am ready to bring forth the consciousness of the One Love into outer expression, so enfold me in your own Heart's Flame of Your Sacred Fire Love that is the end of all distress in my life so the divine may come forth", it will be done!

Sanat Kumara's Sacred Bloom—the Rose...

I, Sanat Kumara, wish to offer you the Sacred Bloom of My own Heart's Flower to Life. The Ascended Host love to create their own flower, or to specialize and make unique any of the mighty flowers that life and the Great Central Sun gives into outer expression. I do not think that your Beloved Akasha has shared with you that the original birth and creation of the Sacred Rose, is a creation of the Great Central Sun itself. It is the gift of the mighty Cassiopeia to this particular System of Worlds. To all Planets of this System is the rose. The rose is one of the most sacred blooms and it is the sacred bloom that I have chosen as the flower of my heart. And I think you may be interested that I have given the command that my Sacred Heart Flower Bloom take on particular qualities.

The stem of my rose is made up of the pure essence of jade. My rose itself is the softest pearl white, and in the centre of my rose I have placed a pink diamond; a pink diamond that is very common to Venus. Pink diamonds have begun to show up on *your* Planet and this is evidence that your Planet is receiving more light from the physical sun, the Great Central Sun, and the Ascended Host that are allowing wonderful new gems of light to come forward into manifestation. So, Beloved of the Light, hold an image of my rose - a long-stemmed rose, the stem made of the finest softest jade - the rose itself a lovely and beautiful soft pearl white in colour and in its centre a dazzling pink diamond. And this, Dear Hearts, I offer to each of you as the Gift of Life of my own Ascended Heart's Flame. Imagine receiving this rose into your heart.

Ask the Ascended Master's Consciousness to come into the human form

There is much help that each of us in the ascended state can give to your outer lives. The environment of the mind can only function in a supreme state of perfection when the physical brain is filled with as much light as is possible. The environment of the feeling side of life once healed and held in harmony, can only function in its supreme capacity when the physical body is holding the highest vibration of Love's Eternal Presence.

A short while ago those of us who represent the Lords of the Flame of Venus observed that Akasha had made a special journey to the home of your precious Mary, Mother of Jesus the Christ; where she had made a special request for the Students of Light under her Soul Journey Dispensation. That request was for that mighty gift of the Ascended Masters Consciousness that many of the Ascended Host have offered in the past from time to time to those who love the light.

Beloved Mary, in the year 1963, and one more time in 1966, had given this gift to the world through the dispensation of the Mighty Saint Germain. And as every time before, so few had taken this gift up and used it. And there was great delight in the Heart of Blessed Mary that Akasha would take up that gift and offer it to the students who would care to use it. And very simply indeed, it is the *Ascended Master's Consciousness*, that has within it all the use and the understanding and activity of the Sacred Fire, the Cosmic Light, and the record of the Victory of Ascension and Attainment over all things in this world.

Enter into a willingness to sit or lie down quietly, very still; in full command of your attention, fully relaxed, sending forth a prayer call to your beloved Higher Self, your 'I AM' Presence and the Ascended Masters to fill yourselves with the Ascended Master's Consciousness, knowing that it comes from the light of the Ascended Masters Heart's Flame and comes to you as a projection of that light, into your physical brain, the physical heart, and the central nervous system of your human forms, and to some degree even to your own Heart Flame. As you engage in this practice and make it common to your daily experience, will this give you a wonderful activity that will assist you in your momentum of releasing the greater powers of life into your outer hands and into your daily activities. Try working with one of the Ascended Masters that you know, such as Beloved Jesus, calling upon Him to fill you with His Ascended Master's Consciousness.

Once you make the call, sit or lie very quietly for ten minutes, open and receptive and rest in the silence. Finish with gratitude.

As you commit to a ten minute use of your time each day in this meditation, filling yourself with the Ascended Master's Consciousness, this will give you the assistance to heal yourself and others; and to increase the light in what I already indicated is the finer use of your mental faculties within the brain. Equally this will expand the light in your heart and assist greatly the good health of your physical body. It will produce, in your lives, much happier manifestations and experiences.

Give yourselves permission for your Beloved Presence, the Ascended and Angelic Host

To add to this, I ask that each of you pay a little closer attention to the thought processes and to the feelings that you experience, with the realization they are the most important building blocks of future moment manifestation. I ask you, I invite you, in prayer, to call upon my own Ascended Heart's Flame of My Sacred Fire Love's Miracle Mantle of Life and Mastery, to enter into your thoughts and feelings, so that you can have the finer activity of the Sacred Fire Love to Life as a raising condition inside the mind, the feeling, the physical brain and the physical body and that you can more quickly identify and let go of patterns of thought and feeling that, of their very nature, create future limitation.

By identifying those thoughts and feelings can you have, and call forth, my Sacred Fire Love to change those thoughts and feelings into much happier ones. Happier thoughts and feelings truly allow you to give yourself life direction, the evolution of your soul, and your rightful place to take your stand in the sovereignty of light, and be that Creator God Being that you were intended to be. A being who has released into your outer life—through command—all the Sacred Fire Love of Our Miracle Mantle of Love's Mastery that we can hold inside you, that we can hold around you, that loves to command all human limitation dissolved and consumed so that the beautiful light inside you can process your thoughts, your choices, your decisions, your feelings and your desires, and the images that you hold in your mind into outer tangible manifestation much more quickly.

As you do this, my Dear Heart, remind yourself that the interior of you is the primary building place of future experience and manifestation and give yourselves permission for your Beloved Presence, and the Ascended Host to offer you and to place in your world what we know your Presence wants for you in terms of perfection, and what we know you are going to require to manifest the wonderful new ideas and decisions and desires that you have and hold. This way your projects, your Fields of Dreams, and your experiences can all have the Desire to Life, the Command to Life, and the Sacred Fire Protection all the way to their absolute manifestation without limitation.

Prepare yourselves for Grace

That which is *not* the light will come into a place of exposure and create many problems. I ask you to take a few moments for the command that the Mighty Violet Flame, or the Sacred Fire Love of an Ascended Master's Flame, come in, through, and around you; come into your dreams, your plans, your goals, your projects, your homes, your workplace, your automobiles, and into all that your

41

energy goes to. Ask that our Sacred Fire Love to Life hold the protection around you, your loved ones, your families and everything in your life, so that you may enter in the great Resurrection Days that are ahead of you; and go forth out into your world to be that great beacon of life that is dedicated to setting the world free. And it starts with allowing your own Field of Dreams to be even much greater than what you have considered.

How will you do this? Well, my Dear Hearts, by going back to your Presence, walking through your Field of Dreams, your goals, your desires, your vision for your life on Earth, and saying to your Presence, "Now I am just certain that you, my Beloved Presence, are perfection. And I am just certain that you have your own ideas for my life down here on this Earth; you have some of your own things that you would just love to bring into manifestation that I may not have taken into consideration, or am aware of. So let it be known, God of my Life, I desire of you and I give the command that all you desire in my life come forth as a direct manifestation of your own Heart's Flame and Sanat Kumara's Heart Flame to life—that what you desire in my life come into tangible manifestation by the Sacred Fire Love's Command to Life, and be protected at all times."

This, I feel, will open the way to the great creative expression of your lives as Violet Souls, and that which are the new things of perfection that must come to your world. My Dear Hearts, you have got to prepare yourselves for Grace. I encourage each of you to come to that place of final release of life as an experience of difficulty, an experience of struggle. It is a strange thing that I have noticed in the human being, that often before a human steps into a whole new experience of much greater freedom, much greater liberty, and a much happier and fulfilling life, that moments before this, you will allow yourselves to experience just the opposite. And I assure you it is an oddity to our consciousness and not an odyssey! However, it is what it is.

We come from Realms of Light to lend you our strength. We lend you our courage. Sometimes, when your state of illumination is so much greater than what has been the immediate past, it requires certain cosmic assistance to undo the residue of yesterday's unhappy human moments. Often when you would think you were free of problems things seem to surface again. And so whatever reasons are behind those things that create a temporary obstacle or a temporary hold on your life, I assure you that we can give you great assistance! However, for us to do so, in prayer and meditation, you must ask!

Go beyond what you have dared to dream

I will add my voice to the final preparation for a great new cycle of resurrection that is touching the Earth at this time. A cycle that allows ascensions to take place in the people of Earth, where a certain amount of love and service to the presence of God and to life has awarded the outer life—through momentum—those *Dispensations* in which the last of the human limitation can be set aside, so that you are free to express the glory of your own 'I AM' that you had in the Great Central Sun before you began your great pilgrimage of lifetimes on Earth.

Prepare yourselves to go beyond what you have dared to dream. If you are to be the Light Bearers to Life, if you are to be the true Torch Bearers of Light, if you are to be the Way-Shower for others, life in all its glory will prepare you well. And it will fit you into a new Cosmic set of garments, it will fit you into a new Cosmic feeling and assertion and knowingness of yourself. There are garments of light you shall wear in the physical body even unascended. Coming for each of you is a whole new way of comfort; of being comfortable in your physical forms, comfortable in your understanding of your right use of mind and feelings, and comfortable in your belief and your acceptance of your ability to command life and manifestation in your world.

You have many interesting phrases that we have observed, and presently you have no idea of the gratitude that we send to the Great Central Sun for the Cosmic permission that it gave to us a long time ago to take up some of the worded 'expressions' of the ancient languages; and finally to take up new worded expressions in your present Earthly languages that become mighty receptacles of light, that when you do your prayers and calls, it will release into your outer lives what will set your life free.

Take command of your attention two to three times a day, and open the way to your own Presence and to us for the release of the greater good into your lives. But also at this time decide what you do *not* want in your life, or who you do not want in your life, or what types of individuals you do not want in your life. And I have looked for a human expression, and I think this one will serve the purpose; in which in the privacy of your own inner thinking, as you understand what you don't want in your life that yet might be knocking at your door, to say to those things, "Get out of my life!"

"Get out of here! There is no place left for you! I have offered everything inside me and around me, to be filled, blessed, and to be taken control of, by the Sacred Fire Love to life from my own God Being and from the Ascended Host. Therefore, limitation, confusion, tiredness, that which blinds me, that which seems to create obstacles in my life, that which seems to create uncertainty or any challenge or loneliness on the path of life—I speak to you! I have taken my stand for eternity in the light, and I am my own Master Sacred Fire Heart's Flame to Life, and I command you, get out of here! Get out of my life and be consumed in the Ascended Master's Sacred Fire Heart's Flame and their Miracle Mantle of Love's Mastery. Get out of my life! I will not give you any more of my power or my attention!"

Such is my Oath; such is my Way of Life!

And then, often sit at the end of your bed and raise your arms to God and your Mighty 'I AM' Presence, with the desire that it come forth and glorify you, and glorify your life. Now, let me see here, I, Sanat Kumara, have another idea. How about an exchange program? Some of you are going through the last battle of the little self with the big self, the little 'I' with the grand 'I.'

So as you turn your attention to your Presence with your arms raised, you say:

"Now, my Presence, let's have an *exchange program*. I send up to you that little rascal, the little 'I,' that seems to get me into trouble more often than I wish, that seems to delay my passage into the true Creator Being that is my right to life. And so I offer this little self up to you and exchange it for more of the great 'I AM that I AM.'

"I hold this heart open, I hold my mind open, I hold my feeling side of life open to receive now the great 'I AM' that You are into this outer life experience. I tender to You, Mighty and Glory of my Life, I offer up to You the end of fear, the end of doubt, and the end of disbelief.

"I Am, by the very nature that my Heavenly Mother and Father have created, a being of God, Light, Love and Creation. I get to state clearly what is in my life and what has no right to be in my life any longer. And I release into your own Heart's Flame Sacred Fire Love to Life—and all its control in, through and around me—what has no right to be in my life any longer.

"Goodbye fear, confusion, uncertainty! I arise upon the wings of my Violet Soul. I Am the great raising and resurrection of life. With great ease and grace I Am raised and risen. I raise my right arm and I reach into that mighty treasure house of the God 'I AM' that is presently living in great realms of light. And I draw back that treasury of light, I draw back that treasury of love; I draw back that treasury of Sacred Fire Love that knows no boundary into my outer self, and I send it forth out into my world with the command that it take its permanent toll and take up its place in my outer life until my ascension.

"*From this day forth, I am come!* I Am come into this world. I Am come to love this world free of all chaos, disintegration, all hatred and selfishness, and the tragedy of all appearances of lack. For me, I Am the Presence that reaches up into my own Divine Treasure Chest and releases down into my hands and use that Cosmic Love and life's energy that instantly loves to fulfill my dreams, my goals, my projects, my desires. I do not wait for a response. I reach up and I draw back the Cosmic Love Supreme that loves to manifest as all I desire in my outer life.

"*Time, space,* I have toiled with you for centuries. Long have you been my enemy, yet you are a configuration of energy created by beings of light long ago. And I release you, time; I release you, space of the spoils of human creation. I command you to cooperate and to be the fulfillment of the Sacred Fire Love's Mastery, that loves—as I draw it down into my life—to manifest my dreams, that loves to manifest my experiences and all that I dare to dream for myself.

"Long have the Masters of the Great Ascended Host loved and loved and loved the Earth, and I shall not tolerate that there would not be those amongst unascended humankind, those who join them in their love to life. I command that my Life be the Sacred Fire Love to all Life in the outer World. I command it! Not only in moments of being filled with the Ascended Master's Consciousness will I draw down into my Earthly experiences the Divine Love that is in this Universe. I shall crown, I shall anoint my Earthly experiences, even those that seem so mundane—I shall anoint them, I shall bathe them with this greater love. I shall hold the energy of my world in sacred space and release into that energy a great wave of my own Heart Flame's Sacred Fire Love's Mastery to Life.

"I shall release into my life *Sanat Kumara's Love* that He offers; that my world shall become a Miracle Mantle of the Sacred Fire's Love to Life. I shall use this Miracle Mantle and it shall flow through me out into the world. I am risen. I draw upon the great Cosmic Powers of Life. And wherever I command 'Peace be still!' all human discord is silenced and the Divine Flame of Life is released to reveal its authority of health, of supply, of companionship, or whatever manifestation I desire to come forth.

"Mighty Presence of Life, I have yielded to great beliefs of the necessity of longstanding durations of time and space. It has spoiled my journey through life. Today is my hour of redemption. Today is my hour of reconciliation. I draw that Sacred Fire Love of my own God 'I AM', and the Ascended Host, and command the whole sequence of time and space that fills the Earth's atmosphere—and the atmosphere of my own outer life—be loved free of all human limitation, causes, thought and feeling. The whole sequencing, the whole networking of the time and space of this world, now is filled with my Sacred Fire Love of my own Heart's Flame Command to Life.

"Duality cease to be! I Am the Flame of Life. I wait not for one moment longer. I Am a Flame of Life Eternal. Time, space, you are my friend. You are given as the great sequence of manifest energy. You are given as the great configuration upon which I can lay out the map of life what is my ascent into my glory, and royal rightful place to Life. And in my Ascent to Life, 'I AM' in me is the sweet fragrance as I walk upon this Earth—as I love, as I offer love, as I create and join with the fine creations of others. I shall live each day my Sacred Heart's Flame Miracle Mantle Love to Life that does not allow any limitation, allows only the light of my own God Being to produce perfect manifestation.

"Feelings, O great Feelings! Great Goddess of Life! How I have slept; how I have compelled a nightmare within thy great Stream. I release you of all discordant emotion, Mighty Feeling of Life! Great Goddess, Thou hast served me as my feeling side of life. I give you all the Sacred Fire Love of my own Heart's Flame. I command you—my own feeling side of life—"Be released this moment into the full state of Harmony! Be released this moment into the Sacred Fires of Eternity, and return to the great Goddess that you are and be on Earth that Divine Reflection of the Holy Mother who art in Heaven in the Great Central Sun.

"My Mind, how I have allowed a shadow to be upon you. And yet this shadow no longer needs to be, for I call into you—my mind—my own Heart's Flame of my Sacred Fire Love's Mastery to Life. And I enter into you and I cleanse you with the Sacred Fire where never a shadow can appear again to life. May you, my mind, the gift that my Heavenly Father in Life's great Heaven has given me, may you now become the awareness and illumination of 'I AM that I AM'. I Am the consciousness that is now free. Goddess and God, I am born 'I AM', I am born the individualization of

life and my Flame is free to take its liberty through choice and the desire of life to go forth.

"Now of my physical countenance, and I say to you, '*O physical body*, long have I lamented the use of physical bodies; long have I felt entrapment in physical bodies; long have I held consciousness and desire to be free from physical form; long have I assailed you and assaulted you with the desire not even to experience myself within you. Mighty physical body of life—thou great elements of which you are composed—I give you now my Heart's Flame of Love, Mercy, and Forgiveness. Wash now clean all that has not been Love's Eternal Presence; wash now clean all consciousness of discord and duality.

"Come, my physical body, come daily to my own Heart's Flame Eternal Well of Life, and wash yourself of all duality. Prepare yourself to be my living garment, my temple, the temple of the Most High Living God, the 'I AM that I AM', for I am ready to enter and to live fully in my outer life from the throne room of my God Being; forever connected to my Ascended Self and to the Great Central Sun—the Source of Heaven and Harmony—never to be separate in consciousness again. I return to my Holy House—the future place of glory, a great portrait of life that waits for the 'I AM that I AM' to come forth and dance through life.

"Within me is a great *orchestra* of sound and light; within me are the great colours of life; within me are the Sacred Sounds, Sacred Chimes and Sacred Light of Lights. I am ready as a Creator Being; I am my own Sacred Fire Heart's Flame Command to Life. And I am ready to cast upon the elements of this world a portrait of the Sacred Fire's Love to Life that loves to materialize perfection and beauty, that loves to experience heights of ecstasy, joy, and happiness, that heretofore I have not even experienced in the first two Golden Ages when life was so good on Earth.

"Thus is my commitment to life; thus am I renewed. Through the Cosmic Light, the Miracle Love and the Sacred Fire—the powers of redemption and the greater powers of the Universe are upon me. And as I am redeemed I come into this world now to offer the light, to give the Sacred Fire, and to redeem this world. As the Masters have sought to love this world free, I will go forth in all natural expression—I will go forth and I will love, and love, and love knowing that I am a Mighty Flame of Life that is greater than all the appearances of this world. I will go forth and I shall not stand down. I am a blazing Presence of Liberty, of Justice to life, and 'I AM' the Flame that loves Life free.

"*Life!* Oh World! Long you have stood to be the portrait of the Individualized Flames of Life that take on physical life in this world. I am returned to my divine home. I look no further, away from my own divinity. I beg not for life; I am that life. And I give myself the gift—the gift of willingness, allowance and permission to set aside through Cosmic Dispensation, time and space as I have known it. And I open the Flame of my own Sacred Heart Centre to birth through me whole new ideas and experiences of time and space without limitation. I go forth—I am Pan; I am the giver of life; I am the artist; I am the dancer of life; I am the mind and heart of God; I am the great orchestration of Life's Eternal Embrace; I am the Flame of Liberty; I am the great Cosmic beings of light who have taken Sacred Office to the great qualities of light and I am those qualities expressing through me more and more each day.

"*Such is my Oath!* Such is my covenant now and way of life! I am free! And I give my own Heart's Flame of Freedom to all life. I am—and I always have been—a Miracle Mantle of my own Heart's Flame Sacred Fire Love to Life. And upon that Mantle is the Sacred Fire Mantle of

Sanat Kumara that is offered to me, and I am ready to go forth and to embrace the second birth—the true rebirth, the true redemption of my life. And I am in that place of great earnestness to experience life's beauty; to experience life that is not compromised with the duality of this world. Let the journey begin—I am come home!"

May the gift that I have shared with you, may it find resonance within your heart. May you rise into the glory of the being of light that you are. You are ready for what life can do for you. Know that we love your Master Jesus, for He is the fulfillment of a divine plan that I, guided by the glorious beings in the Great Central Sun, gave to the people of Earth. He is the first in modern time to open the way to the great knowledge 'I AM' in His mighty statements to life. And it is through His life, His ministry, and those of you who have come to love Him, that for us the door is now open and we can enter into your lives if you will only turn your attention to us and hold it there for ten minutes a few times a day, and let us fill you with what we know will set you free!

The blessings of our Heart Flame are upon the Ascended Jesus Christ; for He is the one who opened the way for the statement 'I am always with you, I have never left you.' He opened the way for that statement to finally be *realized*. It is through that statement and that Cosmic Authority, that each of us comes to you. Hold your attention upon us and love us as we have loved your world, and then command us to fill you with the light of God that never fails. Then, Dear Heart, make it your Oath to Life that you will do *your* part—love God first and then your world, the Earth; and the world that you live within—all that is your special interest to life, make now the effort to love your life free of all that has been the absence of love.

51

We hold you in a Miracle Mantle. We enfold you in a Miracle Mantle of Our Sacred Fire Love's Mastery to Life. God bless you! God bless you! God bless you, for you have chosen the light. You have chosen life. You have chosen a return to worship God in the highest way of your *own free will*. Thus you have fulfilled what life obligates you to, and therefore your freedom is upon you. You have found *The Greatest Power in the Universe*, the Beloved 'I AM' Presence and its Great Sacred Fire, ready for your use.

God bless you, I AM Sanat Kumara.

CHAPTER ONE

I Am Akasha and I greet you from the Heart of my Love for Humanity and the Earth. I invite you to allow an expansion within your consciousness and an opening within your heart to receive the many blessings and gifts that are offered you in this book. May the Light within your heart ignite within you all that is offered here. I bring you greetings from the Ascended Host, some of who come to speak with you about *The Greatest Power in the Universe*. It is my desire that your journey through this book, and your personal application of what you discover, set your life free in all ways that you can possibly imagine.

The subject I would like to begin with is 'The renewal of your power of attention and intentions.' We will begin this by placing our attention on that which is greater, and that is the *intention* of the Company of Heaven and the *attention* that they hold upon the human race and the Earth at this time—to seize every open door and every opportunity to come forward, to assist everyone who is seriously seeking the light, desires to fully awaken and wishing to experience greater freedom, happiness, health, creativity, passion, success and abundance in their daily lives.

The renewal of the power of attention and intentions

The intention of the Spiritual Hierarchy who live in the higher dimensions beyond your third dimension on Earth is to assist every human being; starting with the few who are awakening at this time and growing that few into hundreds of thousands, hundreds of millions, and eventually into the billions, awakening humankind, assisting humankind to be free of the fear, density and limitations in the human structure that is opposing the desire to live free and happy lives that are filled with higher purpose. The Ascended and Angelic Host desire to free the human self of the history of centuries of lifetimes of limitation that your feeling side of life remembers, and therefore remain obstacles in your life.

The intention of the Spiritual Hierarchy is to assist human beings to once again remember that there is a higher purpose, and that you were not thrown out of Heaven—you did not fall from grace, you made a very *conscious* choice to enter into physical realities, a physical universe. The intention of the human race is to become living Gods, living Goddesses, and fully awakened Beings who have come from the Heavenly Mother and the Heavenly Father who live in the Heart of Creation at the centre of the Universe in a place we call the Great Central Sun. That is quite a concept, isn't it? And yet it is not a concept, Dear Hearts, it is a Truth.

It can be very difficult to intellectualize an idea of Beings so *great* in their light, that if they were to present themselves in the fullness of their light, their light would be such a blazing Presence, it would be so brilliant to your sight that literally—like the story of Paul, told in the bible—the experience would literally blind your physical eyes.

54

There are Beings in the universe that are capable of creating light around their physical bodies, and projecting light, even greater than the light that your physical Sun radiates to this particular System of Worlds. Isn't that amazing?

This is the evidence and the testimony that life knows no boundaries; life desires to grow; life desires to expand. And when one accepts with deep gratitude and the right state of humility and humbleness the power and the authority that has been placed within their hands; a power given freely through recognition, love and the applying of one's own personal effort, a power waiting to be directed, and when one takes up that mantle of sovereignty and leadership and begins practicing directing their inner God Light, not only through themselves, but into the world for manifestation—miracles happen.

It is then you are walking upon the highest path—the highest path that the human race has long forgotten, the upward Path of Ascension.

The journey from the Great Central Sun

This is the first journey of the Children of God, the journey from the Great Central Sun. Your lives did not start with your first lifetime on this physical Earth, or on some other physical System—your life began in the Great Central Sun. The Great Central Sun at the centre of the universe is so large, it is difficult to even fathom it. The size of your whole Solar System is smaller than the size of the Great Central Sun—you have to take the size of your Earth's Sun, and multiply it a thousand times, and you might come close to the size of the Sun that is at the centre of the universe. That is why it is called 'The Great Central Sun'. It is there that the Mighty 'I AM' Presence lives as the distinguished Creators of this Universe, the Distinguished

Creators of all the Life Streams that come forth from them—what humanity calls God.

You can evolve a Heavenly Body of Light around yourself that literally becomes a Sun's Presence

There are words that have been used in the religions of the world that attempt to give a higher understanding of Deity, of that which represents the Godsource. Words such as the *Electronic Presence,* the *Great Mighty 'I AM' Presence,* words such as *God, Spiritual Force,* words such as *Heavenly Mother, Heavenly Father* or *'I AM that I AM.'* These are all words that correctly represent the Eternal and Immortal Presence that lives in the Great Central Sun. Not only can you evolve into a Being of such great, great light—you can evolve a Heavenly Body around yourself that literally becomes a Sun's Presence. Your God Parents of your physical sun have done so. They are called Helios and Vesta; Helios and Vesta—the Cosmic Twin Flames, the Ascended Masters in your Earth's Sun—created the physical Sun.

These two great Twin Flame Ascended Masters *draw* the light forth from the Great Central Sun. There are many Great Cosmic Beings that live within the Great Central Sun with the Infinite Mother/Father 'I AM' Presence. These include the Mighty Elohim Creator Beings and the two Beings in the Great Central Sun who are responsible for this Solar System—the Mighty Polaris and Mighty Poseidon. These two Beings *project* the light to the sun of this Solar System to sustain life, harmony and perfection. So too, are there great Beings who project light to other Systems of Worlds.

It is your Beloved Ascended Helios and your Beloved Vesta in the Earth's Sun, and those Beings that are known as the Sisters and Brothers of the Golden Robes who are having an experience in the Earth's Sun, who receive the light from the Greater Sun and project that to the Earth. They work with Helios and Vesta from the inside, from the very centre of the Earth's Sun, in building and maintaining that Star, and then projecting the greater light from that Star to the Planets that are part of this System.

In order to experience Life in the physical Universe you require a physical body

So, tremendous attention is held upon the focusing of great Powers of Light to systems of worlds. Yes? In the Great Central Sun, where you once lived, you had spiritual bodies; and those spiritual bodies were of an electronic nature. Unlike the atom, the electron cannot be re-qualified, it remains in a state of perfection and in a way it is the very *heart* of God-Life. And so it is of such a vibration of perfection, that density of imperfection at that state of vibration does not register.

The atom, of which velocity and vibration can change according to the quality that has been imposed upon it energetically, can shape itself as the forms and the experiences that you have in this world. However the Electron cannot. So, oftentimes, your Higher Self has been referred to as the Mighty 'I AM' Presence, or the Electronic Presence, or it has been referred to, in metaphysics, as the White Fire Body. These are names that appropriately identify this great Presence that is your Divine Self that is above you. And when you lived in the Great Central Sun, you lived in a garment similar to the garment that your Higher Self presently wears—an Electronic Garment, a Spiritual Garment of Light.

When you made the powerful choice to leave the Great Central Sun to experience life in the physical reality, you came into an understanding that this was an evolution and

57

a journey; that in order to experience life in the physical universe, it is a process of entering into a chosen physical System of Worlds, in this case your present Solar System and Earth and acquiring for yourself a physical body, so that you could begin to grow the light of your Godself in that physical body and then cause that physical body to be lifted up into the Ascended aspect of yourself.

The Mid-Self, known by many names...

The Electronic Presence of your Higher Self has never entered a field of limited density as you know it, rather, has always remained in Perfect Realms of Light. That Aspect of yourself is a Perfect Being, because that is how your Heavenly Mother Father made you. However there is also a Mid-Self of you, known by many names. That Aspect between you and your Electronic Presence—your Higher Self—*I* refer to as your *Higher Intelligence*, or your *Christ Self*, or your *Higher Mental Body*. The older religions of the world, not knowing what they are referring to, refer to it as the *Holy Spirit*. In truth, the Holy Spirit is the Divine Feminine Aspect of the Christ Self.

Your Christ Self is up in your Lifestream just above you, and your Beloved Higher Self *above* the Christ Self, has remained Eternally Ascended, so it is correct to suggest to yourself that, "Two-thirds of myself is already Ascended." Because the human attention is too often drawn to the past, to the un-ascended human self, and all its trials and tribulations and all its embodiments on Earth, I feel that it would help you to remind yourself, "Two-thirds of my being is already Ascended." Try to realize you are a multi-dimensional being and we are not speaking of a Force *outside* of yourself, we are not speaking of a God-power outside of yourself.

Although it is yet a linear perspective to you, it is truth that even though you have this Christ Self, and the great Electronic Presence of the Higher Self above you and you seem to be in this world, you are not in truth *outside* of those two great aspects of yourself. The consciousness in which you can say, 'I AM'; the consciousness that gives you the ability to think and feel, that gives you the ability to experience senses in the physical body—all of that consciousness comes from the Ray of Light that descends down from your Beloved Great God Self down your Lifestream through your Higher Mental Body. That consciousness is within the light, and that light descending into the human form is anchored into the human heart. You as a Being of Consciousness are still within the light of your own Great God Self.

Time and space is an educated matter, it is an educated matter of *intention*

And so, there you lived in the Great Central Sun in your spiritual bodies. And you made a conscious choice to enter into a physical universe, knowing that in the first lap of that journey you would expand your light and become One with your 'I AM' Presence. The journey was intended to be of a short time, but forgetfulness of purpose became part of the human consciousness.

Isn't that amazing, Beloved, to think that after fourteen million years you are still in the first lap? Except that you are at the end of that first lap. And this is why there is urgency. This is why you sometimes sense urgency within yourselves, because you are literally running out of time on this Planet.

Time and space is an educated matter, it is an educated matter of *intention*. It is an intention given to the developing 'I AM' Race—to give themselves so many years to come into physical bodies and grow the light in these bodies until they would lose the gravitational pull of the Earth. And then raise up, through the atmosphere, up the Light Ray, and up into the Body of the Electronic Presence where your physical body and the Electronic Body of the 'I AM' Higher Self become One. Then you are finished the first lap of Life—you are an Ascended Human Being, you are a Great God Being with Power and Dominion over all Earthly Life and physical matter!

Planet Earth delayed *Her* Ascension into a Fifth Dimensional Vehicle

This destiny was a destiny that was intended to be fulfilled millions of years ago, and your Earth herself has a destiny too. She has her own Ascension Plan—to raise the matter of herself and her Planet into a Fifth-Dimensional vehicle where only perfection exists. She has her destiny, which is to achieve this Ascension. And so she has delayed her own Ascension because human beings forgot the Purpose of Life, forgot the Higher Divine Plan of Life therefore requiring more time to evolve the Divine Plan.

A Divine Plan to save the Earth and to awaken Humanity to its higher purpose has been unfolding for seventy-five thousand years and is complete in May 2012. Yes, a Divine Plan many years unfolding comes to a conclusion in your Earth year 2012.

Angels and Cosmic Beings are coming to the Earth now

So once again, the people of Earth find themselves in a very critical time. It is because of this critical time that you are in, that the Angels and Ascended Beings of Light are being sent to the Earth. It is worthy of your contemplation to understand that the Spiritual Hierarchy—such as

Archangel Michael and the Great Beings—the Goddesses, the Elohim Creator Beings, the Mighty Chohans—are Ascended Masters who have taken up great Spiritual Offices of tremendous authority. These are all Cosmic Beings of Light. And your Planet, forgive me, Dear Heart—but your Planet is a very, very small Planet and yet important in the affairs of the Universe.

Archangel Michael is the Archangel of the First Ray, not only to your Earth, but to your entire Universe

In light of this, and in light of the tens of thousands of worlds that exist that have Greater Life than the Earth has on it—contemplate well—why would a Being of such vastness such as the Archangel Michael be coming to the Earth?

In the religions of the world there is a suggestion of the Thrones around the Mighty God Presence. Seated in those Thrones, Dear Heart, are the great Cosmic Beings who project the full God qualities from the Great Central Sun, and give those qualities to the universe. Archangel Michael is the Archangel of the First Ray of Divine Love, not only to your Earth, but to your entire universe. And why is it that He is here?

You have called him here, because the critical time period that the Earth has entered into has demanded His Presence. There must be something that corrects the Earth and her destiny plan; and corrects the path that human beings are walking that is not in alignment to that destiny. Human beings have *compelled* the Archangels to come to this Earth. Human beings in the past have even compelled Michael and Beloved Raphael to take on a *human embodiment* in former ages in order to lift humanity out of its own self created darkness and limitation. And they took on a human life to try to avoid the destruction of the human race that had already almost happened twice.

Once again we are in a critical time period, and it is critical for the Angels *to come as close as possible to you*; to remind you of your destiny, that you are a Spiritual Being and you have only a *portion* of your real Spiritual Beingness living within these physical bodies. Because when a physical form is created for you, if you bring the Full Electronic Presence of yourself into a physical form, that form could not sustain it. Your physical form must grow *gradually* in the light so that it can learn to contain that light. Realize that only a portion of your Divine Self came into this embodiment; enough for you to be conscious of yourself and to begin to build the light of your divinity within your physical bodies. If there are not greater numbers awakening by the year 2012 and if the numbers who are awakening now do not become free of the limitations that are expressing in their lives and begin to demonstrate the Higher Power of Life as Jesus did in His life, then this will impact the ascension process of humanity and the Earth after 2012.

The *Purpose* of Jesus' Ministry was to walk through everything that would happen at *this* time

It would be good to re-read at least the first four Books of the New Testament; there is sufficient Truth there. The Purpose of Jesus' Ministry was to walk through everything that would happen at this time. He would come and remind you of the Purpose of Life; walk through experiences that you would have; walk through the challenges; walk through what needs to be overcome. He, by remembering the Purpose of Life, came to prove to life that you are greater than what is appearing in the world; to the point of even allowing the physical body to be destroyed, then coming into that body again and raising it. The crucifixion is not part of your Higher Purpose, but every step of Jesus' ministry was—it was a mission that was literally lived for what was coming in two thousand years, so that you would have the record of his resurrection, freedom and ascension, of knowing what to do in your own lives, to set your lives free!

The Ascended Masters will yet remain invisible

This is why the Angels and Ascended Masters are here, to help a portion of humanity to be free of discord and limitation; to teach you once again how to raise the light within your outer selves and to begin to achieve a state of enlightenment; a state of illumination; to begin to demonstrate a Higher Power that the world calls a phenomenon; that the world calls a miracle. To begin to walk and live on the Earth in your higher Christ Consciousness and to increase in numbers, so that those who are the Spiritual Hierarchy to this world can give the permission the Ascended Masters require, walking again on Earth and being visible, giving the assistance humanity requires over the next century.

This is what they are waiting for. They are waiting to step through the atmosphere, visible to each of you. But understand, the Great Cosmic Law at this time will not allow the Ascended Masters to step through the atmosphere—and lower their vibrations—so that you can see them. The Higher Laws will not allow them to do this, and they will never disobey the Law.

In former ages, three times the Ascended Masters have come; three times they have reminded humanity of the purpose of life. They remained for up to eight, nine hundred years, teaching, improving life. Two Golden Ages that even surpassed what humanity is presently experiencing, was the result of the Masters walking with Humanity in former times. Then, under Cosmic Law, Dear Hearts, the Ascended Masters would have to leave the Earth, to see what human beings would do with the knowledge that had been given them.

After a period of time the light would began to diminish, and human beings would go back to their old belief systems. And so the Great Cosmic Law has spoken, "No more!—You will not walk amongst them again until a portion of humanity, literally of their own will, begin to raise themselves into their own Christ Consciousness. You can give them help but you must remain invisible; unless the desire to see their own Great God Presence is so great, that you can reveal yourselves to them."

Desire to see your own Beloved Presence first

Many of you desire to see an Angel or one of the Ascended Masters. I have suggested ways, techniques, that you can practice, but the greater truth is—unless you desire to see your own Beloved Presence first, an Ascended Master or Angel cannot appear to you in the physical.

That means we are not speaking of vision, we are not speaking of a phenomenon—we are speaking of a place where assistance has been given and your physical sight is raised, your eyes are opened, and you see the Master, you see the Angel standing in front of you. This cannot be done unless you have held within this life—or you are on record of having held within *another* life—the desire to see your own Beloved Higher Self; to see your own Beloved Angel, the Guardian Presence, that stands above you.

So, desire to *see* that Presence. Desire that the Angels come to you and purify the atmosphere between you and your Presence. Desire that the Angels blaze their Sacred Fire Love through the brain, through the sight. Desire that Rays of Light penetrate the brain, so that you can be caused to see your Great God Presence. Once you have seen your Higher Self, the role of Dispensations—the role of Cosmic intervention, the role of Cosmic assistance to you—completely changes. It is almost without limit, the assistance that the Angelic Host and the Ascended Host can give you. Isn't that something?

It is impossible for discord to connect with you without your attention

And so if that is the truth—and it *is* the truth—then, "What do I do with it? Where do I start with these things?" The answer is always *desire*. Be Olympian with your desires! Never give up! Review them each day. Take some time. Know what your intentions are. That is why I referred to the renewal of attention and intention; keep your intentions fresh.

What are your desires? It is not that your attention has to be held on your desires all the time, because you want to let that go and let it manifest; but you do want to energize those things once or twice a day. "What is my intention? What are my desires?—Oh, yes, well, I desire to see and know my Beloved Higher Self as quickly as possible. I desire to have the Sacred Fire Love of the Angels blazing through my being and world to help me purify and harmonize my outer self. I desire to rein in my mind so that I learn to control my attention."

Why is it so important to control your attention? Well, Dear Heart, I will give you this in light of what is taking place on your Earth. And this is truth, although many will find it a stretch—it is impossible for discord to connect with you without your attention. And if your attention is not held upon discord, it cannot connect with you. Some of you may feel that I have been repetitious in this matter of the power of your attention; I say you haven't seen anything yet, because it is the greatest gift.

Contemplate often, "This is where my power is. Now my heart is open. Now I am awakened. Now I am a Student of Light. Where is my power? My power flows through what I allow my thoughts and feelings to be held upon, what I am giving my attention to. Because now I know, even though my eyes are not yet trained to see energy, I know that my energy goes to anything that I am holding my attention upon; whether it is something that I am holding my attention upon in my mind, in my feelings, in my body; or whether I am holding my attention on something out there in the world."

You have to re-train the mind—what is my Vision...my Field of Dreams...my Spiritual road map?

You have to re-train the mind; re-focus the mind. Because you see, Beloved, you cannot go from the old age, the darkness, and into the Seventh Golden Age, and live as a Seventh Golden Age Being—fully awakened—and continue the old thought processes. The way you reference and associate things in your mind, the way you focus your intentions and attention, you cannot take that old way into a new Seventh Golden Age individual that you are destined to be—you have to reshape how you use your mind.

And so, a little bit of exercise will help you to do this. And the exercise that I feel that perhaps is best to use in getting such mastery in your mind is—having a *clear mind*. When you have a clear mind, you have intentions that are clothed with your feeling body; and the clothing of that magnetic energy upon your thought forms is the first stage of manifestation. The idea is to have right thoughts; the idea is to have inspiring thoughts. And that is why I encourage each of you, 'What is your vision?'

Have you written a Vision Statement for your life? "What is my vision for my life? What is my vision for the Earth?" And I invite you to follow through on that Vision Statement which could be simply a letter, a covenant, that you write to yourselves and that you would follow that Vision Statement with a Field of Dreams; that you would give yourself some time to realize, "What is it that I want to manifest in my life; what is it that I want to create; what is it that I want to experience?" That would not be based on how much education you have; that would not be based upon what the intellect thinks is possible for you but really, what is *my* Field of Dreams.

And then I encourage you to create a third thing— a Spiritual Road Map. Perhaps consider creating a Spiritual Road Map that could take you to the year 2014 or later—a Seven Year Spiritual Road Map that includes many of the means and the ways that you are going to achieve your vision and your Field of Dreams. What is that Spiritual Road Map, what is on your Tree of Life? What are the tools, what are the applications that you are going to use to accomplish your vision and to bring into manifestation your Field of Dreams? I say to you, Dear Heart, this is an excellent Threefold process for yourself.

Write a Vision Statement for your life and the World.
Write your Field of Dreams.
Create your Spiritual Road Map.

And I encourage you to do all of this with passion. What do you want to manifest, what do you want to create? Include relationship, include money and supply, include career, and health in the body. If you want to change the aging process, write *that* in your Field of Dreams. Or become an artist and create a beautiful portrait or a chart.

Then do your Spiritual Road Map. "What kinds of things can I do to guarantee that I am living my vision, my Higher Purpose; that I am creating and manifesting my Field of Dreams? What kinds of things can I put in my Spiritual Road Map that gets me there?—I can start to meditate each day upon the Inner Presence within. I can remind myself that I need to renew, that I need to learn to master my mind; stay in my Heart. I know that I can begin to appeal to my own Great God Presence, that I can invite Angels to walk with me each day. I can do these things and it doesn't have to be hours and hours each day, but perhaps fifteen minutes each day. This is where I will gain my momentum." And then will be the unfoldment.

Start training your mind to visualize the Higher Self of those that you interact with each day

I will offer you another exercise—begin to imagine the Golden Light of the Higher Self standing above those whom you are compelled to deal with each day. Imagine seeing the Golden Light of the Higher Self, even though the Higher Self may be hundreds of feet away or twelve feet away, it doesn't matter. Just start seeing the light of the Higher Self about five to ten feet above the human form. Stop dealing with the outer selves; stop dealing with *personalities*.

Now this is not so important, Dear Hearts, with each of you, and with the student body of awakening souls throughout the world, because most of you are doing constructive things. Yet, if you want to help, if one of you turns to another and says, "You know, this is an area that I am having a problem with." Well, the other can start seeing your Higher Self standing above you, and call upon that Higher Self to come into this condition that you have spoken of and correct that condition. But I am speaking mostly of the people out in the world, the world that you have to interface with; the people that you connect with at work, the people that you see on the bus, or the people even that you interact with in a very close way, in a daily way—lovers, companions, children. For the people that most need this blessing, are the people who do not have this knowledge.

Start training your mind to visualize the Golden Light of the Higher Self of those that you interact with each day. Now you know that your Higher Self is a Being of absolute perfection. It is not so important that you visualize the absolute details of the Higher Self; rather you can simply visualize a sphere of golden light above the person or even around the person. Hold your attention upon that Higher Self, and command the Higher Self come forth into the individual and correct every condition; you do not even have to name the conditions. You have no idea how the Presence of that person is going to thank you!

You might ask, "Well, why won't the Presence just come in?" Dear Hearts, if the Presence could just come in and correct every condition in a person's life, you would not have the chaos, you would not have the insanity, you would not have the wars, you would not have the destruction that is in the world. The Presence does not come into individuals because the Presence is not even recognized as existing. And if you do not recognize that you have a Presence, there is certainly not going to be any invitation, and the Presence cannot come into your outer self—your own Higher Self cannot come into your body unless it is invited!

Although two-thirds of you is already Ascended—the Authority for Life is at the point at which you *experience* consciousness. You are not experiencing consciousness in your Christ Self, you are not experiencing consciousness in the Electronic Presence of your Higher Self—you are experiencing consciousness in your physical life. That is a Universal Law—the authority for life is where you experience consciousness. So even though two-thirds of you is Ascended, a Perfect Being capable of producing nothing but perfection, that two-thirds aspect of you has no authority to express in the outer self unless you begin inviting it to.

These are not difficult things. This is not so advanced that the mind cannot grasp it. It is just a matter of retraining the mind. It is a matter of exercising the mind. It is a matter of remembering these higher truths. "Oh, yes, if I want more of the light, more of the love, more of the joy, more of the perfection, more of the happiness of my Higher Self... oh, yes, what did I not do today? I didn't invite it to come and express through this outer self. I didn't acknowledge it as the God of my Being, a Being of great Perfection."

What is your Presence doing?

You might ask, "Well, is my Higher Self just up there twiddling its thumbs?" Absolutely not! Your Higher Self—and this is difficult for the intellect to yet grasp—your Higher Self, is generally around seven to fourteen feet above your physical forms, and yet, your Higher Self exists only in a Realm of Perfection and Endless Light, creating many activities of perfection for the universe. That is why, Dear Hearts, it is truth to say—there is only one place, one space, one now. To try to grasp this concept, you can think of a paper cup where you can have five or six of them stacked inside each other, so that they are all occupying the same space, yet each one existing a little higher than the other. Yes? Indeed!

In truth and as one transcends time and space, there is only one place and that place is *here and now*, however there are many Dimensional Realities that are occupying

70

the same space. You do not tune into those realities; you do not find the gateways into those higher realities until you shift the vibration of your mind to the vibration of that Realm of Light that you wish to connect to. And since there is not enough light in the human brain and mind—even though you have the knowledge now—the brain does not turn on the power sufficiently for you to connect with those realities.

So, even though the Presence of your Higher Self is in a Realm of Absolute Perfection, yet it is only twelve to fifteen feet above you. And what is your Presence doing? It is waiting for its ascending physical body so that it can enter anywhere in the physical Universe. Right now your own Beloved Presence exists more in the Electronic Realms of Light. And from these Great Realms of Light, from the Inner Planes, it participates with Ascended Beings of Light such as Helios and Vesta of your Earth's Sun. It participates with the Great Central Sun in the maintenance of light to this System of Worlds. Or it might even start participating in the building of the Inner Levels of other Systems of Worlds. But it cannot come into the outer physical atomic world—it must work at the Inner Planes of Light because the outer world requires a physical body. It is still waiting for its physical body, the ascension of your embodiment on earth which closes all embodiments in the limiting physical world.

It is impossible for anyone to battle you if you are visualizing the Higher Self

That is why we are entering a very, very important time. I could speak to you probably a thousand days on the blessings that would come to you if you would begin to train yourselves to start seeing the Higher Selves of human beings that you are compelled to work with. Now you can just imagine a perfect Being of great golden light standing above the human self and that will be fine. Your world has the potential of entering into another war, and unless the will of humanity changes a few degrees to avoid this, the men and women of your nation and other nations of the world are compelled back into war.

And I say to you, Dear Heart, not only do you have the power of prayer, it is just as powerful to take a moment and visualize the hundreds of thousands of women and men who are compelled to go to war, to fight on behalf of whatever cause, and visualize above those hundreds of thousands of those in your armed forces, hundreds of thousands of Beings of Light. Just see the Beings of Light and see the Light Ray. See the Beings of Light twelve to fifteen feet above the form. Just visualize them in beautiful golden garments with a beautiful halo; and then visualize all the beautiful Golden Light Rays coming down through the Lifestream into the outer self, down into the crown of the heads and into and out from the heart centre of all these men and women. Just see it. Just practice that in your mind or create some visualization in your mind of seeing the Higher Selves of others. Imagine you are in a theatre, looking at everyone seated. Imagine all the Light Rays rising up from each person, and all the beautiful, Perfect Higher Selves standing above each one.

Now your attention is upon the Higher Self and it is not upon the outer self. Because your attention is upon the Higher Self, you draw to you the qualities and the blessings of the Higher Selves of those individuals, rather than drawing to you the *personality* energy of their outer selves. And especially with what seems to be happening in your world, if every human being on this Earth would take five minutes to visualize the armed forces, and all those who unfortunately are compelled to war, and see the Higher Selves of each one, this could be a great blessing to them.

You would not even have to make a prayer call, you would not even have to ask for the protection of them—just your attention held upon the Higher Selves is an invocation to the Higher Selves to come forth. It is always just a good thing to qualify *why* you are holding the attention; to call upon the Higher Selves to bring *protection* to those men and women who are compelled to go to war.

But more specifically, Dear Heart, you are often compelled to enter into 'battling something' or compelled to confront other people's discord. Human beings are doing that almost every day. And I say why should you? You are Students of the Light. You have *chosen* the light. Why should you entertain something that is a discordant condition that is the great destroyer of Life? You can go into any courtroom any day if you want to see human beings battling each other. You can go into the wrong place at the wrong time and see the viciousness, the discord, and the arguments in which human beings are going at each other. You are making choices that are harmonious and constructive for yourselves, and this is why I say, you do not have to do this so much with yourselves unless you want to help each other with something specific. It is this condition of human beings battling each other *out there*. And if you take time to train your imagination to see the Higher Selves above the personality selves; this stops the personality from expressing through them. It is impossible for anyone to battle you if you have created the habit and gained the momentum of visualizing the Higher Self.

Oftentimes, when you are required to lobby individuals, you are coming up against the personality self, and this is where the resistance is. If you really want to get cooperation, whether it is from governments, corporations, families or whoever, whether you have important meetings or you are meeting investors, if you want cooperation—because you have a good and constructive idea—then before those meetings take place, in the morning before you go out into the world, visualize the Higher Selves blazing its golden light of love in and around those individuals. Because for any good and constructive idea, there is only *one* 'I AM'. And the 'I AM', the Higher Self of those individuals, will be in agreement with you.

So, you take a moment. You know you have a board meeting today, you have a number of individuals to meet, and you just take that moment. "At one o'clock today I have a very important meeting and, yes, I am going to be meeting two, three people. So let's just imagine those people in that room... Oh, yes, there are the three beautiful Higher Selves that are above these individuals, and I am connecting to the Higher Selves of these individuals to come forth in this meeting. I give all power to the Higher Selves, which are always in agreement with each other..." The Higher Selves never differ from each other. What every Higher Self wants—every good idea, every constructive idea—is your own Higher Self expressing through you, Dear Hearts. So take that moment. Connect with the Higher Selves.

Oftentimes human beings are trying to impose the Light on a *human* concept

There are stories written by the thousands, of individuals who suddenly, under a compelling activity, changed their mind—were going in one direction and then changed their mind. Your world is filled with thousands of stories such as this, and oftentimes, it was not the Higher Self but an Angel that stood in the atmosphere of that room, and the *Angel* compelled that person—"Well, what are you going to do? What decision?"

You cannot *impose* the light on a *human* concept, like the tragic marriages and divorces of the human race. You do not have marriages and divorces in the Great Realms of Light. When you find your Twin Flame you do not have to marry your Twin Flame, because your Twin Flame is the other half of you. So you do not have these marriages and divorces in the Great Realms of Light, because you are already married. You can't get away from her, or him. And you do not want to get away from your Twin Flame. So this condition called marriage and divorce, this is a human concept. And oftentimes human beings are trying to impose the *light* on a human concept.

Or human beings will argue, human beings will march, human beings will go to Congress and Parliament. The whole issue that took place years ago—the issues of womanhood, motherhood and abortion—this is all going to come up again and again, over the next years. And that is tragic, because what are individuals doing?—They are applying a man-created morality, according to their religious views, upon a very important subject.

That is like taking the Light of God and saying, "This is my man-made concept and I want that light applied to that concept." And the Ascended Masters just do not do it. They will not do it. Because if an individual is living according to the great love and the 'I AM' of their Presence, problems disappear. These things just do not happen when the light and divine love in perfect balance are expressing. And when they do happen, there is no judgment from the spiritual hierarchy, no judgment at all. If an individual invokes the light *within oneself* anything can be changed and transmuted.

All I am saying, Dear Hearts, is, that human beings will battle each other, and they will even bring religious beliefs into what is right or wrong, and go head to head. Why should you do this? Why should you not start appealing to the Higher Selves instead? It just takes a little bit of practice.

So, how are you going to remember this? Perhaps you are going to go to your local office store and get those little yellow notes, and you are going to put them somewhere to remind you. If you have a diary on the desk, put that little note down, "Did I visualize the Higher Selves of others today? Did I take that time? Did I visualize the God Presence of others? Did I take time to do that three times today?" Don't try to do it all day long, or for hours. Start with a little. Say, two or three minutes, four or five times a day. Sometimes you are moving from one place to another and you are not the operator of the vehicle; so you are sitting back, very casually, in your seat, in your airplane or your bus, and you are reading a good book. Well, perhaps a more useful use of your time and energy might be just to sit back and visualize the Higher Selves above everyone in that airplane. Just visualize the Higher Self of each one. You want safety of an airplane?—that would get you safety!

The Higher Self will project sufficient Sacred Fire Love to correct a condition

So where is your attention? When your attention is on the greater, the greater comes into your life. That's it!— When your attention is on the *greater*, the greater comes into your life; when your attention is on the *littleness* of life, the littleness finds expression through you. Remember, Dear Hearts, what you place your attention upon will find expression through you. So, start with a little practice. Make a commitment of a few minutes several times a day, to keep visualizing. Close your physical eyes, use your imagination, visualize it. Ask your Presence to help you. Ask your Presence that every time you start imagining the Higher Selves of others, to help you to get that imagination, to get that feeling. Don't try to do anything anymore without going to your Presence and saying, "Now, help me

76

with this." And remember, once you have poured your love to your Presence then you can ask others of the Ascended Host to help you too, such as Akasha & Asun, "Come in and help me with this. Help me to visualize. Help me to remember to see the Higher Selves, the Light of God in and above others."

It only takes one individual in physical reality to hold the attention upon the Presence of another. Because there is only *one* of you here this is an automatic will. It is automatic authority. It is an automatic invitation. This is why the Presence doesn't come forth unless it is invited. You must use your free will and I am sure you will love the results.

Now, let's increase light and love's presence, let's raise the energy here, "I hold the attention upon the Beloved Electronic Presence of this person—let's call him John—and I call upon that Mighty Presence to come forth into John, to come forth and to correct everything in his life. I know no truth about anything that is limiting John's life. I only know the Great God Presence within him and above him. Once I have done this, I might see this beautiful Presence of Life descending down and standing right in front of John. So now I do not see John, I just see this glorious Being of Light standing in front of John. And then I see that Being of Light backing in to the space John's body occupies. And so you see, I am connecting with the Lord God 'I AM' of his being. And I am in full alignment with the Cosmic Law. I have not connected with anything in John's *personality*, I have not connected with anything that is going on in his world—I have connected to his Ascended Self, and I have called his Ascended Self to come forth into this physical body."

The Higher Self is not going to come fully in, but the Higher Self will project sufficient light; the Higher Self will project sufficient Sacred Fire Love and Purity to correct the condition that is going on in the individual, or project enough Sacred Fire or Light to create for the individual what you want for them as long as it is good, right and constructive. You are not interfering with another individual, if what you desire for them is what their Great God Presence wants for them—which is perfection. I feel that with years of this work, Dear Heart, you know, you have studied metaphysics, you know now that you can have everything in life. Life, when it is fulfilled, is not barren. Life is not without relationship. Life is not without beauty, Life is not without home. Life is not without money, resources—Life is abundant!

The correction of old erroneous belief systems

So you already know. You have corrected old thoughts of lost will. You have corrected old belief systems that to be spiritual is to be poor, to be spiritual is to renounce the world. That was a long time ago, and that was a *phase* to get you disconnected from the attention you gave to the world, that was held for so many thousands of years; that in being so connected to the world, your Inner Light diminished because your attention wasn't upon it. So for centuries of time there were mystics who came to the world, inviting you to renounce the world, to get your attention away from that, and to turn back within, so that you would be re-empowered by growing your inner light.

Never was it suggested for you to be outside of this world, or that materialism was bad. The world is *here*, you are here to prove God. You are here to prove that God loves to fulfill itself; that God loves to glorify its creation. And in a physical world, that glorification takes place when you have a life that is evident of fulfillment, with great Perfection; you live in beautiful homes, you have wonderful garments to wear, you have all the money and supply that you could ever require or desire in your life; you have all the opportunities; you have great joy, great relationships and harmony, and a great healing taking place.

So I am hoping that you are with me on this one and that you are not buying into the belief that Spirituality must yet consist of renouncing the world; that you must yet go through some barrenness or through some state of poverty. Because it is not truth, that belief gave you a *temporal* God experience. But you are not signing up for a temporal God experience; you are signing up to fully awaken to your God Being and fulfill your Divine Potential. This world was given to you to demonstrate 'I AM'. And as you remember and start to express your 'I AM' Presence, you can use thought, feeling, intention and attention, choice and decision to qualify energy, to clothe energy; to cause energy to manifest in your world as you so desire it, especially in the area of money and supply, health, healing and relationships.

Human beings created a very conscious experiment—to learn all that you are...and to learn all that you are *not*

To further encourage you to begin to master your mind; to see the Higher Selves of others, I will go on record here that these two areas—healing and supply—will be two areas that will be corrected first in your lives. Call forth the Higher Selves of others into every condition in their lives. Call forth the Higher Selves of others to come forth so that those others will assist you in your projects. Then, Dear Heart, what will begin to show up in transformation, opportunity and change, will be in the area of healing on all levels of being, and in the area of money and supply. So, those are the first two areas that you will start receiving some blessing back into life, because the holding of your attention upon someone's Higher Self is an invitation to that Presence to express through that Self, rather than the outer personality self that is yet engulfed in a belief in two powers.

There have never been two powers except the appearances in your world make you believe it is so. It is just that human beings have taken their Energy—taken the *one* Life Stream that comes forth from their Presence and into their heart—and out of this one Life Stream have said, "We will take this Stream and we will create *two* Streams." But *God* did not do that. *You* used the God Life—One Life, One Presence, One Power—and because you were given free will, you said, "Now we will create two streams of consciousness, of belief—one stream will be good, one stream will be bad, one stream will be *negative* polarity, one Stream will be *positive* polarity. And through these two streams of polarity and duality, we are going to learn all that we are, but we are also going to learn all that we are *not*. This will bring us back to the One Stream, because when we come back into the One Stream, we will experience our mastery and this must include our physicality!"

It was a very conscious experiment; it was a very conscious decision. So when you are appealing to the Higher Self, this is an invitation to the Higher Self to come into expression. And will it not thank you? Will it not bless you? Will it not be so grateful? For it has been waiting for its physical garment. It has been waiting for centuries— thousands—millions of years. The invitation means that the Higher Self of that individual can start releasing Rays of Light into the brain through the great Shaft of Light that comes through the Life Force. And the individual who could not in a former moment see the benefit of something; could not perceive the cause and why they should assist; in a moment, the person has a change of heart!

What happens is that the Higher Mental Body sends forth tiny, tiny Rays of Light into the brain—which is the hardware interfacing with the software, which is the mind. Now, those tiny Rays of Light pierce through; and remember, the light contains the threefold activity of Love, Wisdom and the Power of the Presence. So as that light penetrates through the hardware system of the brain, and enters into the cavity of the mind, the software of the mind receives that impulse; the wisdom within that light is a sudden emergence, in which that person has an inner knowing that they are intended to support you, or join you in a project. Isn't that wonderful?

Will you be Olympian?

The magic here, the magic is getting past the three week mark. Your Christ Self is always watching you, it will not join you until you make greater effort—it simply provides you with the Life Force. You have free will to do with its Life Force what you desire. So, when *does* your Higher Christ Self join you; and your cause is so worthy that It actually will increase the Life Force?—Where you are now in your evolution I would say about a twenty-two day mark; twenty-two days of actually exercising your mind, and actually making yourself see what we have been speaking of.

Your Higher Mental Body, your Christ Self, must discern, "Now will this just be something that my outer self is going to try for three, four days and then let it go?" Remember, the Higher Mind—your Higher Intelligence— is your Discerning Intelligence; so one of the first things that it desires to do, is to discern if this wonderful thing that you are now trying is something that you are going to maintain.

Will you be Olympian? Will you try it every day; or after five, six days, will you be like most human beings and say, 'Oh, this isn't working.' Will the pressure of the world convince you that things 'out there' need to be taken care of first? As long as things 'out there' need to be taken care of first, you are missing the point. When you train yourself, "No, the Inner Work is what produces the outer"—That is when you will see the results!

Welcome to the Greatest Power in the Universe, the 'I AM' of YOU!

Namaste, Beloved of the Heart.

CHAPTER *T*WO

I Am Akasha and I greet you out of the Diamond Heart of My Love and the Love of the Divine Mother.

The Great and Mighty 'I AM' Presence in the Great Central Sun—the Heavenly Mother and the Heavenly Father—are truly the Cosmic parents, if you will, of your own Great God Presence. They are the Cosmic parents of each of you. The first thing that I wish to bring to your attention is that those who are the Supreme Creators of your universe that your System of Worlds belongs to, invite each of you to accept that the Archangel Michael is their First Son of the First Ray of their Twelve Rays that govern their universe.

A Message of the Divine Mother

I bring to you a message of the Divine Mother, that Her children of light upon the Earth find greater acceptance within the divine representation of Her Presence in the human form. And you know what that divine representation in the human form is, Dear Hearts—it is your heart and feelings, the Divine Feminine.

Her Message is that within each of your feelings there may be a greater acceptance within your feeling side of life— the Divine Feminine—of her Son the Archangel Michael; who holds all the qualities of the First Ray that governs your developing universe. And as you find acceptance of this Great and Mighty Being of Light and of Love, then this opens the way for His authority and His freedom to come forth into your own lives. I would like you to consider opening your feelings to this acknowledgement, that just as yourselves are children of light, that the Archangel Michael is one of the First Born among angelic souls, and he is of the First Ray who offers his authority to those of humanity who seek to assist the civilization of Earth and freedom at this time.

I offer you here a letter written in the Living Fire of the Language of Light, a letter written directly from the Archangel Michael, which I wish to reveal to each of you.

Divine Desires! To live your Higher Purpose—Your passion! Your calling!

Archangel Michael's Letter

Beloved of the Light, Beloved Friends of Akasha & Asun, and their Dispensation—Soul Journey: I greet you from out of the Flaming Heart of my own Cosmic Blue Flame, and I come to you under that authority. As I join the Great and Mighty Saint Germain of The Violet Ray in his quest for greater association with each of you, I come to you that you might find the freedom that is found within the heart of your own Great God Presence. It will bring you into the Full Higher Purpose lived, the Divine Plan of your own lives fulfilled and makes you a Living Instrument that those of the Spiritual Hierarchy might use in the most wondrous way, to do for the world which it requires at this time. I greet you.

You know, Beloved of the Heart, it seems that the Spiritual Hierarchy, even to the Students of Light at this time, is of such great distance away. Yet in the great truth that is found in my Ray, the First Ray, is the truth that is well worth contemplation at any time—and that is the Truth of the Oneness, the Unity of Life that is found in One Life, One Flame, One Consciousness, one Fire Element, One Time and One Space. And it is because of that greater unity that we know and experience—and that we are all authority of—that we can come to you in many ways. Whether we stand in the midst of you on Earth; whether we stand in the very atmosphere of a gathering or whether we project the likeness of our Beings, it makes no difference as to the quality that we wish to bring forth and the assistance we can bring you in your lives.

If we have the *will* of human beings, there is not one humanly created evil that we cannot silence

You have before you a wonderful Cosmic Journey, towards greater Light and Freedom on Earth. You have chartered yourselves through murky waters and you are moving yourself towards a Stream of Life; a stream in which I, Michael, will join you in the rowing of your boat, if you will, and will add to you all that is required in your freedom.

I do not know if you have considered it, Dear Heart, but those students of the Mighty 'I AM' Presence who have come under an understanding of the existence of the great Angelic Host, the Ascended Host, and a Divine Plan for the Earth and humanity itself—*you* are the only ones we can use for the freedom of the Earth. You—and to perhaps a lesser degree those human beings who do not have this knowledge but are living constructive lives to the best of their ability—you are the only ones who are willingly, and of your own volition, turning your attention to an understanding of self, of life; seeking that which raises you out of the discord that has almost destroyed this Earth and humanity three times. It is only because we have *you* who are aware of our Presence, Dear Hearts—which is yet a very small portion of the greater numbers of humanity—that we can assist humanity at this time. It seems that the Angelic Host are yet an unreality to most human beings on this Earth. Yet I say to you, Dear Heart, if we have the *will* of human beings, if we have the desire of human beings, then there is not one humanly created evil in your world that we cannot cause its absolute silencing and annihilation!

If I am called forth with enough desire, I can walk into the atmosphere of any city and my own Light would forbid any evil taking place

There are very important events that are unfolding in your world. Always, behind the scenes, we have watched with great patience—because the Cosmic Law demands it—those who meet in conference rooms in great offices, in governments, corporations, in the United Nations or the countries of the world. We have watched what takes place in many conference rooms, where those who are in positions of influence—governments, presidents, prime ministers—too often have made decisions that are against *life* itself.

Yet I say to you, Dear Heart, if I am loved enough, if I am desired enough, if I am called forth enough, I can walk into the atmosphere of any city that is having a conference where world leaders are gathered. I do not have to go anywhere near that conference room—I can just walk through the atmosphere in that city, and my own light would forbid any evil taking place in that conference room! Such is the power and the authority of the Sacred Fire Purity that I carry to the Earth under the Cosmic Blue Flame!

We cannot, under Cosmic Law, give more than is the present energy accumulation of those who desire us

So you see Dear Hearts, is not your world yet a testimony to the insufficient desire, the insufficient knowledge, the insufficient will of humanity, to rise beyond their own human desires, and to begin to desire of those who can be the correction of everything that is wrong in your world? And yet we cannot, under Cosmic Law, give more than is the present energy accumulation of those who desire us. There is not one prayer, one call, which is left unanswered under the Dispensations that the Spiritual Hierarchy has given. We have also collected—and the Legions of Angels have collected—the prayers and calls of those who do not know us but who are constructive.

Invite Us to correct the cause of conditions with Our Sacred Fire Purity and Power

You see, Dear Heart, when we are called upon and we know that if our help will change a condition in your life, we cannot help you if you go back to the same creation, or what causes those conditions. We are under Cosmic Law now. We cannot come in and heal you; we cannot come in and correct conditions in your world if we are not invited to correct that which is the *cause* of those conditions. And it is not just I; you can call upon your Beloved Mother of your world, or the great Cosmic Master of the Gold Flame, the Mighty Jesus the Christ, whose miracles are almost uncountable. You can call on many of us.

Too often, healing of bodies, healing of what is wrong in individuals' worlds, has been performed and yet the *cause* of those conditions has remained within those human selves because the Sacred Fire was not called forth to remove it. And now, under Cosmic Law, We are not

87

permitted to heal anyone unless you desire that the cause that created the condition is to be healed as well.

So you see, even though we have All Authority and All Power, yet we cannot demonstrate it in your world; we cannot give that power; we cannot offer that correction unless we are called forth and the desire for the removal of the cause of the condition is included in your prayers and in your calls.

My Angels gather the constructive and the dynamic calls, prayers, and decrees of students of the world

There is a Legion of my Angels—who are under the authority of the Cosmic Blue Flame Angels—who gather the constructive and the dynamic calls, prayers, and decrees, of students throughout the world. We take these calls and prayers up, and we take them to our great Octave of Light. We take them into my own Cathedral of Light in the City of Shambala—the Golden City in the great Realms of Light above the Sahara Desert. And there all of these prayer calls are taken in to my own Cosmic Blue Flame; where those calls are harmonized, purified, and multiplied millions upon millions of times.

And yet, Dear Heart, with all of that multiplication of the energy from those who turn to us for assistance, and know of us, it is only seventeen percent of the 'human will factor' that allows us to respond by a Cosmic Power or Authority that could correct conditions.

It is for this reason that you yet have chaos in this world. It is for this reason there exists a degree of humankind— and we estimate at this time about thirty-five percent of humanity—who literally want another war. Dear Hearts, if there are thirty-five percent of human beings who want war; they definitely do not want us. They definitely do not want their own Great God Presence. And it is because of these things, that we often, under Cosmic Law, are not given permission to stop the terrorism, to stop the destructive element that yet finds its way through the human expression.

Under the great Cosmic Cycle that is now governing your world, already tremendous intervention has been given, even where it has not been asked. And it is because, Dear Hearts, of you. It is because of you who have become aware of our Presence, accepted our Presence. Those of you who consciously know of us, work with us, call us in, are estimated between twenty-five and twenty-eight million on the Earth who apply, who turn their attention towards us. And then there are those others, twenty-three to twenty-five million, who are slightly aware of us and make *some* application.

The tragedy is that there is still so much of the human consciousness that is creating more and more mistakes; that oftentimes it is one step forward, two steps back, or two steps forward, one step back. We are not really able to use the energy of those who are 'kind of', 'sort of', looking to us or who most often look to us only when their lives have been filled with so much limitation that they are seeking that Cosmic Power to release themselves from that limitation.

When you call upon Our Sacred Fire Love

As I begin my letter to each of you, it is to salute you; it is to thank you with my own Blue Flame. To thank you, and to personally offer each of you an anchoring and a sustained expanded Action of my Cosmic Blue Flame, in, through, and around you. This gift offers a greater Harmonizing and Purifying Presence to your outer selves, that will allow the Liberty, the Freedom, Protection and the Perfection of your own God Presence 'I AM', to find its expression as the totality of all that you are; that the limited human consciousness simply fades away and you awaken to the Glory of the 'I AM' Divine Consciousness that each of you truly are.

This is the Gift that I offer each of you who are seeking in all ways to awaken yourselves; to harmonize your outer selves; to walk with the Angels; that you might be free. We offer you great Gifts, Dear Heart. These gifts—their ability to be an expanding and a formidable power in your lives— will require only your acceptance, your remembrance of them and your willingness to use that Sacred Fire Love of my own Heart's Flame that I offer each of you. In your prayer calls, command that Sacred Fire Flame into your lives and worlds as the *undoing* of all human accumulation that is of struggle and discord. Use that Blue Flame, Dear Heart, use that Cosmic Blue Flame and call it forth; command it to be a Protecting Action to all your manifestations!

Many of you have wonderful plans and you are moving into that Stream where you are living your Higher Purpose. But often yet, you are working on creations, manifestations, or projects, that do not have the sustained protection of my—or others of the Ascended Host—our Sacred Fire Love. And I wish you to understand that when you call upon our Sacred Fire Love around your homes, yourselves, your manifestations, and your projects we literally enfold that in a Sphere of our Sacred Fire Love. It stands between your manifestation and the vibratory action of human consciousness that is in the atmosphere. It keeps the vibratory action of the 'negative polarity' that is in your atmosphere from intruding upon yourselves, your loved ones, your projects or *anything* upon which you call the Sacred Fire Heart Love to come in and around your lives, your worlds, and your manifestations. You are yet to experience the Sacred Fire Purity and Love from the Angelic and Ascended Host, and when you do, you will realize you have opened your life and world to one of *The Greatest Powers in the Universe!*

I, Michael, Am in your memories

O Children of the Light, hear me well, for, I, Michael, am in your memories. Today you are advancing in the Mighty Indigo Soul's evolution. Many of you are preparing for your advancement into the Violet Soul. This is a tremendous open door to the *greater* powers of your own life coming forth into expression through all of you, Dear Heart. There have been many who have said this truth, but I shall repeat it to you because it has been spoken even by human beings, 'With great power comes great responsibility.'

And the greatest responsibility you have as Children of Light is to be willing to harmonize yourselves and purify your outer selves, that there may be no more obstacles to the light. Then the Glory, the Power, and the Perfection of the great God 'I AM' of your beings, comes forth into living love, living joy, living power and expression through your outer lives, awakening your brain, healing all the elements of your body out from limitation and into the authority of Divine Love, Consciousness and Will!

I say to you, even when I am in Counsel with the Spiritual Hierarchy on Saturn, yet your call to me through your own Heart Flame—with sincerity, with focus, with your attention—your Heart Flame sends forth its Ray of Light; and that Ray of Light comes to whomever that you place the attention upon. And if it is me, it matters not if I have returned to the Great Central Sun, it matters not if I have returned to my Seat on Saturn—I will receive your call. And it is upon a Ray of Light that comes to us in your call that *we* send back to you the qualities of what you most need to set your lives free.

We want you to telephone God more often...

Again I shall emphasize—you precious students of life who are awakening to the true glory of your lives are a sampling of the student body throughout the world through different paths and faiths, through different schools of higher thought and knowledge who have become aware of our existence; and to a lesser degree those who do not know us but are constructive to life, are the only ones where we can do through you what the world most requires at this time to be free of that which destroys life.

Do you understand now how much we depend on you for the freedom of all humanity? Not just humanity—we also depend on you for the freedom for the Powers of Nature and the Forces of the Elements; and the Earth and Her Divine Plan. And we depend on you for the freedom of the Divine Plan of your Higher Selves to come into full expression in this lifetime for each of you. Do you see how we depend on you for the freedom of the Mighty Saint Germain who is the authority for the Three Americas, for *His* Divine Plan to be fulfilled?

You are the only ones, Dear Heart. So we want you to come close to us. We want you, first of all, under Cosmic Law, to depend more upon your own Beloved Great God Presence. We want you—as we heard your own Beloved Akasha & Asun say to you recently—we want you to telephone God more often. We want you to call *us* more often in your prayers because you are the only ones that we can use to save the rest of humankind. And the numbers of you must grow.

How will those numbers of humanity, who are helping, grow?

How will those numbers grow, Dear Heart? Have you thought of that?—It is because the Radiation of your own Great God Presence, the Radiation of the Angelic Host and the Ascended Host has begun to form around you, and the great qualities of our Heart Flame has begun to express through you!

Each of us carry the Great Central Sun's Magnet's Presence; and if I am invited to do through you what your loved ones, your country, your humanity, the Powers of Nature, your world most requires at this time—then, Dear Hearts, I will project my Heart Flame up into the great Cosmic Gates in your Life Stream that are governed by your Christ Selves, your Higher Intelligence. And there your Higher Mental Bodies will open those gates, allowing our Cosmic Blue Flame into *your* Life Stream; where literally my Blue Flame will come down your Life Stream and join with your own Love Flame that is found within your Heart Centre. Then, Dear Heart, *My* Heart Flame is *one* with *your* Heart Flame.

Now my Flame can go out from you, carrying the Great Central Sun's Magnet's Presence; and through you I can do things in the world that the intellect is just unable to even perceive or even conceive at this time. I can do things that even you will be unaware of. And as this opportunity comes about—as my Flame joins your Flame and becomes a Magnet's Presence of the Divine Plan of Life that is pouring forth through you what the world most requires— then that must come back to you as a mighty blessing of life; and that blessing will seek to lift and raise you into the Divinity that you are, that you might find your freedom in this lifetime.

Will you care for it? Will you so thirst the desire for freedom in this lifetime, not the next lifetime, *this* lifetime? For I say to you—in the memory that is within each of you, you know me, the First Ray; because each of you began your evolution on this Earth on the First Ray of Light and Sound. Today you are in the Indigo and the Violet Soul. You have journeyed and graduated through the six Rays that have governed your Earth in the past. Today you are Indigo Souls evolving upon the Violet Ray that is governing your Earth. And you have an opportunity before you to *graduate* into the Violet Soul—for as Violet Souls, upon the Violet Ray that is now governing your Earth, there is nothing that can stop your freedom in this lifetime if you strongly desire it!

You might say, 'What am I going to do without my human desires?'

I promise you, Students of Light, I will not disappoint you if you call forth my Heart Flame. If you call upon me to appear in the atmosphere of your life, and to strike my Sword of Blue Flame into all the accumulation of the limited human consciousness that has created a density in your human lives, and all the accumulation that is in your outer world—I will strike my Sword of Blue Flame, and I will set your life free!

I will strike that Sword through the feeling side of your lives, so all that is of the negative polarity may be removed; so then the Divine Love that is found within the Feminine—the Feeling Side within each of you—may no longer be bridled, may no longer be parenthesized, may no longer be blanketed, so that love may come forth as the greatest support, the greatest foundation of life and love's manifestation!

This is a Mighty Dispensation. This is a very powerful Dispensation. And it cannot be given, under Cosmic Law, unless you hold the desire that 'I am through with limiting human desires'. Now some of you have questions upon this, and you say, "What am I going to do without my human desires?" Well, Dear Hearts, you will probably be free of all limitation! In the great passing of the human into the Divine, your human desires will not be *cut off* and be *replaced* with Divine Desires—that which is Divine Desire brings you into *heightened sensations of love* in all aspects of your life. There is no sacrifice. It is a very gentle journey.

It is a gentle journey that *embodies* the Holy Spirit

It is a gentle journey that embodies the Holy Spirit; to be considerate of all that has been of a human desire. And it is a journey that is ever so gentle, that *evolves* your desires; so that certain things that you had as human beings—of interests and desires—simply fade away and they are not there any longer. And in their place are the Divine Desires of your own Great God Presence. They are not desires that are *out* of this world, they are desires waiting to be fulfilled *in* this world. For you have come into this world to find yourselves, you have come into this world to illumine your physical bodies and to rise back up into the Spiritual Body of your Mighty 'I AM' selves.

So you see, Dear Hearts, to be free of the limiting human desire is to be free of that which is the polarity of negative and positive, for you have lived this journey for a very long time and it has served you extremely well. This offering is not available to everyone. There is not more than a fraction of humanity that this Dispensation could even yet be offered to at the moment; for that which is the human desire is still a road of experience, a world of evolution, a world of lessons in which individuals are learning about themselves the hard way. This could change if their desire for freedom was great enough.

The Great Book of Names in Archangel Michael's Cathedral of Light

Each of you have made a powerful choice; all of you who are making a choice to become awakened and whole again, and this includes those who are aware of us in different schools of enlightenment. In my Great Cathedral of light, the Archangel's Cathedral, which your Beloved Akasha has spoken to you of, this is where the Great Book of Names exists. And those whose names are in these Great Books, Dear Hearts, are those who have sought the light, who have sought to stay close to the light; those who have registered attainment in the soul, the feeling body, and the great causal body of the 'I AM' Presence. And when that seeking of truth and light has gained an attainment and momentum, the names of those souls are written in the Archangel's Cathedral. And when your name is recorded in those books, it demands an extraordinary and wonderful amount of assistance be afforded each of you in your physical lives.

Even if your names are in those books, you might yet be under the temporary veil. You might not yet remember that attainment—but the attainment is there! And it is *because* that attainment is there, Blessed of the Heart, that you have literally come into that place where you desire your freedom; you desire your ascent back up into, what I call, your normal Higher Consciousness. Or what the Mighty Saint Germain and your Beloved Akasha have addressed as—your Christ Consciousness. That is your real Inner Desire. And *human* desire is not of Christ Consciousness. Human desire must entertain the polarity in this world, to identify the truth of your being; for it is the polarity that you have been born into. You are graduates from the human school now, Dear Hearts, and you have entered into the Great Mystery Schools of Life. The Greater Knowledge of Life must be given to each of you so that you might find application of that knowledge in your own lives.

It is for this reason, that each of you, within your prayers, your meditations, might contemplate and might remember to hold within yourself "Lord of Life, I hold within myself this day but one desire, and that is to be free of the limiting human desire and to be filled with Divine Desire. I desire but that which my Beloved Great God Presence desires to do through this outer self. I desire only that which my Beloved 'I AM' wishes to do for this outer self, and I desire that my world be that Cosmic landscape of all that my Great God Presence desires to manifest its great love and life into my world. Let me feel only this, Mighty Presence of Life. Beloved Archangel Michael, sweep your Cosmic Blue Flame through my being and world, and take out all desires that limit me, that I may know only the desire for Divine Desires expressing through this outer self..."

My Angels of the First Ray place that Cosmic Blue Flame around all constructive manifestation

Fear not, Dear Heart. You will not have your desires taken from you. You will find your desires will move through phases, will go through heightened states. You will find yourself coming into a new awareness of desiring, of feeling, with greater passion. You will find my First Ray over-lighting you, bringing forth that Ray of Initiative, of Initiation, of new beginnings, new feelings, new desires, new ideas, ready to come forth through each of you.

You will find that anything that is in your world that is of excellence, anything that is in your world of great

97

perfection—whether it is in the architecture, whether it is in the world of art and the great, great, paintings of the Renaissance; whether it is in the world of music, the world of engineering, the world of modern communication—here is the excellence of civilization, the civilized mind. And there is not anything constructive that has come forth in the modernization of your world that has not had one of my Angels of the First Ray, placing that Cosmic Blue Flame around that manifestation, around that creation, that it may have the protection that it requires and that it deserves.

There is yet that which is in your world, Dear Hearts, which for centuries of time has had the perfection and the protection of Our Cosmic Blue Flame. Back in the days of Armageddon—when your human race so desired another world war that came forth in 1914 and again in 1939—our Legions of Angels went to work to identify the Holy Shrines of the temples, those sanctuaries on your Earth of all the major religions. We went into consideration of all the ancient architecture in your world. We considered some of the ancient palaces and states of government houses, whether in England, France or whether in Mother Russia, and gave these our protection where it was possible to do so.

All over the world, we sent forth our Legions of Angels, and we sealed those 'sites', if you will, that the All Seeing Eye of the Elohim Cyclopea revealed to be most important to the future of humanity and the history of the human race. And it is only for that reason that those sites in Russia, in England and in France and other places, that those sites did not go down in the horrific bombing of those two world wars. And I say to you, Dear Hearts, *that* is a Cosmic demonstration of what my Legions of Angels can do when we enfold Our Sacred Fire Love Protection from our Octave into anything that has been created in your world!

It is not just structures that we protected. Many great paintings and many ancient manuscripts came under our Sacred Fire Love in which we held back the vibratory action projected by the destruction of war and the discord that was sown in the past. And I say to you, Dear Heart, this is what we desire. We desire a greater open door to your world that we might come forth with Our Sacred Fire Love from our Octave of Life. We desire to protect everything that is good and everything that is constructive in your worlds from that which is the destruction that is yet being unleashed by some of humanity, and will be unleashed, because there is not *enough* of our Angelic Host in your world.

So will you do it? This connects back in my Living Letters of Light to you—that we depend on you. We depend on this tiny portion of humanity to receive your will, to receive your prayers, to receive your call. Put us to work, great, great Children of Life, because we do not require the sleep that you do. Yes, we enter into the Great Central Sun. Yes, we enter into Sacred Sites where we drink the Waters of Life that sustain the Sacred Heart Flame within each of us. But we do not rest!

Even when we go into the Great Central Sun to be reinvigorated with the Mother and Father's Flame we send forth projections of our likeness throughout the world. We sustain the action of our world while we are visiting with the Seven Mighty Elohim, while we are visiting with our Brothers and the Great Goddesses, our Sisters, and our own Twin Flames—we never leave our work unattended, Dear Heart.

Call upon the total accumulation of all your good to now come forth into expression through you

There is much that is yet to unfold in your world—in your personal lives, in your business affairs, in your families, your loved ones, in your upcoming futures—in the fulfillment of your own Higher Purposes, and to the Divine Plan that is yet awaiting fulfillment in your lives. Freedom must come to the Powers of Nature and the Forces of the Elements, to the world, and to all humanity that is constructive and we are yet waiting greater calls, greater desire—the Command, for that freedom!

Call upon the accumulation of all your prayers, all your decrees, of all your meditations, the great accumulation that is on record, not only in this life but in every life you have ever lived, for this, Dear Heart, is why you have an Etheric body. It is that body that is unseen to you that remembers all your efforts towards God, Life, Love and Liberty. Liberty, too, is of My Ray.

Call upon the total accumulation of all your good, of all your prayers, of all your meditations, of all your calls to God to now come forth into expression through you. Ask that the prayer, you are now about to give forth, be equal to one billion people giving that call. And then turn to us—turn to your Presence first, and love and bless your Presence, then to us—and call upon Michael; call upon my Legions, call upon the Angels of the Cosmic Blue Flame, call upon the Angels of the Cosmic Christ Blue Lightning, and call upon the Angels of Cosmic Illumination, Legions upon Legions of these Angels to descend into your world and the world to protect yourselves; to protect your lives, your loved ones, and everything that is good and constructive—your projects, the unfolding of your Higher Purpose, the unfolding of the Divine Plan of your lives; to protect that which is constructive within humanity, to protect everything that is good in this world. Call upon us to enfold all of that in Our Sacred Fire Love from Our great Octave of Light...and just see what we will do!

Command us! Command me! I only need the will of a certain amount of humanity, and I say to you that all of you—if you are of *one Will, one Heart and one Desire*—can become a Commanding Presence; *demanding* that I stand in the atmosphere of your Crystal City of Vancouver, New York, Paris, Cairo or any city, for the removal of that which is discordant; for the removal of that which is the selfishness behind the discord. You have not yet considered it, Dear Heart, but the discord which finds expression through the lives of human beings—the discordant behavior, the addictions, and all that lowers a human life to the living of life less than that which an animal lives, that lowering—what is behind that is always selfishness, which in your world is called evil!

There is no *Cosmic* evil, there is no such thing

Do not confuse my word, because there is no *Cosmic* evil, there is no such thing. And many students—I have observed this—get confused when we speak of the sinister force, when we speak of the evil that is in the human world. Yet we speak, knowing the great truth—there is no good and there is no evil. And when we say these things, we are speaking in Cosmic terms. We would never create *good*, we would never create *evil*—Our Heart Flame only knows perfection. It is human beings who have created good and evil. This is human beings' reality, but it is not a capital 'R' reality, it is not the big *Reality*, it is only a reality that is in this world. And because it is only a reality in the third dimension of Earth and it is not born of perfection, it can be undone.

So be very clear. That which we refer to as 'evil' or the 'sinister force' that is in the world, is simply nothing more than the generated accumulated discordant energy of human beings that has coalesced together, that has gathered together, that seems to be a tremendous power that is influencing the lives of human beings. And behind all discordant desires there is that core, if you will, of human evil and the sinister force, which is a core centre that is feeding the discordant desires that live through human beings' lives. Ultimately, it is selfishness on a mass scale.

You do not yet contemplate the power that any of the Angelic Host can wield in your lives. Even an Angel that is not an Archangel—a great Cosmic Angel—can stand in the atmosphere of your city and do tremendous work of releasing that Cosmic Sacred Fire that forbids the discord that finds its expression through human beings. But to the *degree* of success of a Cosmic Angel's work and how many peoples' lives it can touch depends upon how many of you are reaching up and are opening the door.

The door to the Fifth Dimension, the door to the Realms of Light, is open

Let it be very clear—as your Beloved Akasha has stated—the door to the Fifth Dimension of Earth, the door to the Higher Realms of Light, is open. The Great Archways are open. There is only one place that the door is sealed—and that is within human consciousness. And each of you have the power to open that door as simply as placing your attention upon us in sacred remembrance of the power and glory of God that is the very *essence* of your lives; the invitation for that glory to come forth, and the holding of your attention upon ourselves or any one of the Spiritual Hierarchy to descend into your lives to stand in

102

the atmosphere of your homes, to release the Sacred Fire Love from our Octave of Light, into, through, and around you—and any manifestation—as an eternal sustained action that forbids any discord from touching your lives or your creations or all that you are yet to bring forth into your outer lives. We will do it! We will not disappoint you, Dear Heart. And the more that you desire the Divine Desires of your own Blessed Higher Self finding its expression through your human selves, that, Dear Heart, is a tremendous Cosmic Dispensation that opens the door to us.

Then you will find our own Sacred Fire enfolding you and gently passing through your being and your world. And you will find a very gentle change and transformation; you will find the gentle lifting; you will find the newness of life; you will find the confusion disappearing. You will find yourself lifting into a higher consciousness, and a new place of clarity. You will find a light—you will find moments of *no thought* where your resting is upon your divinity and a flash of light so brilliant comes forth within your mind and there is never again a confusion or a distortion that could be an obstacle to the divine thoughts of your own Divine Self expressing through you!

Then your lives shall truly become, as spoken by the Mighty Saint Germain, a new stage of wondrous unfoldment. You shall be in the world but not of it, as your Master Jesus prophesized. And your world truly shall be a stage where the *will* of the 'I AM' within each of you, to shake a spear at human darkness, has become strong, has become resilient—and your world is a manifestation of joy; a manifestation of supply; a manifestation of beauty, a manifestation of rich relationships.

Divine Desires bring forth the creativity of your inner genius

Divine Desires do not take you out of this world, in what you call 'the change called death'; Divine Desires do not bring about a life of boredom—Divine Desires bring forth the creativity of your inner genius; Divine Desires bring forth that of which the world is in awe.

Anything that is of great excellence—whether it is the modernization of civilization; whether it is the great technology that is advancing your world; whether it is the new art; the new music that is coming forth—is being enfolded with our Sacred Fire Love that is keeping the vibratory action of discord away from those things, allowing the creativity to channel through human lives.

All of those, whether they be the Mozarts, the Beethovens, or those who have been great Greek philosophers in your world; whether it be those who came through the doorway of India and brought forth the great ancient texts, all of this came forth with the Sacred Fire protecting those things, and they have lasted for centuries and centuries of time. And now in your new modern age, many wondrous things will come forth that have never been on Earth before.

Precious of the Heart, let me not ever hear any of you saying that you do not need the Sacred Fire Love of our Heart Flame because if you yet believe this, you do not have the complete knowledge of the Ancient Mystery Schools; you do not have the knowledge of your own great God 'I AM' Presence and what it can do for you; you do not have the knowledge of the Cosmic Resources that can set your life free.

You are aware of the great resources that you as human beings have used to accomplish something, to create something in your world. Rise, and test me! Challenge me to use Cosmic Resources. Have Faith! Because just as each of you have resources at hand to get the job done— to bring something into manifestation—we have *our* Cosmic Resources, and I am quite certain that the unprepared human eyes would be blinded if they were commanded to see some of our Resources released into their life.

Great assets of your Soul will come forth that give you new talents, new abilities that you did not have before

Test us. Call upon us. Challenge us to enfold your lives and all that you wish to bring forth in our Sacred Fire Love, even if you do not yet quite believe or feel that miracles exist. There is not one miracle that has come into this world that is not a manifestation of our Sacred Fire Love that simply purifies the vibratory action of what needs to be corrected, allowing the full Presence of the 'I AM' to manifest as the miracle in your lives. I offer you my own Sword, and the great Goddess of Liberty offers you Her Flame of Liberty, for each of you to become a commanding Presence in your life.

To be an instrument of Divine Desire is to be so raised, that you are a channel of God's Love, a channel of God's Healing, a channel of God's Great Creativity expressing through you. Do not be so certain, Dear Heart, that you yet know the Divine Desires of your Great God Presence expressing through each of you. Because if you desire the Divine Desires, you will be so raised that all of a sudden there is power in your voice, there is a commanding Presence that gives you the ability to be a spokesman, to be a great singer or other great assets of your soul will come forth that give you new talents, new abilities that you did not have before.

Your Divine Desires, expressed by each of you, brings excellence into this world—that which human beings love.

Human beings love good music; human beings love good art. Now I know I am using that word 'good', but I am using it in the sense of excellence; I am using it in the sense that it is that which causes you to reach up. In all things there is the great ladder and evolution of life, and anything good and constructive is a stepping up, is a rung upon the Cosmic ladder of upliftment.

Reach for the Cosmic Heights of Attainment, desire to be instruments of the Great Creative Genius under the Divine Desires of your own Mighty 'I AM' Presence. Call upon us to enfold you in our Sacred Fire Love that keeps back all the discord, and that just purifies and harmonizes your outer self so that which is the *greater* might find its expression through you.

Look forward to your future. Look forward to being open channels; look forward to the new; look forward to new ideas, new talents, and new interests. And then, engage your life, and just see the fulfillment that will come to you. Engage your relationships; and see how—even in your relationships and even in the world of intimacy—our Sacred Fire Love can bring you into states of intimacy that even your own present sexuality has not even begun to express in your lives.

So you see, Dear Heart, do not ever fear that exchanging your human desires for the Divine Desires is going to create a life of boredom, or that you are going to be taken out of what seems to fulfill you now. It is because of the persistence to have human desires that actually limit you, that the darkness in this world has been here so long, and I know there will be many on your Earth who will beg to differ with me. And that is fine; for all of us in the Ascended Host are in one agreement with that which are the opinions of human beings—we just do not consider them, at any time!

**To live your Higher Purpose—Your passion!
Your calling!**

Your Beloved Akasha has suggested to you that each of you have a Higher Purpose; that your Higher Purpose is that which is lived every day in your lives—it is your passion! It is that which makes a difference in this world. She has often referred to it as your ministry; and as I come to you I shall refer to it as your *calling*. For it is truth that each of you has a calling; and that calling evolves, it graduates, as each of you evolve and graduate through life. That calling is found within the original *electron*, the *permanent cell of the physical heart*. That calling is known within the Life Stream that is given to each of you from your own Beloved Great God Presence. And that calling is that particular thing you have come to do in this world, which you can do so well, so perfectly, and in such a way and manner, that no one else on the Earth can do it quite as well as you can.

I am able to assist each of you if you grow within yourselves a desire to *live* your calling this lifetime. A desire to be aware of it; a desire to feel it; a desire to know the quality of your calling, how it comes into expression, how you might live your calling each day and all that is required to bring it forth into manifestation in your lives. If you desire this, you must speak to the great 'I AM' of your being, your Spiritual Selves, your Divine Selves. Call this forth, and then call upon Michael or one of my Angels— especially here the Angels of Cosmic Illumination—to enfold you in their Sacred Fire Love to harmonize and open you to full awareness and full feeling of that which is your calling.

Ask the Angel of the Cosmic Blue Flame to come to you to purify the very elements of your body, your mind, and your feeling nature; so that calling can find its creative expression, and you can begin to channel the gifts of your divine natures. For within everyone's calling there are *gifts of light,* there are very sensitive qualities that can express through the personality self in such a manner that brings them forth in a way that is unique to the soul that it is expressing through.

I, Michael, will assist you—my Angels will assist you—if you call upon our Cosmic Blue Flame to enfold you, to harmonize you, to purify you, to open you so that which is the calling of your life in this lifetime might come forth as quickly as possible into your knowing into the life that you are living. Then it will be done. What do you think of this gift? It is a good gift. Oftentimes, the student asks, 'Well, Michael, how often do we call this forth?'—You call it forth until you have it! May your Light be a blessing of greater freedom to all humanity!

CHAPTER *T*HREE

I, Michael, continue now with the next part of my letter to you, Dear Hearts, and that is I wish to speak to humanity through each of you now; for many of you, I feel, are accepting what I have to say. And it is through the oneness of the human emotional body and the feeling nature of life, and the oneness of the mental body that the vibratory nature, the quality of what I wish to express, will reach more of human consciousness.

And so, I Michael, say, *O Humanity, reach up, try us.*

Oh blessed humankind, you yet hold within yourselves a feeling of practicality and importance in your relationships with each other. You have placed a quality of practicality on your relationships with your careers, your experiences in your world of form. And there is within yourselves, human life, a belief that it is impractical to spend time or attention upon the Angelic Host; or that you feel that it is impractical, that it is impossible to reach us. There are ideas that have qualities to them, human qualities, that you have woven into the fabric of your humanity, where you have accepted that there is this distance, even if you accept our reality, that there is a great distance between you and us. It is through the great Unity of Now that there is in truth no distance, and yet there is distance. And all distance comes into the one moment of Now, through

109

the power of consciousness, the power of the heart, and the power of your attention, focus and concentration and energy vibration.

It is this belief that it is impractical and that one is being silly and foolish in their hopeful prayers to the Angelic Host, which keeps us from assisting you. Because what could we, Beings who live in realms of great light that are physical too—and yet not physical in the way your world is—do for you? How practical is it that we could enfold your lives, that we could come into your world of form and experience, your relationships, and make a difference? And that is a tragedy, because the Ascended and the Angelic Host are so needed in your lives if you want your rightful freedoms.

I do not wish to confuse you, because it is truth that your own Beloved Higher Self—the great God 'I AM' of each of you—is All Power and All Authority, and fully capable of producing perfection in your lives. But the tragedy of human life in this day and age is that the average human being has sown so much discord, so much belief, and so much limiting quality and feelings into the human emotional body, that these feelings—based on perceptions and concepts and feelings of lost will—become an obstacle, so that the perfection and the power of your own Great God Presence does not find its expression through each of you.

And so, I, Michael, say, 'O Humanity, reach up, try us.' Because it is what is sown within the human emotional and feeling body that keeps the perfection of your own Great God Selves from coming into full embodiment in your outer lives. You can call any of the Angelic Host, or any of my brothers—Raphael, Gabriel, *any* of the Archangels—to assist you to be free of everything that is not Love's Eternal Presence, and we will come to you!

We come to you and we evaluate the energy around your bodies

We come to you and we evaluate the energy around your bodies, the auric field, and the immediate atmosphere. We evaluate the emotions that are most obstructing your freedom. We evaluate the lost will. We evaluate what you have hidden from your own self. We evaluate the denial. We evaluate the will to be free of these things, and depending upon what is found there, is our Sacred Fire Purity released underneath you and through you.

When our Cosmic Blue Flame, which usually holds a touch of the Pink Flame, is drawn in, through, and around you—and qualified to be a sustained action—it passes through you and begins the purification process. Just as the physical power of fire in your world consumes things that it passes through, does our Flame from our Octave of Life consume and melt away the vibratory action that is less than love, allowing perfection to come forth in its place. Unlike the physical fire of your octave, the Sacred Fire of our Octave is not harmful. There is no amount of Sacred Fire that would ever be too much in your life. Are you ready to start using and enjoying *The Greater Powers of this Universe?*

Call for more Light from your own Higher Light Body Christ Self *and* the Ascended Host for *safe* increase

Yes, it is possible, through your focus, prayers and meditations and upon your decrees, to raise the Light in yourselves to a certain frequency vibration. But if you do not call forth Our Sacred Fire into your lives—even though your calls for more light are given forth from you—that light will only expand to a certain place within yourself. Because if you do not have the Sacred Fire that purifies and

111

harmonizes your outer self, then there is an opportunity that you would use the increased light or Life Force in an adverse way, a way that would compel suffering back into your life.

It is for this reason, Beloved of the Heart, that your own Christ Self, that hears your calls for more light, can only increase that light to a certain degree; unless your call for the light is equal to your call for the Sacred Fire Love from Our Octave and from any of the Angelic and Ascended Host. When you equal your calls for light, when you equal your calls for the opening of the higher centres of your bioforms—your physical body—with a call for our Sacred Fire Purity to come into you, your expansion of light will be safe.

With calls for the Sacred Fire of Our Love, whether it be the Mighty Saint Germain's Violet Consuming Flame, whether it be Beloved Mary, Mother of the World, and Her Rose Pink Flame, whether it be a Three-fold Activity of the Violet, Pink and Cosmic Blue Flame, or my own Cosmic Blue Flame—any activity of the Sacred Fire that is called forth, coupled with the desire for more light, will allow the light to safely increase within your being as the Sacred Fire purifies the elements of your body, the human brain, the field of mentality and the field of emotion. As the purification of the outer self, the harmonizing takes place, the fields of mind, the fields of feeling, the fields of the brain, the elements of which the body is composed, are purified and raised in vibration. It is in this raising that the light you call forth can be a light that is sustained—a light that can come forth as much as you desire it to be. And within that light is intelligence, strength and love.

Go to your Christ Self and Us and call forth the Cosmic Light directly down your Life Stream

Then there is the *Cosmic* Light. The Cosmic Light is that which you can call forth from your Higher Christ Selves and the Ascended and Angelic Host. This is different from the light that you call forth from your own Great God Presence, because anything that you call forth through your Life Streams from your Mighty Higher Selves must be placed under your will. This means that you have the opportunity to qualify that light, to qualify that energy how it will act in your lives, how it will express through your outer selves. The *Cosmic* Light is always the light that comes from the Angelic or Ascended Host. It cannot be requalified—it retains a state of perfection and it retains the quality that the Ascended Master Being has imposed upon that energy.

When you call upon your Christ Selves and invoke the full Cosmic Power of Light into your feeling body, it silences anything that is not love until those things are consumed. Your own Christ Self then reaches out to one of us to qualify the light that It will bring into your feeling body. And we must respond. We love to be obedient to the Law, and the Law demands that we respond to your Christ Selves. And when you go to your Christ Self and you call forth the Cosmic Light directly down your Life Stream, understand that this is different than an Ascended Master Being standing *outside* of you and projecting that Cosmic Light *to* you.

Please realize that anything that comes through your Life Stream and down through the heart and into your own Divine Flame, has access pathways into the feeling body. Which means, Dear Hearts, that if you wish to have the Ascended Masters' Cosmic Light directly from your Christ Selves, that Cosmic Light will come down through your

113

Life Stream, through the Crown of your bio-forms, into the Heart Flame, where it enters the Cosmic arteries, the pathway into the feeling body. And this is much quicker, if you will, in the results that are produced.

But you see, if you call it from your Higher Mental Body, your Christ Self, then your Christ Self must reach out to one of us for that Cosmic Light. Because the only place that the Cosmic Light can come from, is the light of a Being who has lived in a Third-Dimensional reality and gained its Ascension up into the Fullness of its Divine Self—an Ascended Being, an Ascended Angelic Being.

If you wish to know that we are not impractical, if you wish to know that it is not so impractical to work with the Angels, then, Dear Hearts, take my suggestion and reach up to your Christ Self. "Mighty 'I AM' Presence, Beloved Higher Mental Body, my Christ Self, I call forth Your Full Cosmic Powers of Light into my feeling body, and out into my world. Let it be the silencing of all struggle and all discord that has ever registered in my being and world, all accumulation of it, so that my own Heart Flame might find its expression into my outer life."

We project Our Sacred Fire Love from Our Octave according to the will of humanity

In ages past, the mass of humanity realized the practicality of reaching up to us when their suffering was so great that they asked for help. The help came, and then they were grateful for a short time. The tragedy of human life is that so often human beings turn to us in an hour and in a moment that is very late, and too often it is *too* late. Under the new Cosmic Laws that govern the Seventh Golden Age that the human race is now under, the Great Beings—the Great Cosmic Beings in the Great Central

114

Sun who govern your System of Worlds—now command there must be a portion of a human beings' energy that is turning towards the light voluntarily. Not because of suffering, not because of limitation, but because of the joy and the love for life and light and liberty, and there be a desire to be raised up, back into the truth of their being. And if that exists within you, Dear Heart, then we can do so much for human beings.

Today there is great preparation. In any given moment, unknown to the totality of the human race, or even to the student body, there are numbers of us who are walking in the lower atmosphere of the Earth, projecting Our Sacred Fire Love from Our Octave. According to the will of humanity we attempt to protect that which is constructive and that which has great opportunity for the future. Tremendous work has been done in the last two to three years in anchoring Our Sacred Fire Love around hospitals, churches, synagogues, mosques and around temples and other places considered sacred. And yet, there is only a portion of Our Flame that is ever used by those who enter into those holy shrines. Tragically there are, within the mass of the human race, concepts of the human mind and various belief systems and a tremendous guilt that keeps human beings from receiving the blessings that we offer.

You are not yet completely healed of those difficult situations of what has been brought forth into this world. Akasha has suggested that the desire for our Presence and our Angels to come into closer association with each of you will bring great freedom into your lives. Affirm often "I walk with Angels, even though it seems that they are invisible to me, yet I walk with Angels in this world. And I demand that the Angels come into close association with me, more and more each day that their Sacred Fire Love lifts me into whole new heights of attainment, illumination and enlightenment, of all that I Am and all that desires to come forth into expression through this outer self. I love and thank the Angels for their Presence with me."

Struggle—ask its cause, effect, record, and all memory of it to be removed

Much has been given to the technology and the advancement of modernization of civilization. Not too much more can be given without the desire for peace and liberty amongst human beings. There are millions of the Angelic Host that are standing ready to respond to all who invoke their Presence. Rise and use your minds in the most constructive way. Remember that if you call to us for Assistance, you call to us to be free of that which is limiting you. But when you return your attention back to that thing that is limiting you and you allow yourself to feel the quality of that thing that limits you, you are not allowing our help to come to you. Even *Our* own Sacred Fire Love cannot come to you then; for what you *allow* yourself to feel, you are clearly stating to the universe that this is what you wish manifest in your world.

It is for this reason that when you ask our Sacred Fire Love to remove all struggle that has ever registered in you, you ask its cause, effect, record, and all memory of it to be removed. And always, Dear Heart, when you are requesting the Cosmic Powers to relieve you of a condition, ask that it be *replaced* by the Ascended Masters' Cosmic Light Substance that can never be re-qualified. There is no point in leaving that space that would be purified open for more discordant quality.

The human feeling body…Majestic! A spectacle of Light

We know what the human feeling body looks like and it is majestic! It is the most wonderful spectacle of light. Some of you in former attainment, or in temporary heights of being raised, have seen the human feeling body. I say to you, Dear Hearts, your feeling body is much more attractive, much more beautiful, than the physical body has yet gained in it's attainment. It is spectacular to behold! Even though there is yet discord that is registered in a human beings' feeling body, if you could see the light structure of the feeling body, you would be forever, forever grateful and in awe of the great expression of the Divine Feminine that has been given you. And you would have the desire never to taint or to colour your feeling body with discord again.

As each of you came to Earth long ago upon my Ray and you descended in your first and up to your hundred and tenth life experience, when Earth began, fourteen million years ago, when you descended into physical bodies upon the first Ray, your feeling bodies were the carriers and the expression of Divine Love. It was not until the end of the Second Golden Age that the human feeling body began to take on discord, due to the attention being turned away from the light.

Once again you have an opportunity, O People of Earth, a tremendous opportunity to restore your feeling bodies to exquisite expressions and vehicles of Divine Love—that love, a portrait of the great Magnetic Energy of Life that just loves to clothe your thoughts, loves to clothe your mind, and then projects that clothed energy out into your world for manifestation.

There is not any healing that takes place without the Sacred Fire Love of the Higher Self and of the Angels

Akasha has taught you well of the need to harmonize and purify your feeling body of that which is not love; so that your thoughts are qualified only with Love, Wisdom and the Power of the Presence that is within you, finding wonderful manifestations in your outer world. And how will you do this? There are many today to show you how much life loves each of you, Dear Heart. There are many in the world today that do not have this knowledge that each of you is so fortunate to have, yet they are out there in the world as practitioners, as healers. And when an individual, when a student looks for healing, and goes to these ones and finds that there is a healing taking place in the feeling body, there is not any healing that takes place without the Sacred Fire Love of the Higher Self and of the Angels.

This is how much life loves you, that even those who do not have this knowledge do not yet realize—even though they may acknowledge that they are channeling great Universal Energy, yet there is very little cognition or gratitude—that there is no such thing as a healing without the Sacred Fire Love of Life from Our great Octaves of Light or from the great Goddess Temples that exist in the belt around your physical sun. And yet, healing takes place. But I assure you that there is not any healing that takes place without the Sacred Fire Love.

So already there are those who have the intent to be healed, a desire to be free. There are those who stand forth today as practitioners offering healing modalities, such as the art of re-birthing, Universal Healing Energies that come from the Mighty Orion, or the energies of Reiki. There is not one of these delivery systems of healing through the practitioner, in which there is not the attendance of an Angel of the Sacred Fire that is releasing and holding the Sacred Fire around the practitioner and around the student; allowing the healing to take place.

Angels of the Cosmic Christ Blue Lightning of Indestructible Purity and Power

So now, Dear Hearts, hold gratitude for this great Sacred Fire Love that is freely offered into your use. Find the ease, find the joy; for you are not asked to pick up and do something, you are not asked to do hard work here—you are asked to turn your Life Stream, to turn your Hearts, and to turn your attention and your focus first to your own Beloved Great God Presence, and then to us. Call upon us. Call upon me to stand at least once in the atmosphere of your home, to anchor there the Eternal Flame of My Love. Call upon my Angels to come to you to anchor and enfold you in the Cosmic Blue Flame. Call upon my Angels of the Cosmic Christ Blue Lightning if you feel that you are being bothered by an intrusion, if you feel that there are astral or psychic energies touching your Life Stream.

Today the astral or psychic realm is charged with the energy of human good and evil. You will not find our perfection there. There is nothing of our Divine Love about that which is psychic; there is nothing of perfection about that which is astral. Human beings have taken those energies, that were once a great opportunity for life, and destructively qualified and bound them. And if you are being touched by destructive lines of force—in which you have energy streams between yourselves and other human beings who won't let go of you when you wish to be free of those human beings—you call my Angels into action.

If you have lines of energy between yourselves and manifestations in your world that are limiting you; if you feel that you have walked in valleys of darkness or the dark places of cities where there is much discord, and if you feel that energies of those things have touched you or gathered around you, if you have walked in chambers of great dance halls where there is the booming music with many astral forms hanging about in the atmosphere and if you sense that one of those forms have walked home with you, then, Dear Heart, you call the Angels of the Cosmic Christ Blue Lightning of Indestructible Purity and Power.

And you command those Angels to release that All Christ Blue Lightning; first of all into the atmosphere around your body, second to the auric field, third into the mental body, fourth into the brain, fifth in the physical body, sixth into the feeling body, seventh into the etheric body. Or you might say *my entire being*; as long as you know, remember, you are the authority for your lives, as long as *you* know what you are referring to.

And say to those blessed Angels, "Enfold me now in a Dome of your Cosmic Light, and release a shattering of your Cosmic Christ Blue Lightning of Indestructible Purity and Power into my being and world; shatter, dissolve, and consume, any discordant energies or any energies that are trying to gather about me that are wrong energies. Clear my being and world of astral energies, carnate energies and wrong energies and take those things right out of me. And I bless you. I bless you Beloved Angels for this transcendent service to my Life Stream."

Those Angels *desire* to work in mental institutions, those Angels desire to step forward and free human beings from the addictions that come into the elements of the body. And yet, there is very little work for them, because there is not the desire of human beings for Angelic assistance. You can be free if you choose to walk with the Angelic Host. You can choose the words of the great Cosmic Son who came to you as Jesus " 'I AM' an open door..."

" 'I AM' an open door to Archangel Michael. 'I AM' an open door to His Cosmic Christ Blue Lightning Angels. 'I

AM' an open door to his Angels of Illumination now made manifest in my being and my world; anchoring their Sacred Fire Love in, through, and around me, that just stops all that is wrong in my being and world—stops it right there in its tracks, liberating the Inner Splendor that has long been imprisoned in this outer self." And just see what kind of response you will have!

Beloved Children of the Light, again I say to you that Akasha has been perfect in suggesting to you that it is not about hours and hours of meditation time. That is not what we are asking of you. We are asking you to connect with the God of your being, to turn your attention to us, perhaps ten to fifteen minutes, three times a day. Gain your momentum, gain your consistency, and your life shall be an open door where we will come into your life. Begin to use daily, the Greater Powers of the Universe that we are privileged to offer you. Won't you try, Beloved?

We have but one desire, and that is to set your life free of all that is limiting you. What else could we desire? For the Angelic Host to your world are the Emissaries of the Great Central Sun. And who is the Great Central Sun, Dear Heart?—That is the home of your Heavenly Mother and Father, and it is the home of those Life Streams who have not yet chosen to have a physical reality in a physical universe. And it is they who watch, through the All-Seeing Eye, the physical realities that are unfolding in your Systems of Worlds; it is they who send the Legions of Angels to your world. And so they are great Causal Emissaries that come with great powers that are offered into your use.

The worded expressions of Ancient Prophets can resonate with you

There are the teachings of the Mystics who have come to the Earth so long ago. These teachings were clothed in a certain way, in certain worded expressions. And because each of you have some previous lifetimes when some of the Mystics, some of the Ancient Prophets, were on the Earth—and you feel very close to them—sometimes you must go and find those worded expressions; they have a feeling to them because you were there at that time. And when the Master Jesus said, "Of my own self, Lord, I can do no thing, I am nothing without you. Thou art the only Power and Glory. Come forth and glorify yourself through this outer self." If that touches you, if that resonates, then use those words. Find the words that carry the vibration of Divine Love and Promise, for this is Sacred Fire Love of God's Heart. Others of you will be touched by the words and comforts of the Buddha or the Prophets of various world religions. Unfortunately most of their teachings have been altered by man.

That is why, in the great current Dispensations on the Earth today, all of that which has been the occult and the ancient metaphysics—all of that which was the ancient manuscripts of the first religions of the world—are being drawn back into manifestation today under Cosmic Law. So if your resonance connects with that which has been in other schools of higher knowledge, this can be brought forth and used for your freedom in this life.

Your life can be anything that you desire it to be. The Sacred Fire of our Love from our Octave, drawn in, through, and around you, can liberate yourselves if you make a choice. And I, Michael, challenge each of you Blessed Children of the Light to be free of knowing anything about limitation; to be free of that which is the destroyer of the human form, to be free of knowing anything about lack.

I would also like to say here that he who was Joel Goldsmith, who was Usa, the Messenger's teacher when he was young, was over-lighted by the Archangel Raphael and his Twin Flame, the Beloved Mary of this world. And

Joel Goldsmith was quite correct as a teacher, of streaming the ancient religions together and understanding what has been given. This one was correct in many of his great statements that he issued forth. And whether you are drawn to his work or the work of others, it is for each of you to realize that nothing in this world can be a power unless you continue to accept and agree with it. As Joel taught his students to say about limitations, "I do not know anything about you. You are nothing. You have no power." If you do this too, then, Dear Heart, something new can take place in your life.

As long as you constantly talk to each other about limitation, as long as the feelings and the intellect of your mind suggests that you know something of lack and limitation, then you are an open door for that lack and limitation to be drawn into your lives. And you might say to the limitations—"Whether it be lack, or whether it be confusion, or lack of opportunity or career, it matters not what you are, you are a human concept and appearance and I have entertained you long enough!"

Remember the words of your Mighty Jesus, Who loves you so much. "Get thee behind me!" Who was Jesus speaking to? The voice of the antichrist! Jesus was speaking to the voice of the altered ego; Jesus was speaking to the voice of the human intellect that would give power to the things that you have feared long enough. And each of you can use your own words. Or you can use Jesus' words, "Get thee behind me!" You can use the words of Joel Goldsmith and say, "You are nothing. You are a human concept, and because I have believed you, because I have feared you, because I have given you my attention, I have energized you. That is the only reason you are in my world, and I say—now I take the power out of you. You are nothing. Be gone!"

That is a treatment you can give to the appearances that seem to limit you. And then you focus, reminding yourself that the truth is you are 'I AM'. " 'I AM' fully here, 'I AM' here and 'I AM' there, and 'I AM' is in full manifestation in my life, opening all channels of good into my life; opening all channels of creativity; opening all channels of companionship; opening all channels of money and resources and opening all channels of career and opportunity in my life." Decree it in the name 'I AM', with feeling.

There is a means to have all the money and supply...

There is a means that you might have all the money and the supply and the resources that you require in your lives. Remember, as your Akasha has taught you well, of all the Cosmic Elements of Earth—Air, Earth, Water and Fire—Fire is the First Element of Life. It is that first element out of which the light comes forth. It is the Element out of which *all* Life comes forth. And since all of the Angels are Divine Flames—that is exactly what they are—they are Divine Flames of the Sacred Fire of God—you can request that the Angels place that Sacred Fire in yourselves and in your life and in your worlds.

Now, what does that mean when you say 'your world'? It is the world in which you interact, it is the world that you know, it is the world of friendships, it is the world that you come and go in your life. And you can command the Angels of the Cosmic Blue Flame, you can command the Angels of the Violet Flame, to manifest that Sacred Fire in yourselves and in your world as all the money and all the supply that you could ever require, as you also command those Angels to anchor Their Sacred Fire Love in, through, and around you, to harmonize and purify your outer selves.

You see, Dear Heart, why do we constantly refer back to the harmonizing and the purifying of the outer self? Because you have been on the Earth centuries of lifetimes, and that is a long time for discord and belief in good and bad, and experiences of lack and limitation, to weave themselves within the very fabric of your human lives. And the only way that you are going to stop having these experiences—further qualifying your energy—is by having the Sacred Fire Harmony and Purity of an Angel's Presence.

The Sacred Fire Love of any of the Angelic Host, commanded in, through, and around you, can harmonize and purify everything within you so that there is no longer any qualifying that is of a discordant nature. Never forget that every moment you are a qualifying being; and your qualifying is in accordance to the thought and the feeling and the spoken word that comes forth from you. Every moment you are qualifying the Life Force within. And it is desirable from this day forward to decree, and to make a covenant with thyself, that all the energy within yourselves and all the energy that ever goes forth from you is qualified with Sacred Fire Harmony. Let that be your decree, let that be your covenant. It will take care of the now, today, and it will take care of tomorrow.

And then you hear us calling for not only *harmony*, but *purity* in your outer selves. And that is to invite the Sacred Fire Love to purify all the energy within yourselves, the etheric body, and your worlds, that belongs to yesterday and all lifetimes behind you; to allow the Angel to pass her or his Sacred Fire Love—for it has all power and illumination to do so—through yourselves and all former creation. And then to help the *maintaining* of the purification of your human self today, so that the perfection and the tremendous power that God wants to release through each of you can come forth.

Invoking the magic of former legends through stories...

There are many today who are invoking the magic that has been found in former civilizations. Today, in the world of those who write—those who write stories, those who write books, those who have the authority to write screenplays—many today are being touched by a Higher Power that is encouraging folklore and the magic of former legends to come forth into manifestation. There is not anything in this world that is of legends of greatness—stories of those who would fly upon magic carpets, stories of Atlantis—that is not born in truth; the great quality of that truth broken down by human distortion and then placed in folklore as just child's imaginations. Yet, all of these belong to civilizations of the past in which all of these things have been in former manifestation.

It was a wonderful time. It was a wonderful time in north-eastern Africa, it was a wonderful time in Arabia, and it was a wonderful time in India and in the Himalayan valleys and a portion of China and Tibet and South America in former ages; in which in the Third and Fifth Golden Ages, human beings had much more illumination and much less density in the world. It was a wonderful time in which indeed, Dear Hearts, you would move yourselves around on flying carpets; you did not even need airplanes. And you had the capacity to create bubble-like Domes of Light, in which the temperature of that atmosphere would be controlled in the bubble of light which you would place around yourself. Yet there is much greater that is to come in this new civilization that is forming in this present Seventh Golden Age.

There is not anything that the human mind is capable of conceiving that cannot be manifest somewhere

So there is a growing fascination, and in this growing fascination the motion picture industry will continue to be used to bring forth mind expanding motion pictures that speak of magic; that speak of Higher Powers that human beings use and motion pictures that reveal human beings with tremendous auras of light. And this will speak to the remembrance; this will speak to the deeper memory; this will speak to the possibility and potential that exists within each of you.

There is not anything that you could ever conceive of in thought that is not possible for manifestation somewhere in the universe. This is a great and mighty truth—there is not anything that the human mind is capable of conceiving that cannot be manifest somewhere in the universe!

The diversity of the next seven years of your Planet— the Light has spoken!

Well, Dear Hearts, your Planet—its atmosphere—is yet choking with human discord. Yet you have arrived at a time—where through Cosmic intervention, the Harmonic Convergences, and the great outpouring of light—that today even with the discord on this Earth, there are millions who are turning toward the light and there are billions who are holding a desire for greater peace on Earth today.

So today, Dear Heart, you have *diversity*. Today you have nations such as in Africa, in which life that is lived in those nation states is to such a diabolical degree that it should not be accepted by humanity, and yet you have possibilities of human beings living lives of such great light, such great Freedom, such Joy, such manifestations the likes of which have not ever been on this Earth before! Such is the growing diversity of the next seven years of your Planet. And the Light has spoken—none, and nothing, can stop the true Student of Light from now achieving any height of spiritual attainment and any height of manifestation of abundance and opulence. No limit to the wealth of the world will come to any student who is seeking the light, seeking to be an instrument of the Divine Plan that will save this world!

So you see, Dear Hearts, in this next seven years there will be great diversity on this Planet; from the worst of human chaotic conditions—in which human beings are living in conditions unspeakable—to those human beings who are living lives of fulfillment, lives of perfection, and lives of great opulence. And there are those who will say, "Where is the fairness in this?"

The Light has spoken, and you are in the twelve-year cycle favoured by the Ascended Jesus Christ. You are in that twelve-year cycle in which the words "The courageous and the illumined will inherit the Earth" will be fulfilled. Your bible has not interpreted and recorded these words correctly where the bible suggests that He said "The meek shall inherit the Earth." He actually said—"The courageous and the illumined will inherit the Earth." This speaks of every heart, every voice, who stands for sovereignty of individual liberty and harmlessness; and who will not allow themselves to be imprisoned by the discordant forces of those who hate the light.

You are in the years in which the prophecy of Jesus the Christ will come into manifestation

Those who seek freedom, those who seek freedom of life, the freedom of worship, and the freedom to attain their victory in life—you have entered the last final years; those years that lead to the full manifestation of the words of Jesus the Christ. Jesus looked upon the Field of Certainty to see into some of the future. He did not gaze upon the Line of Possibility or that which is Probability; but rather, as your Akasha has stated, there is in the upper Realms of your Earth's atmosphere the great Line and Field of Certainty. And no human being may break that line; for it is the very undoing of the structures that support your Third-Dimensional Reality.

And so you see, you are in those years in which the prophecy of Jesus the Christ will begin to come into manifestation, in which the courageous and illumined will inherit this Earth. And the great wealth—as prophesized by the Mighty Saint Germain—will begin to be transferred into the hands of those who love the light, who stand for the light; those who awaken each morning and declare, "I come into this day, in God, with God, by God, and for God. And 'I AM' God-Free, God-Illumined, God-Victorious and God-Supplied, this day and every day!"

It is out there *in the streets of everyday life* that your Light be a Blazing, Flaming Presence of the Light

You are the authority of your life, Dear Heart. Waste not your time with the littleness of life. Waste not your time for those who are against the light. You are not responsible for them. If you walk away from those who are against the light, Dear Heart, God will not leave you alone. When you stand for the light and stand sovereign—and know that God is the Majestic, Conquering Presence of Victory within yourselves—you shall attract the Legions of Angels around yourselves; and they will attract to you companions, They will attract to you people who support you and love you. Come forth into the light and declare your sovereignty in God. Look forward to your lives; you are all here with a great calling. The world is waiting for you; even those who are in 'the great sleep of human consciousness' they yet know that you are coming. They know of the calling that you have, they are expecting you to assist them to awaken to their own God Divinity.

It is not in the caves of the world, it is not the ancient Mystery Schools, it is not the Himalayas where your light is needed—it is out there in the *streets of everyday life* that your light be a Blazing, Flaming Presence of the light. Seek to become an outpouring of the Fiery Flame of Life, seek to be an outpouring of your God Parents in the Earth's Sun. And I know that you have not contemplated that the Ascended Helios and Vesta—the Twin Flames of your own Earth's Sun—are your God Parents to this System of Worlds; the same way as those who are of the Great Central Sun are God Parents to this universe. Seek to be an outpouring of Beloved Helios and Beloved Vesta of their Twin Flame Presence and be a blazing Presence of Light to all Life in your world!

'I AM Come', 'I AM' that Light that cometh into the world that Lighteth up every man, woman and child

I say to you, each of you can become such a Blazing Presence of Life so that which is discordant, that which is sinister and that which is the evil in this world, *dare* not even look in your direction. But you must desire it! And you must declare to the God of your being and those who are the Cosmic Beings—the Goddesses, the Archangels, the Mighty Elohim, your own Helios and Vesta of your Earth's Sun, and your own Great God Presence—to make you on Earth a blazing outpouring of the Sacred Fire Love and its Light; illuminating everything in your life, loving the Powers of Nature, purifying the Forces of the Elements, healing everyone who crosses the pathway of your light!

Desire it, declare it, and demand it— and you shall see how my Legions of Angels will respond to you! They will crowd your homes; they will love you; they will care for you. They will desire that the Flame of Liberty and the Flame of Freedom be found within your beings and worlds. The Powers of Nature, and the Forces of the Elements, They will bless you. They will bless you because your light has come into the world and you have fulfilled the word of Jesus the Christ; for the light within you that is being broadcast out, the light is saying, " 'I AM Come', 'I AM' that Light that Lighteth up the World. 'I AM' that Light that cometh into the world that Lighteth up every man, woman and child." And you will be the Fulfillment of the Law.

I came to the Earth in the Name 'I AM' and I came to pour the Light of the Spirit 'I AM' into a physical body

There is not anything that will fulfill the Law of Life other than the Sacred Fire Love of God's Heart that is Our Sacred Fire Love, which we offer you as freely as the air that you breathe. All you have to do, Dear Hearts, is enter into your mindful use of prayers and calls. Command and demand us; be serious, be full of heart and joy, and say to us, "Now Michael, I have heard your call. Now I wish to ·rise into my calling. Beloved Michael and your Angels, be so close to me, let me feel your Presence. Touch me. Let me know with absolute certainty that you are enfolding me in your Sacred Fire Love that just crowds out everything in me that is of discord and limitation and opens the way for the Divine God and my Christ Self to come into Full Expression through this outer self. I thank you.

"I desire that I truly get on with the business of why I came to the Earth in the first place, for I came to Earth to receive a physical body. I came to the Earth in the name 'I AM', and I came to pour the Light of the Spirit 'I AM' into a physical body. I came to expand my light, to love my physical body into ascension. I came to raise my body up into the Spiritual Body of my God 'I AM' Presence, that I might go forth anywhere in the universe as an Ascended Being, a God Being, Free and Victorious. And I have now joined the Great Cosmic Federation of Great Life Streams and Great Systems of Worlds, and I AM Victorious and Free." That is a Great Covenant, Children of Light!

Without the opening of the Seventh Seal of the Earth by the Mighty Saint Germain, without that taking place, if there was not the Sacred Fire Love that was brought to your Earth since the year 1929, if you had no intervention from the Angelic Host, from the Ascended Host—then the average life span on the Earth would be twenty-seven years. That would be the limited life span, because your atmosphere and the Powers of Nature and the Forces of the Elements would be so poisoned with human discord. And so you see, much has already been accomplished so that you have the opportunity to live in physical bodies with a greater life span, to experience life in a physical reality. And a portion of that reality continues to be cleansed by the Angelic Host—enough for life to be sustained here until greater numbers reach up and desire that light of their own free will.

Archangel Michael's Blessing

I, Michael enfold each of you in my own Cosmic Blue Flame. May it find its Eternal Presence within each of you. May your heart desire it. May your own Inner Love Flame, your Heart Flame, command it to go forth out into your world to liberate you from all limitation. May it bring you into right relationship with yourself and with God. May it bring you into right relationship with each other. May it bring you into right relationship with your world, the Powers of Nature and the Forces of the Elements.

May it bring you into right relationship with the vision of the tomorrow land. May it bring you into right relationship to those Precious Gods of the Earth—long forgotten by human beings—who are yet here, deep within your mountains, doing everything they can to save life on this Earth. May it bring you into contact with the Mighty God Meru, may it bring you into contact with the Mighty God Tabor, and may it bring you into contact with the Mighty God Mercury, and all the Gods who are beyond the visibility of the human eye that are doing everything to balance the Powers of Nature and the Forces of the Elements so that the atmosphere of your Earth may be a place where human life can continue to embody and become free.

God Bless you unto Eternity. I shall only know for each of you the very desire of your own Heart's Flame; that you be raised in these physical embodiments, you be raised into your full Ascension under the original, or first, second or third Dispensation for the Ascension of your lives, that this take place in this lifetime for you at the end of your embodiment and service to the Earth. This is my Desire for each of you. And I offer to each of you the Sacred Fire Love of My Heart to this Victorious Attainment of your Life.

We, the Angelic Host and the Ascended Host, we love you; we bless you, and we thank you. We greet you in the Mighty Name, the Holy Name, 'I AM'.

I AM MICHAEL

✷

CHAPTER *Four*

I Am Asun, and I greet you out of the Diamond Heart of our Love. Well, Dear Hearts, you are here in this world to demonstrate all that you are, the Truth of your Being, the very Light of the Christ 'I AM' that is the true essence and the very true spiritual identity of your being.

The Power that you have to qualify each day

When there is the identification of all of your intentions, of what you wish to bring forth, and you understand that it is the holding of your attention upon a thought—upon a feeling, in which you are able to clothe the energy of that thought/feeling to bring about manifestation, all that is taking place here is the power of qualification, which is one of the greatest gifts you each have. It is a gift that is used unconsciously by the entire human race. When you make a conscious choice within yourselves to *consciously qualify* your day with the Sacred Fire Love of the Mighty Archangel Michael and any of the Angelic Host, you will find great assistance to come your way.

Let not that which is the Cosmic Resource of the Ascended Host be such a stranger in your life. It is not too long now before the manifestations of the Sacred Fire will be seen in your Earth's atmosphere; specifically first will come forth the manifestations of the Violet Ray. You know, Dear Hearts, it is a very interesting thing, all light comes forth from the Sacred Fire, but when light becomes so blazing, so bright, then that light manifests more fire! So, the fire manifests the light; just as you have a candle flame and that flame creates light. When the light becomes so bright, it is filled with the electronic pattern of the Fire Element, and then it bursts into another flame. Such is the great continuation of life!

And as you make a choice, you realize, "Through my thought, through my feeling, through my spoken word, I am always qualifying energy as to how it will act and express in my life and in my outer world. I am not yet capable as a human being to directly produce this Sacred Fire Love—this Sacred Fire Love is produced by my own glorious Higher Self; it is produced by the Angelic Host or any of the Ascended Host. My duty at this time, until I am risen into the glory of my Higher Self, is to call upon that Sacred Fire Love from my Great God Presence, the Angels, the great Archangels, and the Ascended Masters; to enfold me in that Sacred Fire Love so that I can purify the outer self of the density that has accumulated—the perceptions and the concepts and belief systems that have accumulated in the vast library of the human intellect, and to purify my feeling body of everything that is not love. This is why I call forth the Sacred Fire Love!"

When you know that God is within you, within your bodies, as the Heart Flame that maintains life in your body, you know that you have a direct pathway to your own Great God Presence. When you reach out to Beloved Michael or any of the Ascended Host, it is your Heart Flame that flashes a Ray of Light to that Being of Light; and what you are calling forth goes out upon that Ray of Light and is received by the Ascended Host, and then the quality that you are asking for in your life is drawn back to you.

So, Dear Hearts, why not begin to use this gift that has been brought to your attention; for there exists the

Sacred Fire Love that is sufficient to cleanse and purify this world and all humanity, if only human beings would reach up for it. When you are doing your morning prayers, begin to qualify your day, "I qualify all of this day with Archangel Michael's Sacred Fire Love. I call His Sacred Fire Love into my being and world, into all of my thoughts, my feelings, my spoken words, all of my plans, all of my Field of Dreams—all that I wish to bring forth. I command Archangel Michael's Sacred Fire Love, his Cosmic Blue Flame, and his Cosmic Flame of Illumination to come into all of my interactions with humanity this day!"

Illumination

The Flame of Illumination, Dear Heart, is a mighty qualified flame. When you call upon the Cosmic Flame of Illumination, that Flame comes into the human brain, into the mental body and into the feeling body and it seeks to find that which is obstructing the illumination from taking place within you. When that Sacred Fire Love is within you, it is literally the same as walking into a darkened room in the evening and turning on a light switch—you turn on the light and the darkness is consumed. There is no struggle, there is no light saying, 'Darkness, come here! We are going to battle it out.' You just hit the light switch and on comes the light. It is no different when you call forth the Sacred Fire Love; that Sacred Fire Love just burns out the human discordant creation. There is no darkness in the great Realms of Light. There is no imperfection.

Gold and the Ascension Thrones

What is going to clear the way? What is going to open the corridors and clear the pathways to your Great God Presence? You do not have any *human* resources—your science is not yet advanced to the place that you have the technology in which you can use a machine that has been created to purify the outer self. However, this is coming. Those of you who have studied mighty Saint Germain's works have come to understand that in the Royal Tetons there is that which is termed 'the Great Ascension Thrones'. These Thrones are made out of pure gold and contain within them certain gems that come from the Earth—diamonds, rubies, sapphires; and these Gems of Light that are united with gold bring about the Raising Activity of Gold.

The marriage of the Earth's Sun pouring its light rays into the Earth creates the substance called gold. Gold is one of the *Greater Raising Activities* of energy into a higher vibration presently taking place on Earth. That is why there is a portion of gold in the Earth that will never be brought to the surface, because that gold is used to continue the lifting of the Earth into a higher vibration of light. A certain amount of gold is given to be brought to the surface; the monetary use of gold and the cosmetic use of gold are but the lesser activity.

But the *greater* activity of gold is the *raising of vibration of energy* that gold provides to the human form—the body—and to atmospheric conditions. That is why the Ascension Thrones are deep in the Royal Tetons. Beloved Lanto, who is the great authority in the Tetons, and his Ascended Master Beings that come under His authority, are always watching humankind. They are waiting to help advance science. In order to give the knowledge as to how to create these Ascension Thrones, they require greater numbers of constructive minds within humanity. However as human beings are yet showing that they are willing to use technology in war, in destruction, this technology for the Ascension Thrones is being withheld by the great Ascended Host of Light.

138

They wish they could have given you this information back in the seventies and eighties, but a great shadow appeared again in your world in the seventies; and as long as these shadows keep being generated by human beings who are determined to have the war energy, then this greater technology is not given. It is somewhere between the year 2014 and 2028 that the knowledge of the creation of these Ascension Thrones is intended to be given to humankind. This is part of the Divine Plan. Until you have those Ascension Thrones—in which, literally, you can raise yourselves and free and purify the outer self of the density that has collected within you as a result of having lived in a third dimensional reality—you do not have any means to completely purify the atoms of which your bodies are composed, nor to purify yourself of certain limiting desires that the human body depends upon through habit.

When you have become a blazing Presence of Light, everything you touch can turn to gold. Can you imagine being of this world and everything you touch turns to gold? It is absolutely possible! There is not anything that has come into matter, into form—whether it be a glass or whether it be one ounce of gold—that is not a qualification of life's energy. It is just that the substance of gold is a Cosmic Qualification by great Beings of Light. They qualify the rays from the Earth's Sun into the Earth itself where it merges with Earth's elements to produce a substance that is called gold. You would have no gold, you would have no gems of light in the Earth, if the Brothers and Sisters of the Golden Robes inside the Earth's Sun were not qualifying the Rays of Light from the Earth's Sun to penetrate the Earth Mother Planet, and produce this substance called gold. You would not have it.

Problems with refraining from eating red meat without the use of the Sacred Fire

There are many lofty ideas out there in modern metaphysics; and there are many great truths. But you cannot apply those truths successfully when the mind, the feeling and the body has not been *prepared* for them. One of those truths is the subject concerning the eating of red meat. As long as there has been the taking in of red meat into the body, if one was to cut this off without use of the Sacred Fire, then injury could be done to the physical body. That is why there have been some vegetarians who have found that their energy system has been weakened; or problems have come about in their outer self as a result of becoming vegetarian without the use of the Sacred Fire— because the physical body *remembers* the taking in of meat.

Your physical body has a consciousness; but that consciousness is a developing consciousness. It is developing according to the thoughts, the feelings, and the habits that are clothing the elements of which your bodies are composed. When your body's elements are conditioned to a thing, through your thoughts, your feelings, and to a substance that you put in the body, if that substance is placed in the body over a long period of time, then the body's elements *depend* on that substance. Take that thing away, and the body can become quite upset.

So you see, even though it is an ideal to raise the light energy of the body, it is not to the body's advantage to go through the lifting and raising while there is yet the taking in of red meat. It is a truth that the taking in of red meat disturbs the body's cells and brings about the aging process. It is a truth that the fear that an animal experiences at death, even though you may say, "Well, the flesh is dead," that fear is imposed on the cells of the animal flesh; and then that is taken into your physical body and is made active within you.

So there are all sorts of healthy reasons as to why you might eventually get off the use of red meat. But to do so, you do not have the advantage of remembering, "Oh, yes, well, I did get off meat five and a half lifetimes ago, so because of this I do not have that consciousness of taking meat into my body." There are people who have done it very easily; there are people out there who are completely repelled by the taking of meat into the body, and chances are they are human beings who have removed themselves from the use of red meat a very long time ago, and so they are ready for that—their whole *consciousness* has gone through a transformation.

This is why it is not wise to 'should' on other people! That is why you really cannot take a book of metaphysics and apply it to all people. You can only apply truth to yourself. But I say to you, if it is brought to your attention that red meat slows the vibration of the body, and you think that you can continue to eat red meat and still see your Higher Self, you are absolutely fooling yourself. It will never happen. Why? Because you have been given the knowledge—red meat slows the vibratory action of your body.

In order for you to see and experience your Higher Self, the vibration of your body and sight must be quickened. Now that you know this, if you continue to choose to eat red meat, then assistance cannot be given to you to raise the vibration of your body and sight. Well, you are not invited to do this alone. You are invited to use *all* the knowledge, "My body is used to eating red meat, and I understand that there is a transition here; so I will call forth that Sacred Fire Love from Mighty Saint Germain and from Beloved Archangel Michael. Blaze your Sacred Fire Love in, through, and around me, and take out of me all desire for red meat, so that this desire does not bother me any more; remove the cause, effect, record and all memory of it." When that Sacred Fire Love passes through your mind, body, and feelings, it takes the *record* of eating meat out of the body consciousness and it opens the body to a certain knowingness of what is an appropriate replacement in feeding your body.

Why are chicken and fish not included in this? There are those things that have greater density and other things that have lesser density. You start with the removal of red meat, then as your body becomes accustomed to it—you are carrying the Sacred Fire—then eventually, under the prompting of your Presence, your desires will change. It is best to let your Presence prompt you, to say to your Presence, "Guide me. Let me know in no uncertain terms when you do not wish me to put any form of flesh in this body."

All is a state of evolution, and evolution is most graceful. It will happen with ease when you include the Sacred Fire, because the Sacred Fire transmutes the energy in your body and brings it to a higher vibration. Keep calling the Sacred Fire each day and say, "Mighty Presence of Life, Beloved Michael and Beloved Saint Germain, blaze your Sacred Fire Love through every cell of my body, my mind, feelings and the atmosphere around me, to purify this outer self." When you keep making that call, and you are holding the Sacred Fire Love within yourself, eventually your desires change. This is the way life intended it to be—that you would not just *cut off* a desire without graceful assistance.

Liquor and drugs create tears in the emotional body

For many of you now, your bodies are being refined. That is why many of you went through certain experiences

142

in which you needed to identify that there are certain substances that you take into the body, that the finer body—the more sensitized physical body—finds harmful to itself, like drugs and liquor. It is not an easy subject, the subject of liquor and drugs. For one carrying the higher frequencies, it is especially the white whiskeys that are so harmful to the human form; they create tears, not only in the cells of the body, but they create tears in the emotional body. The white gins, the white rums, and the white vodkas are tremendously harmful to the physical body. And so, when you carry the Sacred Fire Love in your physical cells, it begins to take these things out. And when you are carrying the Sacred Fire Love in your body, then anything, such as a lovely glass of wine, if there is any discordant element in the grape, that discord is simply consumed by the Sacred Fire Love and you can enjoy a fine glass of wine.

It is not a difficult thing to do; it is just the training, the training of turning your attention to your Presence and any of the Spiritual Hierarchy; and calling upon them to keep blazing that Sacred Fire Love of Love's Mastery and Love's Victory, in, through, and around yourself, and into all manifestations.

Any condition in your life has its root cause within your mind and your feelings

What about those things which seem to trouble you, those things that seem to follow you everywhere you go, things that have become hardened in your life? Today you accept greater responsibility in your lives; and you know that whatever is happening in your life, that the cause, the root, the quality of that thing, is being sustained by something within yourself. We so desire that you are through with not knowing how to deal with something— with not knowing how to shift something; and know you are capable of looking at anything that has been following you, any limitation that seems to have been so present in your life. You can sit down and say, "All right, enough is enough! Let's go in and shift this energy. Let's go in and change what has been creating this condition in my life—let's get that out of this outer self. Let's shift it. Let's transmute it and let's bring about the energy that I do desire manifest in my life."

Whether it is a condition of lack, a condition of walking through life without a partner, whether it is a condition of not knowing the next step in your life or not having opportunities, it matters not what it is. It is to realize that any condition in your life has its root cause within your mind and your feelings, and to say to your Presence, "I have complete intention to pass through this year, to live this year, in such a manner that I can demonstrate to myself that I can call that Sacred Fire Love into my mind and my feeling to remove any belief, any feeling or any quality that is supporting this wrong or limiting manifestation in my life. There is no part of me that doubts that I can connect with that great power. I am lovingly commanding Beloved Jesus', Mighty Saint Germain's and Archangel Michael's Sacred Fire directly into my mind and my feelings, to go after the thought, the belief, the feeling, the quality that is holding this condition of lack, this condition of disease, or whatever it is and dissolve and consume that thing right out of my being so that there is no longer anything supporting it." And then say to the limiting energy that has been manifest in your world, "You have no power to bother me any longer!"

You can take the energy out of the manifestation you wish to be free off, by declaring that it is no longer manifest in your life; and then take your attention off the condition. We will walk through the steps: you have a condition in your life that is limiting you or bothering you and you do not know how to get from *this* place to the place that you are *living* your Higher Purpose and ideals. "How do I get there?" The Sacred Fire Love will do it. It can produce money; it can produce people helping you; it can produce opportunities. It can produce recognition, talent and resources. There is nothing that that Sacred Fire Love cannot do.

Why is there nothing the Sacred Fire cannot do? Keep reminding yourself that all life (light) comes forth from the Fire Element. Of all elements, it is the first. It is the Fire Element that creates the elements of Earth, Air, Water and Ether. Therefore, that Fire Element can create money if that is what you desire in your life. But the Fire Element cannot be called in to create a manifestation in your life while there is yet within yourself, a belief, a perception, a quality that is creating the wrong or the limiting condition. Call upon your Individualized Presence of God, your Higher Self to pour the Sacred Fire Love and Purity through you, "Whatever is producing this condition in my life, I demand you blaze your Sacred Fire Love through my mind and through my feelings and take this right out of my life."

Oftentimes, what persists is the degree of *struggle* that you have thought and felt within yourselves; and oftentimes it is to ask for the thought, the feeling and the struggle around this thing that you have faced, to be taken out of you. Because struggle is a feeling that has become a quality and it is sitting in your body and your feelings, therefore, it is being broadcast to the world where it is finding manifestation. Yes? Indeed. So it is to ask Your Presence, the Ascended and Angelic Host to pour the Sacred Fire Purity and Power through you, to remove all feelings of struggle.

My Beloved God Presence...speak to me concerning all the matters of my life. I am here, I am listening...

The Angels are here; Great Beings of Light are here, to remove from your humanity that which is creating problems in your life so that all obstruction to your freedom is removed; so that the light, the love, the omnipotence, the omnipresence of your own God Presence, spiritual nature and inner light finds its expression through your mind, through your feelings and your world. And when you feel the love, wisdom, and joy of your Inner Spiritual Presence, then you will find that your world is lifted to a whole new place. Your life will have such value to it; such beauty and magnificence. This wants to take place now, Dear Hearts.

Try using the words 'I AM', they are the greatest words in the Universe. Use these words, " 'I AM' Angels of the Sacred Fire Love blazing through my Being and my world, harmonizing and purifying and correcting everything within my Being and my world, opening the way for the Divine Plan of my Life Stream fulfilled in this lifetime. 'I AM' that!" Oh, how magnificent that is!

The future is so different - the future is so majestic, it is so magical; it is so much more than anything that has been. You cannot call to the Sacred Fire Love and its Victory manifest in your Life without it coming to you and producing the most amazing results. It is just a matter of establishing the habit of going within, making your calls, for ten minutes a couple of times a day. And then during the day you keep your attention upon that which is constructive and try to remain aware of your Higher Self Spiritual Presence while you attend to the various activities of your day.

It is possible to live without mistakes

You are in a place of greater authority; you are capable of saying to yourself, "I forbid my outer self making any more mistakes. I just forbid it! Mighty Presence of Life within and above me, see to it that I do not make any more mistakes. I choose to live in my Heart. Anything that is outside of the Realm of Love is a mistake. There is only One Great Law—Divine Love, the natural threefold activity of Love, Wisdom and Power!"

You are growing, you are awakening; and I just know, Dear Hearts, that any one of you can develop *listening* that you can say to your God Presence, "Now you guide me here. I do not want to make any more mistakes where I have to use my energy to correct those mistakes. I am speaking to you. Thou art all knowing. You are the God of my Being. Guide me in every way. See to it that I do not make any more mistakes. Speak to me concerning all the matters of my Life. I am here. I am listening….!"

When you make that invitation, it is to just practice listening in prayerful meditation. You do not have to listen for hours; when you turn your attention to the Greatest Power in the Universe, things can happen very quickly, Dear Heart. Listen as though there is a very gentle friend within that has a very important message for you. Hold a sense of expectation—the qualities of anticipation and expectation are qualities in which you are opening the listening value within yourselves.

It is not so important that you get the answer the first time, but it is important that you open the *pathway* of listening. Then you go on about your day. You may be driving your vehicle, you may be attending to an errand in your life, and all of a sudden it is there, the guidance and the inner direction that you require in your life. Say to your Presence, "Give me all the insights, give me all the epiphanies I require each day!"

Your physical body desires to evolve...to grow equal to the expansion of your consciousness

There is another matter in this—you are heading for a time in which your *physical body* desires to evolve, to grow equal to the expansion of your consciousness, equal to the growth in your mind and your feelings. Call forth that Sacred Fire Victorious Love within yourselves; desire that your body let go of density, that it let go of the aging and that it open to an absolute renewal. Remember, everything is under *your* authority and use, through your feeling side of life where your *will* is stored for your use. Use these great gifts that have been given to you. Remind yourself, "I am connecting with the Greatest Power in the Universe, and when that Power is unleashed; it knows no boundaries; it knows no limitations!"

What is in your *atmosphere* is much worse than the density that has collected in your bodies

The physical body is a very easy vehicle to harmonize and purify. What is in your *atmosphere*, Dear Heart, is much worse than the density that has collected in your bodies. And that is why the Mighty Saint Germain gave humanity the prayer call to call forth the Cosmic Tube of Light from your Higher Spiritual I Am Self around your physical garments; so that the atmospheric pressure of human thoughtforms would stop getting into your mental and emotional bodies.

These conditions that prevail in the atmosphere are horrific. Today there are all sorts of things that are going on in peoples' lungs. It is everywhere because the *thoughtform* is prevailing. Some people would suggest, "Well, it is just the cold weather; it is cold and people are not bundling up so the lungs are being exposed." Ridiculous! It is the *thought* about cold weather, it is the thought about chills and flu that are creating these conditions, it is the human thoughtforms that are gathering in the atmosphere of your Earth that are contributing to these conditions and these become magnetized to people through their fear. However there is not any condition that cannot be corrected with the Sacred Fire Love.

You are always connecting with whatever you are agreeing with, with whatever you are placing your attention upon. Watch your attention. Watch where it goes…and the moment your attention tends to stress about things, or your mind is trying to worry about something—or your mind wants to think about something that is troubling or a condition out in the world—watch your mind! Speak to your mind "You come back here! I am not going to let you focus on that. You come back here! God is the Victorious Majestic Presence. I carry the Sacred Fire Love within my body—I am safe. I do not connect with those things that are destructive! My Beloved Great God Presence 'I AM', enfold me now in your Great Cosmic Armour of Light, your Tube of Cosmic Light substance that protects me from all the wrong conditions and thought forms that are in the Earth's atmosphere and hold your Tube of Light sustained around me at all times, I thank and bless you."

The attention is the window in which you connect with what is in your World

The attention is the window in which you connect with what is in the world. It is so vital, especially in the future, that you hold your attention more upon the Light, or upon Archangel Michael. Hold your attention upon the

Luminous Presence of the Ascended Jesus Christ. Hold your attention upon the Angelic Host and all the healing they can do in your feeling side of life. Hold your attention upon your own Beloved Great God Presence and then the light of all of that will prevail within your outer selves. Again, this is not to take you out of the world—this is to bring you *into* the world safely, but no longer *of* it.

Everything that appears in manifestation is a qualification of energy. So, you will find that your fulfillment in your earthly journey is going to take on greater manifestation if you will simply qualify all your experiences "I qualify all the supply in my life with Sacred Fire Victorious Love and Power. I qualify all my interactions this day with Archangel Michael's Cosmic Blue Flame!" The Sacred Fire is here to stop the *interference* with the Divine Plan of your life. It is here to stop the interfering with your Divine Consciousness expressing through you. That is what the Sacred Fire is here to do; to stop the interference so that in this life—in one life—you have the opportunity to come into full manifestation of the Christ Being that you are, and then you can begin to manipulate energy in the most magnificent and constructive way.

Manipulation! That is a word that has been tragically misused because of human beings' willingness to misuse and to abuse self and each other. The word *manipulation* does not have too much of a positive connotation, does it? And it is because there has been the wrong use of the vibration of *manipulation*. Yet there would be no Universe, there would be no Systems of Worlds, there would be no Powers of Nature and the Forces of the Elements if energy was not molded, if it was not sculpted—if it was not manipulated and qualified to manifest itself in a certain way. So it is the most natural thing to do, to manipulate energy. This is *exactly* what your thoughts and your feelings and your spoken words are doing—you are qualifying, you are manipulating energy. Energy is a very willing servant. We want you to do it *consciously*; we want you to *think* about your Field of Dreams. And we want you to know that there is a greater means for you accomplishing your Vision and your Field of Dreams—use the Sacred Fire Love that is available from your Beloved Higher Self Presence and the Ascended and Angelic Host! We ask you to use it and call it forth into your lives, your loved ones...

The Electrons in your body are waiting to receive the points of Light at the centre of each cell

Call upon Archangel Michael's Cosmic Blue Flame to stop the destruction that is expressing through a human being; or the destruction that is expressing in your lives or that is expressing in your worlds. It will do it! And I will say, Blessed of the Heart, you are not being truthful with yourself if you do not know that in this moment destruction is still taking place in your body. If the body is yet aging—destruction is taking place. The body was not created in the beginning to age and die. Aging took place as a result of the discord sown by human beings. Death was a Dispensation, so that as the bodies aged and became immobile, you would have an opportunity to leave that body and come back in a new one. And try again. Indeed.

So you see, you can call upon Archangel Michael. All the Ascended Host know the Divine Plan for human beings, and when you compel them to release their Sacred Fire Victorious Love into your body, your mind and your feelings...to stop all destruction...they will do so. Then the Light that is yet imprisoned within you can be released into *every cell of your body*. It will bring about a metamorphosis, in which your body energy quickens, and the cells release the activity that is within the Points of Light, which is the

Light Pattern of your bodies; the Points of Light become free to produce a perfecting activity within the body as they ping the electrons that are asleep within your body into activity. That is what the electrons in your body are doing, Dear Hearts. They are waiting to receive the points of light at the centre of each cell. But the points of light at the centre of each cell are not released until they are connected back to the Light within your own Heart Centre by the Sacred Fire.

Your atoms can be qualified with human thoughts and beliefs, but your electrons cannot.

That is why Akasha has given you the Invocation, "I call upon my Golden Heart Flame within me to expand and expand and expand, and to become *one* with the points of light in every cell of my body." Upon that call, your Heart Flame expands, and the great expansion of light activates your Light Body and each point of light. As those points of light are touched, they begin to expand, they begin to pulse; and the light *explodes* within the cell, allowing that light to be released and take its dominion. Then the light flows through the cell and connects with the electrons in your body; once the electron receives the light from the centre of the cell, the electrons become active within the body and the body begins throwing off the aging process. Remember, Dear Heart, your atoms can be qualified with human thoughts and beliefs, but the *electrons* cannot— They are Superior and are a mini focus of the Heart of God. They never take on duality. May your Inner God Light expand each day and make you a blazing sun of great light and love to the world!

✻

CHAPTER *Five*

I Am Akasha and I greet you in the name of Beloved Mighty Archangel Michael, and may His Blessings, which are endless, and his own Sacred Fire Love truly find a welcoming Heart within each of you.

I would like to address your life. Only a short while ago, I suggested that each of you might hold the desire within you that your life be loved free from all limitation. In deep prayer and meditation, affirm "I desire that my Life be loved free of all lack, of all discord, of all confusion." You will notice that sometimes I refer to that word *confusion*, for often it is that which has been projected at you that finds itself lodged within the human mind, that keeps the inner knowing, the inner promptings, and fields of inner activities from coming into a higher state of awareness and enlightenment.

Hold within yourself a Desire to love your Life free

Hold within yourself the desire to be loved free. Remember to remind yourself, to speak to the God of your knowing, to speak to Michael, to speak to all of the Ascended Host, "I desire to be free of all that I have gathered about myself that is limiting my journey and obscuring my vision. My Beloved Great God Presence, Great Host of Light, make it so. Make it so. Make it so."

If you will hold the desire that your life be loved free, then it is that Flame of Eternal Love that abides within each of you that shall be fanned; for that which is the fanning of the Sacred Fire—that Mighty Heart Flame—is *desire* itself. Desire is the fanning of the Spark of Love, and when that Spark of Love is fanned, it bursts into an Immortal Flame. And when that Flame is continuously fanned by *desire*, the Flame bursts into a blazing miniature Sun's Presence where light prevails. Where the light prevails, the mind is drawn up into a state of enlightenment, and it is in this place where you have the opportunity to know your calling, and to live that calling each day.

So put those two ribbons together. Couple your desire to love your life free with the knowing that if you continue to *maintain* that desire, you fan the Mighty Flame of Life within you. Then it is the Mighty Flame of Life within you that brings you the results of that desire.

I offer you the third piece of this, and that is to love and to treasure life, for truly it is a sacred jewel itself; for you have often been referred to as the 'Children of the Diamond Heart', the light that comes out of the Super Diamond Electron of the Heart Centre, where life is initiated out from. Love life, and seek the joy and the true happiness, the true creativity, and all expressions that life affords, where life is not tainted, when life is not lessened, where life is not compromised by limiting human desires. Love life, and seek to desire those moments of greater happiness because the Sacred Fire Love will give you those moments of true happiness and true joy. Not happiness that is fragmented, but happiness that is the outpouring of your own Heart Flame, where there is nothing within your emotional body that can chip away at that happiness, or lessen it.

Light, Love, Self, are but different worded expressions for the One Great Activity 'I AM' or God

The love of life, the love of God, the love of self, the love of light—this is all the same activity, simply under different worded expressions. There is a great unity that is coming forth from out of the heart of the developing human race. It is in this growing unity that you will find the *essence* of what I speak of when I say to you that—*God, Self, Light, Love,* are but different worded expressions for the One Great Activity, 'I AM.' Each of you is that activity, waiting to be fully discovered, realized and actualized. Each of you are removing the blinders of limiting belief systems; each of you have been on a voyage of unclothing yourself of the perceptual values and the spell of a belief in two powers—the belief in good or bad, negative or positive, and by doing so you are opening the way for the Oneness of Life to find its expression.

Love your life! Love your body! Respect your body! This is the first journey in hundreds of embodiments where the physical bio-form, the body, is no longer sacrificed; where the hardened religious belief systems, or fragmented schools of thought, are no longer limiting the journey. When love is allowed to weave itself through the physical, the mental, and the emotional attributes of the human resources—the outer expression—there are heights of joy; there are heights of happiness and attainment that are a thousand times greater than any expression of pleasure that can come to you through the human senses. Of course, will you realize that I am speaking of Divine Love when I say Love, and keep in mind that Divine Love is a threefold activity of Love, Wisdom and Power? I hope you will try to remember this.

Only you, Beloved of the Heart, only you can open the door to this greater love. Mighty Jesus cannot do it for you.

155

The Heavenly Father/Mother themselves cannot do it for you. Such is the authority that has been placed in your hands! We can assist you; however, it must start with *you* and *your* desire. And it begins by reminding yourself that you are not here to be a victim of what has been created in this world—you are here now to *undo* creation that is limiting you. You are here to become the authority for what shows up in your mind, your feelings, your body and your world—to direct energy, through the qualifying of your thoughts, feelings and spoken word, how it shall act in your life.

The idea of imaging, visualizing, is a tremendous activity

You are here on a great journey, and I say to you, the healing that has come about so far is sufficient for the continual releasing of that inner splendour that is hidden within your hearts. Asun and I have often thought that while there is yet a *conceptual* realization to the human thought, then perhaps there are yet some concepts that are worthy of embracing if they create an opening to the greater light. And if a concept, an image, speaks to you, you can use the art of visualization. For example, you can choose an *image* that represents to you the *inner splendour* that has been locked within, that has not been unleashed. You might visualize bars, in the outer chest area, like prison bars, and you see that inner Golden Sun's Presence inside, behind those bars. Imagine your hands taking those bars, like Superman or Superwoman, and pulling those bars back, allowing that which is the *Inner Splendour* to unfold. You can see the light pouring out from you, enfolding you. It is that light that will heal your bodies, it is that light that will bring you into a state of illumination, it is that light that will be the great corrector of all limitation in your life, for it is the light of your own inner Heart Flame. Be creative. See it! Feel it! Meditate on it daily!

It is not *you* who enlighten yourselves—it is you that *direct the process* where enlightenment by the light within can come forth. This is very important. You can study great books and great philosophies to establish some form of evolution but in the end it is *you* who decide. It is *you* who choose. It is *you* who desire and it is *you* who direct. And I say to you, if you direct yourself, and if it works for you to see your own Inner Presence of Light behind bars—and that you could pull those bars apart—then pull them apart allowing that Sun's Presence full expression through you. Visualize it!

The idea of imaging or the idea of visualizing is a tremendous activity for accenting your evolution and the full expression of your inner power. Contemplate it well, because if you are willing to work with this in meditation, the light is registering your great acceptance of this inner power that resides within each of you "I so love my body for the instrument that it shall become in housing the living light that declares 'I AM' the Light that cometh into the World, and I invoke the opening of that light, which is *All-knowing*." When it registers that you are doing everything you can to release the light through acceptance and imaging, then visualization can be a wonderful tool and a useful activity in your lives.

A state of being in which there is an 'Isness' that finds a deep restful and peaceful place within yourself

There is not anything now that you cannot transmute. Oftentimes, it is in these days ahead that you will seek to be in balance in all things—a balance of self-evaluation and a balance of just being and listening, just being with yourself—a balance that engages all your outer activities

157

such as work or a balance of rest and a balance of applying yourself. You can only invoke the truth to come forth so many times—then that truth but waits for the opportunity in which the outer self is in a state of balance and relaxation, where the outer self has created chemistry within itself through introspection and contemplation and quiet anticipation. It can be a magical moment in which you are simply in your joy, such full relaxation knowing that all is well in your world.

Because you have daily invoked this Great God Presence within yourselves to come forth, that great Presence watches every future moment, and oftentimes it watches for that moment in which you are in a state of being peaceful, a state of being that has no human qualifying to it or a state of being in which there is an *Isness* that finds a deep restful and peaceful place within yourself. And it is that place where the *All-knowingness* of your inner power seizes the opportunity and expands in a flash of a second, bringing you into an epiphany, bringing you into an awareness, bringing you into a state of greater peace and illumined consciousness that gives you the insights and inner guidance and the directions for your life and the days that are ahead of you!

Words are vehicles of energy; your words are the vehicles of your thoughts and feelings

Love your life in this lifetime! I say to you, Beloved of the Heart, it matters not whether you are nineteen years in the body or ninety years in the body, it makes no difference, for the Mighty Flame of Life within you—the Soul of your Being—knows no age. You are not sixty-three years *old*, you are sixty-three years *young*. Why do you not change that word? Instead of saying old when somebody asks you your age, say, "I am forty-seven years young."

It has not yet registered fully, this whole subject called *the language of words*. Yet words are vehicles—as Angels are the vehicles of the Sacred Fire to your world, to help you harmonize, purify, and raise yourselves; your words are the vehicles of your thought/feeling matrix into manifestation at a greater pace than the silent thought—words are vehicles of qualified energy and intention. Words are that phraseology in which a phrase of words carries the intent of the vibration of the energy that has been qualified, so that it can come forth into manifestation much more quickly. In the future, you cannot just say, "It is just a word"; because if the Universe hears you saying 'It is just a word', the Universe knows that there is a part of you that is in denial that you truly are the authority for everything that takes place in your life. And if you say to the Universe that you are fully awakened, yet you continue to use words or phrases such as *I hate* or *I can't*, then you are sending a strong message to the Universe. So, your words and messages now have to become very positive and clear if you wish to free yourself of limitation.

You have to be specific as to what financial freedom feels and looks like to you

Many of you in your prayer calls to *Life* are calling to your Great God Presence and the Angels for financial freedom. It is not that your own Higher Self does not know what financial freedom looks like, or that the Angels do not know what financial freedom is—certainly they do—but they are not the authority, *you* are the authority. And the only way that they can give you financial freedom is that you are absolutely *clear* as to what financial freedom feels and looks like to you.

Take the time to sit down and contemplate what financial freedom looks like to you. This is important; this is not something that you do off-the-cuff. This is not something that you say, "Well, I am going to sit down for fifteen minutes." This is something that could affect the next two to three years of your life. This is something that you say, "For the next week this is going to be my contemplation. I cannot continue to call forth financial freedom, and know that I can have financial freedom, and not experience it." That's enough to make you mad, Dear Heart, to know that you can have financial freedom, which is a truth, and to know that you can call forth financial freedom and not to experience it. That's enough in itself to upset anyone.

When you have too much of that kind of activity, do you know what happens? You stop calling. You get frustrated, "It doesn't work for me." It doesn't work for you, Dear Hearts, because—and this is why I repeat myself so often, so that it is going to go deep into your consciousness—*you* are the authority. The paintbrush is in your hands! This world is your canvas! You have to be specific as to what financial freedom feels and looks like for you; if that is obscure, then you will have an obscure manifestation that is less than pleasing. You must feel the will—the feeling—for that freedom.

Some of you are carrying some 'renouncing' energy, because you still have past lifetimes that are very close in your feeling body that were rich in spiritual growth, but you renounced the world to have that. In those lifetimes, it did not give you your freedom; because if it did, you would not be here today in this lifetime. Yes, it might have spiritualized your life, it might have brought you up a peg, a notch in life, but it did not give you your freedom, otherwise you would not be here in this lifetime. When you have gained absolute freedom by the end of a life journey on Earth, you are no longer returned to this world—you have gained your *Ascension.*

160

If you are going to be the artist of your life, you are going to start paying attention to the details

When you love life, you have to be willing to look at where limitation and lack is showing up. It is not just a lack of money; it is a lack of illumination, lack of understanding, lack of loving, lack of joy, lack of companionship or lack of loving yourself in some aspect of your life. Those of you who have found a partner in life who is of equal heart and mind to you, you have no idea how blessed you are; and you are blessed that way because there is attainment in this and former lives that you have worked for. And when there is the effort for attainment, life gives back to you, Dear Hearts.

If you are going to love life, you will have to be the artist of your life—you are going to start paying attention to details. Details are a very interesting thing. Does it mean that you have to be aware of every single detail in the great portrait of your life? Or does it mean that you are aware of the details in the *feeling*, the essence...? What is the *essence* of what you are going to bring forth into manifestation? In identifying financial freedom for your lives, have you built some energy around your ability to be very active, to move around this world in any way with ease and with grace? Are you living in beautiful homes? Do you have every care and requirement taken care of?

Every one of you is created as a very unique expression of God Life. Some of you love to have life serve you back, and others of you love to be the serving. It doesn't matter. It does not matter what you want in life, as long as it is good, as long as it is constructive. It is you that must convince yourself, because if you made a journey home to the Great Central Sun, and if you had the opportunity to sit with your Heavenly Mother Father, and you asked

161

them, "Is it all right to be a billionaire on Earth?" They would say, "Of course it is all right, my goodness, *you* are the authority for your life!" The Heavenly Father loved you so much that He has given you His Mind; the Heavenly Mother has loved you so much that She has given you Her Heart and *the feeling side of life.* And the individualization of them *together*—The 'I AM' Presence—has loved you so much—that it has given you a physical body to unfold your beautiful self and reality!

You are complete to go forth a God Being, and by your thoughts and your feelings do you decree energy to manifest in your life. If you are seeking the light, if you are seeking your freedom in this lifetime, if you are seeking that Angels walk with you, if you are seeking to see your Great God Presence with your physical sight—you are seeking to be here in this world to make a difference. You are seeking to demonstrate and prove God in your life; you are seeking to prove to the world that there is One Master over the hate and the evil that is in this world—and that Master is Divine Love, Sacred Fire Love that each of you can invoke into your lives.

The energy of discount stores

If this is what you desire, why should you not live in magnificent homes—why should you not have the finery in life—why should you not have beautiful technology in your homes in which the sounds of music can reflect in the finest way? Why should you not have beautiful paintings, and vases filled with glorious flowers? Why should you not have magnificent wardrobes that allow you to express the finer energy of your being? Why should you not shop in the finer stores?

There is a tremendous energy of lack happening in certain stores, Dear Heart. You might not like to hear this—all the more reason I'll say it—*everything* has energy. There are certain stores in your shopping malls that sell great volumes of clothes at discounted prices, and I will not mention their names, you know what I refer to. They are big barns or warehouses. There are these places, yes? And those clothes have energy to them...

And then there are those places, in your villages and your cities, where you can go into—those boutiques—and of course usually they have a little bit more real estate tagged to them. Do they not? But they are a finer garment. They have been prepared with a little more loving care, and chances are they are made of fine cottons and fine silks; they are not made of the, forgive me, the heavy denims that are in the world today.

And so, everything carries a vibration of energy. That is the point I was making. If you go to these barn-like places, where you can get all your discounted clothes and you can get three-dollar pairs of trousers, then the energy is not going to be the same. I hear your voice, Dear Heart, and I hear you saying, "Oh, yes, but I can go in and re-qualify it with the Sacred Fire...!" Well, if that's what you want to do with the energy of your life—spend your whole day re-qualifying—so be it! It is an absolute waste of time, if you ask me.

Your Presence cannot deny you. You say to your Presence, "This body is your temple, this temple belongs to you—it is your light that I have come to expand within this temple. See to it that I have the means to clothe this temple in those garments that hold the finer energy within them." Your Presence will not deny you!

Ask Saint Germain—Shakespeare—to give you the inner meaning of Life hidden in cipher code within His Plays

Find within yourself, the sanctuary of your life. Speak to yourself that you are carrying the Holy of Holies within your Heart Centre. Accept the power that is your Presence when you turn your attention towards it when you invoke it to come forth in your life, and you say, "Now there is no failure in my calls, to my prayers. I am now communicating with the Greatest Power in Life. I am no longer outside of life. I am back in the centre of the stream. I am in alignment with truth. I am calling forth the Full Power of my Cosmic Christ Self, my Great God Flame, the Violet Flame and the Cosmic Blue Flame of the Angelic Host—to go before me, out into my world, as the manifestation of all that I desire, all that I require, now made manifest in my life." When you do this each day, and your days become weeks and your weeks become a momentum, and when your glass, your Crystal Cup, is full with the momentum of that energy— wondrous manifestation takes place in your life!

Look at your life! You have been given a stage to live upon. Imagine your life as you are living it now. Imagine that it is a great musical, it is a great play that is playing itself out in the theatres of New York; and there are thousands of people coming in every day to watch your play—your life that is unfolding on the stage. Is there anything that you might want to change, in light of this concept?

The Mighty Saint Germain has given you a tremendous gift in his last life embodiment as William Shakespeare— the Shakespearean Plays. Perhaps you would like to go to the library to read some of these, or the notes around the Shakespearean plays because he has placed the drama of the human theatre that has unfolded civilization after civilization and the whole truth of *why* you are here, in them. But he has also hidden in those plays the future, and the Divine Purpose of Life. With the discernment and the enlightenment that each of you have today, you can go back to those Shakespearean Plays, read them, and ask the Mighty Saint Germain—who wrote those plays—to give you the inner meaning of life that is hidden in cipher code within his plays.

Ask him to over-light you as you read them. Ask that his last lifetime on Earth as William Shakespeare over-light you. Then you would become a very interesting observer, and you would begin to see what he weaved within the theatre of those plays. You would begin to understand what the Mighty Saint Germain as William Shakespeare—William, Will-iam—the Will of the 'I AM', to Shake a Spear—was saying in those tremendous writings that were given to humankind.

You can move around what is manifesting on your stage of life

Then you could shift your attention after studying those works, and then look at your own life and you would look at your life with a transformed state of mind and heart. You would look at your life more in the capacity to stand back as the creator, as the observer to see where life is playing itself out in a manner that you can go in and shift it so that it is playing out in a different manner, a more fulfilling one. I am quite certain that as you embrace the application of what has been brought forth here; you will truly find that the life outside of you is a stage, and you are the Star Being. And each of you is choosing to be co-stars in everyone else's life, that you are celebrating *their* life.

Ah! To live in that place of ease, where energy obeys you instantly, where simply you can move that which is in your life with as much ease as you move the characters in

165

a good game of chess, with no resistance. To know that you are the authority, and that when you decide that you are finished with an experience, you say to yourself, "I have nothing further to learn from this experience. I am at my zero point and I have nothing further to learn from it." That's an announcement to yourself!

I would also make that announcement by asking my feeling side, asking the Goddess energy within my feelings, "By the way, is there anything that I am holding in my feeling side of life that is suggesting that I am yet holding a value on the experience that I am having?" At any moment you can have a curtain call, you can make a new choice. At any moment, when the curtain is drawn—and all those who are watching your life get to take a reprieve and go have a break—you can move the players around. You can move around what is manifesting on your stage of life. It is your life, and all that is in your world is a manifestation of energy that has been qualified by your thoughts, your feelings, and your beliefs.

Each of you knows where you are at in your evolution. There are times during the day that you are more aware than at other times of the day. There are some times during the day when it is appropriate to say—as the great Mystic claimed—to say to life, "Here I am, I am an empty cup." Why did the Master Jesus offer this suggestion? Because the human mind is so filled with beliefs and concepts and thoughts that have nothing to do with the truth, and therefore there is no room for the light to come forth, where the *light* and its *wisdom* might express through your mind.

When your mind is filled with light—when the Light Rays penetrate the brain, allowing the brain into a greater vibration where it can house an expanding mind—then, Dear Heart, you are a direct knowing of higher thoughts

166

and ideals and inspirations that you can act upon all throughout your day. But if you are not at that place, then it is good to sometimes have that ten minutes, where you say, "Lord of my Life, here I am. And I come as an empty cup to be filled with Your Light, Your Wisdom, Your Joy." Then the Light comes in and brings you into clarity, It brings you into a clear mind—you are thinking right again, you are getting directions, you are receiving wonderful new ideas; the field of inner prompting from your Higher Self is expressing through your feeling and everything is working again in your life.

The real 'estate' of the Planet must increase

To love life, is to give yourself every opportunity to achieve everything that your Ascended aspect of yourself—your Great God Presence—desires for you. It is to give yourself the opportunity to live a life of joy, a life of grace, a life in which the real 'estate' of your life has truly taken on greater value—one that cannot be measured in monetary terms. I suggested a while ago that the real estate of Earth, of the Planet, would go through a tremendous change where that which has no real value, will continue to diminish, so that the true value and virtues of life can be found and realized. This is now playing itself out.

Your stock markets have plunged and risen several times and will continue to adjust until there is equal value of what has been placed on the market and its real investment potential. While this happens, the real estate of the Planet must increase. If the stock market is going to be used constructively—because more human beings are making constructive choices and coming back into a state of love—then the stock market must be a true reflection of the growing true real estate of *tangibles* in your world and their potential. There is a need to remove from the stock market and financial institutions that which is destructive, wrong, selfish and greedy.

When this is complete, 'the placing' of the wealth of the world into the hands of those who are constructive and awakening—will then proceed for this is a divine plan waiting fulfillment. Mark my words, Dear Heart, "If there is no real 'value estate' behind something in the stock market, you will lose your money." The only thing that the Ascended Host can support is when there is a product of great value that contributes to the upward progression of humanity. And when I say 'real estate' I am not simply speaking of the value of a home—I am speaking of the value of the Florida citrus crops, I am speaking of the value of farm and agriculture and mining and lumber. I am speaking of the value of human life. I am speaking of the value of the great treasures and resources that this Earth provides when constructive human beings join with the Earth to bring forth wonderful manifestations—it is *that* real estate, beginning with human life and resources, with gold, silver, diamonds, apples, oranges, strawberries, homes, automobiles...anything that is a *tangible*.

Think of human resource, of commerce, think of communication, think of technology, of engineering, think of physics, the arts and fields of invention. Think of the future, whether it be in the area of space technology, whether it be in the area of medicines, whether it be in the area of telecommunications, for this is all future real estate. Tremendous Light is pouring into this ideal. That tremendous Light is a result of more of Life being loved. And it is as a result of the Sacred Fire Love of the Spiritual Hierarchy over-lighting everyone who is constructive.

Those who are of greed and selfishness and have hidden plans against humanity will be exposed

While there are those who want to take the world into a war, or a localized war, there are those who will maintain peace in other areas. There is a separation that will take place on your Earth. And while this takes place, that which has no value will continue to diminish. Those who are of greed and selfishness and have hidden dark plans against humanity will be exposed, while that which is of value—the real estate of life, and all who are of good mind to protect this Planet, to protect the wealth of this world—will find a transfer of power, a transfer of wealth into their use along with protection from the Angelic Host.

To love life is also to love the opportunity to be responsible for the life that you have been given. There is many a great man or woman who has realized that to be given great power, there must be a realization of great responsibility that comes with that power. There are many yet in the world who do not desire accountability and responsibility for their thoughts, their feelings and their actions.

When you enter into willingness for accountability and responsibility, willingness to love your life free, willingness to love the sanctuary of your life or a willingness to be a force for freedom in this world, these are the very fabric of good character that draws to you the Love of the Angels, and Angels will come upon you. Any one Angel who knows of your constructive desires can stand in the midst of your world, release its Sacred Fire, and stop all destructive action that could possibly limit their fulfillment! Any one Angel can purify cities and perform great activities, but cannot do so without the will of the people.

The shadow of darkness seeks those who do not have a vision for humanity

Your Archangel Michael spoke to you of the great thing that requires attention that is visiting the door of humanity at this time. It is the same energy that created the two World Wars. It was that shadow that came again in Korea and in Vietnam that was lessened, because of the growing heart and the growing desire in human beings that war be no longer acceptable and tolerable. It is a shadow that has touched Europe, Africa and Asia many times historically.

And then, do you not see it, Dear Heart, what happens is that years go by once a war is over and then human beings do not stand guard for their liberties; a few years go by, and the sinister force that has not yet been removed from the world seeks to seize upon humanity again. The sinister force has been lessened, yes, but it has not been removed from the world in its *entirety*. It is Cosmic Law—as long as there is one human being who is willing to be discordant, the entirety of the sinister force cannot be removed. However, sufficient of it can be removed so that the mass of humanity can continue to evolve.

So this shadow lurks, and it waits. It waits for human beings to enjoy the modernization of life; it waits for the light to expand, knowing that the light will translate as much happier times, wonderful new creations, colour televisions, computers and many other blessings that ease life into greater comfort. That lurking darkness waits while civilization evolves. Once again, humanity has their toys. And once again, the attention is on the *outer*. That shadow just waits—it waits until enough of the attention is back on the outer and humanity is in an unguarded moment, and then, Dear Hearts, it seizes. It feeds upon those who are weak in your governments of every nation.

That shadow seeks those who do not have a vision for humanity. That shadow seeks those who are selfish, who are there for their own selfish reasons in positions of influence and authority and that shadow gets in them and then they themselves do not even know that they have become pawns in which that shadow will seek to express itself. And then the shadow grows within your parliaments, it grows within your Congress, and then you have those who call for war. Those who have the shadow within them—and do not even understand—find the reason. Well, of course you can find a reason for war if you have the shadow of war within you. You will find, "Oh, yes, I can intellectualize that. I can see why we need to go and attack another nation..."

I say to your nations that stand for the freedom of this Earth, Blessed Hearts, your nations of a United Europe, the United States of America and the Americas and many other nations that love liberty and freedom, there is enough weaponry in the civilized world to keep any country that threatens this world contained. Human beings are too often *led* to believe something else—when already you have a *thousand times* the armaments necessary to contain any destructive dictator or nation that threatens the world; simply through the great technology available in the armies and the navies and the great new aerial ships, the new technology that is hidden within aircraft carriers, the advanced technology of satellites and more. If any of you had the opportunity to walk through these ships you would just be amazed at the technology there!

Washington's Vision

To have those on Earth that would suggest to you that the free nations of this world do not have the ability to contain a renegade nation is absolutely ludicrous, and it is a lie against human life. It is rather that the shadow of war is seeking again to find its expression; and the hatred and evil that finds expression in this world will not be satisfied until the third episode of Washington's Vision has an opportunity to find expression. And this, Oh Human Life, must never happen! The third episode of Washington's Vision speaks of a potential destruction of the Three Americas—Canada, America, South America—which is followed with the destruction of the entire world. The sinister force knows this and wants this.

If any of you care to know more about this, you can do some research. You can research and you can find the Message of the Great Angel that visited Washington in his greatest hour of need, in that terrible war. You can read of the Visions which this one was given, and you can see that the third Vision, if allowed to come forth, would be the end of the world as you know it. And it is for this reason that the war energy keeps trying to come back, to draw America into war, and then for everything to get out of control, just as it did in World War II. Well, fortunately, the light prevailed. Fortunately—at the end of World War II—the advancement of technology was sufficient for those who stood for democracy to stop the spread of socialism and communism that has been in this world.

Call for the release of whole new Legions of the Angelic Host, to stop the planned destruction of humankind.

Where has humanity fallen in the past? Humanity has fallen into a trap when most unguarded. You will guard your lives when you love your life. And you will understand that every Life Stream that is in your great nation Canada—the *Crown* of the Three Americas—is equal to every other life, whether that be a life in Kuwait, a life in Iraq, a life in Britain, or the Asian continents. Your life is *equal* to that life, and to love life is to love *all* of life. And if you will

172

love all of life, you will not care for war—you will become a *commanding presence* for the will of peace on Earth! You will take the time to enter the sanctuary of your being and command the Great Central Sun, the Archangels, and the Seven Mighty Elohim, to release whole new Legions of the Angelic Host into the lower atmosphere of the Earth, to stop any planned destruction of humankind.

Human beings cannot yet avail themselves to the history of war and bloodshed that has taken place in Earth's history. You have your last few thousand years of history that you are aware of, but if you could look beyond that history you will find the destruction of the once great nations of Arabia, Lemuria and Atlantis and in South America; such fine civilizations that existed in former times, and all lost by those who would take humanity into war, time after time after time.

And so, Beloved, we say to you, this discourse is given that you might find within your Hearts the closeness of the Archangel Michael and the protection he offers the world if the will of humanity wants that protection. He has joined with the Great Divine Director who oversees all Life Streams to this System of Worlds. He has joined with the Mighty Saint Germain, Master Jesus and the Great Cosmic Being Sanat Kumara who has come from Venus—to relieve this world of the discord and the desire for war; to silence those things and take them swiftly out of your Solar System so they may not appear anywhere in the Universe again!

Many now are responding to the Call for the upward progression of humanity and the Earth, for Resurrection and Ascension. The Indigo Souls are all returning to the Earth. The new Violet Souls are coming in. All are ready. They are ready to merge humanity with the light, not for another *battle*—the battle of Armageddon took place in the two World Wars. All the forces of light are merging, Dear Hearts; and these forces of light, including the light

173

that is within yourself, they are not merging to gear up for another battle—they are merging so that the light of God prevails on Earth. They are merging so that Prime Ministers and Presidents and Kings and Queens will have a change of heart and will stop taking the children of Earth, the children of light, into war.

The Light will prevail through new great councils and leaders

The light will prevail. The people will prevail. You have today in the United Nations of the world a new Security Council that has been established. The rank of influence and authority that has been won by nations such as France, and Russia and China—these positions of authority that they have on the Security Council of the United Nations—is very, very important authority. It is very important that the authority that they have as permanent members of the Security Council be a *useful and constructive* authority and not an ineffective United Nations.

They know this, they desire this. Unfortunately it is because of this reason that probably nations such as France and Russia and China will be called upon to vote with other permanent members to make legitimate a war upon a nation. This probably will be the last time that the nations that are from the Security Council of the United Nations will be trapped into voting for something that they do not wish to vote for. But if they do not vote, their position in the Security Council will be seen as being weakened and ineffective, and this is not what they desire.

So you see, Dear Hearts, there are tremendous Forces of Light available to the Earth. Archangel Michael is preparing whole new Legions of Angels of Illumination to over-light the leaders, the ambassadors, the great committees, the lobbyists in America, the United Nations and the free nations of the world that there will be a change of heart; there will be the courage and the will to say *no* to the hidden plans that are against humanity, to say no to the destructive forces, and to say yes to that which the good people of the free world—of the entire world—are desiring at this time.

"...Do *through* this outer self..." that's the key! That is the key covenant! That is the key desire!

When you love your life, when you realize that there is a very great need that is knocking at the door of human life once again, you will realize that Archangel Michael has spoken very well to you. He made you realize that the awakened, aware of the Spiritual Hierarchy, are the only ones that they can use to work through to reach greater numbers of humanity. Because you are yet not so familiar with the Great Powers that are found in the Sacred Fire of the Higher Octaves of Earth, you do not yet know what Archangel Michael and the Ascended Masters can do *through* you for your nations, but it suffices to have the desire "Mighty Presence of Life, Great Host of Light, Archangel Michael, blaze your Sacred Fire Love through this outer self, purifying and harmonizing this outer self of all discordant creation, and do through me what you know my country and my world most requires for freedom of the people of Earth and this Planet. I thank you."

"...Do *through* this outer self..." that's the key! That's the key covenant! That's the key desire!—You placing your attention upon the Great Ones, and saying to Them, "Do *through* me what my city, my country, my world, the people of the Earth require, do through me what *you* know they most require to secure the freedom of the Earth and humanity, and to secure the Ascended Masters' Divine Plan for the people of the Earth fulfilled. I offer myself as thy instrument. Do through me what you know the Powers of Nature and the Forces of the Elements require at this time to be free of the tragic discord that is imposed upon them!" The Ascended Masters Plan is God's Plan!

One lovely temperature of comfort in the Earth's lower atmosphere

As long as there are storms, as long as there are hurricanes, as long as there are twisters and tornadoes; as long as there are dramatic shifts in temperature changes—one day cold, one day warm—then you know, Dear Heart, that is an aberration. What is normal and a part of a greater Divine Plan for the Earth, is the warming of the Planet where it is cooler, and a lessening of the heat where there is extreme heat and where there is a desert—a transformation and normalization of an expanding of *equal* temperatures, so that there is one temperate zone within North America, east and west of the Rockies and north and south. Your planet's evolution provides there shall be one lovely temperature that shall prevail—where there is extreme heat in the deserts shall become enjoyable and warm; and where it is cool in other areas will become warmer. It is a natural Divine Plan for one climate for each land mass continent. It is the Divine Plan for all parts of the world—that you will have one temperature for each land mass that is governed by the Great Presence of Life that expresses through the Powers of Nature and the Forces of the Elements.

So beyond the change and the transformation that must happen, when you have an aberration of sudden temperature changes, storms, and tornadoes—this, Dear Hearts, is the Powers of Nature and the Forces of the Elements that have taken on the burden of human beings' discord; and that discord reaches a point where it has to express, and it expresses as the nasty weather conditions that human beings experience.

So, in loving life, in loving the Powers of Nature, life can bless you back. There are many ways in which life can bless you. When you look to the Higher Selves of other human beings, when you see the Higher Self above them instead of the human that is standing in front of you—the Higher Self will bless you. When you call upon Michael and the Ascended Host to do through you what your country and the people of the world require—then Michael and the Higher Selves of the country and the world will bless you. When you invoke Michael and Saint Germain and Mighty Jesus to do through you what the Powers of Nature and the Forces of the Elements require to be free of the discord that is imposed upon them—the Powers of Nature and the Forces of the Elements, they will come and bless you. The Maha Chohan, a great Cosmic Ascended Being of Light who oversees the Authority of the Earth and its Elements, will bless you with more abundance and treasure than you could measure in your life!

When you seek to love life so fully, that your life is about being such an outpouring of light that goes forth from you in all directions, and just loves and blesses all life, then that light, as it goes out into the world, will grow and grow, and eventually it must follow a return path to you. When that light comes back to you it will be so expanded, and it will manifest as everything you require, everything you desire.

The true Law of giving and receiving

I have left you a hint, Dear Hearts; even that which is the area of supply, revenues—forget about receiving. Be conscious of *giving* the light that is found in your hearts. Every day you can command your light to expand out a thousand feet, a thousand yards, a thousand miles or more, as a blessing to all life outside of you that just lifts and heals and is a resurrection to all life outside of you. Then that light and life must come back and bless you and bless you and bless you. You do not have to convince it to, you do not have to ask it to—everything that goes out from source returns to source; that is why each of you in your Ascended State will become the perfection of the Great Central Sun one day.

All the energy of your life, all your thoughts, your spoken words, all your feelings that are broadcast out into the world, are constantly returning to you. And every day can be a day of renewal, a day of rebirth of your intentions and the power of your attention. At any moment you can take a minute and declare to your Presence, "Make of me a blazing outpouring of the Sacred Fire Love, of the Cosmic Christ Light, that just blazes out from me a thousand miles and more, blessing and healing all life outside of me." That one call, Dear Hearts, if done many times a day, that light will go forth and set Life Free. It will obey your command, and it will bless and bless, and all that it blesses will bless you back. That light will grow and grow, and when it comes back to you it will bless you with all that you truly require in life.

This is the true Law of Giving and Receiving. This is the true Law of Exchange. This is far greater in its value than human law, don't you think? God Bless you, Dear Hearts, and Namaste.

❋

CHAPTER SIX

As you grow and evolve up into the very truth and essence of your being, more and more the use of the words 'I AM' will become very important in your life. The understanding of the words 'I AM' as the name of God, of God in Action, as the name of your true Divine Self, as the name of that inner splendour that is within your own Heart Flame, will become realized within each of you.

The thoughts and words that you place behind the words 'I AM', become more important

In your phraseology, the thoughts and words that you place behind the words 'I AM', will become more important. You will carry the fuller power of your own feeling body, and the feeling body's Flame of Divine Love, to empower those words such as " 'I AM' Love's Eternal Victory, now made manifest in my mind, body and feelings."

We see the present evolution of humanity held in a great Flame of Resurrection. The words of the living Ascended Jesus Christ will continue to prevail during the resurrection process because all of you are now under the resurrection, the lifting up and out of chaos, and into the True Divine Consciousness of your being. The use of these words will draw the full power of the Sacred Fire:

" 'I AM' the Resurrection and the Life of my mind and my body; 'I AM' the Resurrection and the Life of my

179

thoughts and my feelings; 'I AM' the Resurrection and the Life of my being and world; 'I AM' the Resurrection and the Life of my creativity, of talents and resources expressing through this outer self; 'I AM' the Resurrection and the Life, an open door into the Light for 'I AM'—the Heart of the 'I AM' Presence." This always invokes the Sacred Fire Element that opens the way for all that you are decreeing to be made manifest in your lives.

A new Unity between Master Jesus, the Archangel Michael, and the Ascended Master Victory from Venus

The Gifts that the Ascended Jesus Christ brought forth from the Great Central Sun recently include a new unity between Master Jesus, the Archangel Michael, and the great Being from Venus, the Tall Master that is known to you as Blessed Victory who is helping Master Saint Germain for the purity and freedom of the Earth. This unity of a Threefold Activity of Beloved Michael, Beloved Victory and Beloved Master Jesus, is offering an out-pouring of light; an out-pouring of Archangel Michael's own Heart Flame of His Sacred Fire Love, and an out-pouring of Cosmic Light Substance already qualified as Victory. So, Dear Hearts, this is a wonderful team of Ascended Masters' Presence. Through prayer, meditation, invocation and visualization, working with Beloved Mighty Victory, Beloved Archangel Michael and the Beloved Master Jesus will truly assist you in lifting yourself up into heights of new attainment and creation in your world.

Another Threefold Activity...Beloved Nada, Beloved Charity, Beloved Mary...

The Ascended Masters' Beloved Precious Mary, Beloved Lady Nada, and the Beloved Goddess of Charity are a new

Threefold Activity who are teaming together to offer the continued purification and the healing of the feeling body, and the purification of the physical heart of the wounds of grief and loss and the wounds of hate, that have gathered around that physical organ. For all of you, tremendous effort and success has already been given, and in months and even years ahead, there will be many who turn towards you for assistance. Beloved Lady Nada, Beloved Mary, Mother of Jesus, and the Thirteenth Goddess, Beloved Charity, will offer each of you, as Cosmic Christ practitioners, their combined Threefold Flame of Their own Sacred Fire Love to assist those who turn to you. They will over-light you.

There are many who will turn for assistance now who are holding within themselves deep wounds, deep grief, and deep loss. It is the feeling of loss that often keeps an individual away from that which is the very thing that could heal them of that loss. Wounds of grief and loss attach themselves to the physical heart, where they become barriers to the freedom of those individuals. In just the same way that you can use this Threefold Activity from these Great Goddesses and the Threefold Activity offered by Victory, Archangel Michael and the Master Jesus you yourselves will become an Open Door, in which the Masters can work with those who turn to each of you for assistance.

All of the Ascended Host are coming closer to the Earth at this time. All are seeking an opportunity to help you to your own freedom, and through you to help the Earth. All of you have, through your own inner intuitions, your own inner feelings, a stronger field of resonance to certain of the Ascended Host. This is because of a former association that you have had with these Beings of Light. Not only a former association, but even future association, where the All-Seeing Eye of Cyclopea might reveal to the Goddess of Harmony—might reveal to the Queen of Light—might reveal to Beloved Serapis Bey, that you would be working with them in future manifestations for the freedom of humanity and this Earth.

Ask yourself, "What is the perfect application for me today?"

In all that I ever offer you, that are the Greater Powers of the Universe, Dear Heart, it is offered as a structured application. Application refers to your approach and your effort in entering in to your spiritual work each day. When you enter in to do your decrees—to do your prayer calls—I suggest two things: "Will I be using the Violet Flame today, or will I be using the Cosmic Blue Flame? Will I be calling forth, or use an 'I AM' realization?" Both can be very powerful. If you have truly accepted these great Powers and Beings of Light, it can be of equal quality, or even greater to affirm, " 'I AM' Archangel Michael's Sacred Blue Flame, His Cosmic Blue Flame that blazes through my being and world." If you have a degree of acceptance within you of your closeness with these Beings—and knowing that they will never fail to answer you—you can change your calls and use them as an affirmation.

" 'I AM' the Luminous Presence of the Ascended Jesus Christ expressing through this outer self. 'I AM' the Healing Presence of Beloved Lady Nada, pouring forth through my hands and my Heart's Flame." Remember, you are connecting with and calling forth the Greatest Power in the Universe when you are calling forth or affirming in the 'I AM', the Great Heart Flame of Sacred Fire Power, Sacred Fire Love and Sacred Fire Purity from your own Beloved 'I AM' Presence Higher Self or from an Angel or Ascended Master.

Are there Ascended Beings that I feel an extraordinary amount of closeness to?

So, sometimes it is good to go within. "Should I be calling forth these powers or should I be putting it in the 'I AM', in the first Cosmic name?" Ask yourself. Your inner feelings—your inner guidance—will tell you. Secondly, it is to ask yourself, "Are there Ascended Beings I feel an extraordinary amount of closeness to? I do not even know why I feel close, but I seem to really resonate with Beloved Mary or I seem to really resonate with the Grand Master Melchizedek..."

Perhaps you have been to some of the ancient Academies of the Mystical Arts and Sciences. Perhaps you have been on the Earth in South America when the King of the Archangels visited the Earth in three civilizations— Mighty Metatron. Maybe you have closeness to Metatron. Maybe you have closeness to the Seven Mighty Elohim, one of the Great Creator Beings. So sometimes it is good to ask yourself, "Is there one of the Ascended Host that I should be working with today?" It might change each day.

Maybe you have a standard that you follow in your calls—you have turned inwards and upwards, you have sent love to your Great God Presence, asking it to enfold you in its Garments of Light, a Tube of Light, and then you work with a certain group of Masters... That might be a general practice for you. But then, you might have an inner feeling, you turn within, asking yourself, "Is there a Being of Light who is trying to connect with me today?" Perhaps you might find—because you have asked the question—that the Elohim of Purity and the God and Goddess of Purity may wish to bring their own Heart Flame of Purity that day!

Feeling trapped in a situation?—the Goddess of Light can help...She has experienced it.

Maybe you feel trapped in a situation that you find difficult to come out of. Do you know who to call in that kind of a situation, yes?—the Goddess of Light. She is the one that was seized in an unguarded moment when she was a princess of the Royal Family in South America, quite a long age ago. She was trapped by the sinister force for three hundred years and held in a tower. Can you imagine doing prayer calls for the Light for three hundred years?

Many of your ancient swamis that at one time lived in the Himalayas in an unascended state, knew how to maintain light in the body for three to seven hundred years. And the Goddess of Light in that lifetime maintained light in her body for seven hundred and twenty-five years. Her body had already been four hundred and twenty-five years young when she was seized by the sinister force; and then for another three hundred years she was kept in that tower in South America, where her Light could no longer influence and help the people that Her Royal Family reigned over at that time.

Of course, you are very blessed and you are very fortunate that today you do not have the dark magicians on the Earth. At that time they were on the Earth, but they are today seized by the Angelic Host and held in the compounds waiting for Ascended humankind to deal with them. So you are very fortunate. But you see, the Goddess of Light was trapped. She found herself in a condition she could not get out of, and for three hundred years she meditated upon the Light within and called and called and called. It is for this reason that when the Universe finally responded to her and she was freed from that entrapment, she immediately gained her Ascension and she immediately

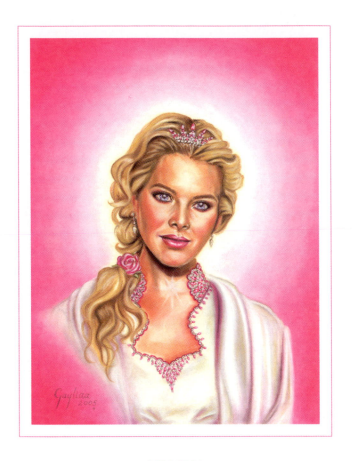

AKASHA

ASUN

was placed in a position of tremendous authority over this world. She is the Goddess of Light.

Now be careful for you can get caught up in all sorts of human concepts, "How can a Princess who was so evolved, who applied the knowledge that we are receiving now, and she had learned to maintain life in her body, how could it be that she could have an unguarded moment in which the sinister force could seize her like that?" You could also ask, "How could it be that it would take another three hundred years before the Ascended Masters would rescue her?" You see how the human can quickly jump to a conclusion? But what did she gain from it?—She gained her Ascension! She gained her complete Freedom and Ascension. And not only did she gain her freedom from that entrapment, she gained her freedom from a Third-Dimensional reality and went on to become a fully Ascended God/Goddess Being, with All Authority and Power over All Systems of Worlds. And then, within thirteen years, she evolved up into that office of Goddess of Light. There is no end to the Spiritual Hierarchy and its evolution. So do not be too swift to jump to human conclusions about things and how a human condition can be transformed into a Higher Purpose.

And so perhaps, if she had an unguarded moment, her own Higher Christ Self knew that It was going to use that unguarded moment. Her Christ Self did not create the unguarded moment, *she* created that unguarded moment. But her Christ Self said, "This has happened and now *I* will take advantage of it." And in taking advantage of it, saw, that if her entrapment lasted a certain amount of time, then she could literally decree her freedom—not only her freedom from that entrapment—her freedom from this world of limitation! And thus she gained that freedom and is now a force for freedom for others.

We speak on this subject because if any of you feel boxed in, if any of you feel that you are in a situation that you find yourself trapped, and you do not seem to have the present illumination as to how you might get yourself out of that situation, who do you call?—The Goddess of Light. She has promised humanity throughout the world, "Call upon Me! I know what that feels like. Call upon me and I will release my own Sacred Fire Love through you that will give you your freedom from that condition that seems to be limiting you." This is just one example of all that with which the Ascended Host is lining up to assist you.

What does the Mighty Violet Flame and the Cosmic Blue Flame do?

As you know, there are many types of Angels and Legions of Angels in this world. Of the millions of Angels that are now in the lower atmosphere of the Earth, more than six hundred thousand of those Angels belong to Archangel Michael. So you can see the authority that he has in the great Heavenly Realms of Light! His Angels are very important. Perhaps you are asking, 'Why the different colours of the Sacred Fire?' Well, you see, you have that Mighty Violet Flame, which we always encourage you to call forth, in, through and around you. It is the Flame of Transmutation. It is the Flame that gently pours through you and begins the purification and quickening of light in the human form. That which is the Cosmic *Blue* Flame is used for going after a condition that is seriously broken, a condition that has become very hardened and density that is frightfully limiting you. The Cosmic Blue Flame is also used to silence and seize that which is evil in this world which quickly seems to be taking a momentum. It is used by the Angels to drive, bind and remove evil, discord and selfishness from the Earth, when called into action.

I'll give you an example how The Cosmic Blue Flame was used to take out a frightful momentum. Archangel Michael and Mighty Astria, with more than two million Angels, entered the Fourth Dimension; entered the astral psychic realm, between the years 1935 and 1947. In those twelve years the Archangel Michael, Mighty Astria, and their Legions of Angels, cleared out the astral psychic realm, which was the Fourth Dimension. They cleared that Dimension out because it was filled with poltergeists. It was filled with discarnate entities and it was filled with human thoughtforms that had become, literally, beastly creations, that had been on the Earth. And so it was a ghastly place! It was this Fourth Dimension, along with the poltergeists and disembodied entities that had remained in your world, that combined force of evil, that held humanity in the darkness in centuries past.

The Fourth Dimension was collapsed—it doesn't exist anymore

It was the Ascended Master Saint Germain, Ascended Master Mighty Victory and the Beloved Archangel Michael, who teamed together to create a plan to clear the Third Dimension and the Fourth Dimension of all discarnate entities; *discarnate entities*—those individuals who had become wholly destructive and who had lost their physical bodies and had no light within themselves to journey back up into the Planes of Bliss where they could prepare for re-embodiment. It was Archangel Michael and his Angels who were dressed in impenetrable armour, Dear Hearts, because that Fourth Dimension existed for millions of years and it had tremendous momentum of discord and destruction. If you saw some of the negative thought forms in *your* world that were in that dimension, well, it would bring about a heart attack instantly, and you would

187

understand why even Archangel Michael would armour himself in impenetrable armour. And of course this is why a tremendous debt of gratitude is due this great Archangel for the tremendous service that he has provided.

I do know and I am aware that in some metaphysics, there are those who refer to the Fourth Dimension as being the Dimension of the Angels and the Ascended Masters. The reason that they are doing this is because they are referring to the *next* Dimension. Well, the next Dimension above yours is the Ascended Masters' Realm, or Octave of Light, but it is actually the Fifth Dimension. It is just that the Fourth Dimension, after it was cleared of all the discarnates, was collapsed. It doesn't exist anymore. This was done so that now, under the new Cosmic Law, everyone who leaves their physical body through *the change called death* must go directly up into the Planes of Bliss where they prepare for re-embodiment on the Earth.

We are also very aware that there are those who disagree with us. There are all sorts of people who are claiming to clear people of discarnate entities and who go into homes and clear discarnate entities. And you can believe them, or you can know the truth. But, Dear Hearts, Ascended Masters do not make mistakes, and certainly the Archangel Michael never makes mistakes. The Archangel Michael decreed in 1947 that from this time forward all those who are losing their body through the change called death now would be escorted by an Angel back up to the Planes of Bliss. That is one of the reasons why today you have millions of Angels on your Earth performing many different activities including escorting Souls back to the Planes of Bliss, where rest, healing, and then re-embodiment can take place.

When there are those who come under the belief that there are discarnate entities that are bothering someone, or ghosts that are walking around people's homes, unfortunately they do not have the fuller knowledge. There is that which will create what *appears* to be a poltergeist or discarnate entity quicker than anything else, and that is intense and extreme human grieving. If you intensely grieve one who has left their body in the change called death, that grieving becomes a *thoughtform*. Those of a certain racial consciousness on the Earth, those of certain cultures, believe in the necessity to grieve and to wail for days and months. Yes?

Thoughts are qualified with the feeling that is going on within. You know this now. Then those thoughts are clothed with that magnetic energy and go out into the world where they become an individual energy, all on its own. And if that individual energy is *continuously* fed, then that energy comes *alive*. And yes, there are tens of thousands of thoughtform-*carnate*-entities. They are thoughtforms of the individual that have come alive due to the individuals who are grieving that person. Meanwhile, the real person is up in the Planes of Bliss.

The Planes of Bliss...where you go to after you leave your body

Well, then I will get an argument from those who say, "I know that my loved one is with me; I can feel her/him walking in the house." I have an answer for that, too. And it is this, if you have a loved one that has departed, upon entrance to the Planes of Bliss, what immediately takes place is an orientation process intended to comfort and inform that one. There are those who appear to them who they will recognize, who assure them that they are safe, that they simply have departed from their physical body but that they are alive, that they never die, just the body is left behind. Once they have been helped through the orientation, the Angels appear to them to explain why they must go into a rest—the Sleep. They go into the Sleep for purification of part of the emotional body. Depending upon the degree of love versus the degree of discord is what determines how long they stay in the Sleep. Some stay in the Sleep for three days, some stay in the Sleep for three years. Some, there are some from the First and Second World War who are still in the Sleep because of their acts. So, how long you stay in the Sleep depends on how you lived your life on Earth.

Once you are awakened from the Sleep, then you are taken to a place where you meet an Ascended Master. It is explained to you that this is an Ascended Being; and if you do know Ascended Beings, you have an association given to you. They will say, "This is a Being like the Buddha; this is a Being like Krishna, Mohammed, or Jesus the Christ, who is Ascended." And then they will present to you the Truth of Life. If you are unable to accept that truth, if you do not believe it because you are still carrying the racial consciousness of your human life, and you say, "No way, I just do not accept this, I know there is only the God of my religion that I left behind," then the Ascended Master will attempt a demonstration to prove what is real. Generally, many at that point will, having seen the proof, then say, "I accept it."

Those who do accept the truth are then escorted into the new Schools of Enlightenment that the Mighty Saint Germain has opened in the Planes of Bliss, where you receive in your Light body the exact teaching that we are sharing with *you*, and the exact instruction that came forth through the Mighty Saint Germain in the last century. This guarantees you that once you are finished the instruction in the Higher Schools in the Planes of Bliss, you are ready to look for the ideal parents for your next embodiment on Earth. Then with the Angel's assistance, you create the ideal personality, the ideal characteristics that will assist you to live what you've just learned when you go back to the Earth.

When you are in the Mystery Schools in the Planes of Bliss between embodiments, one of the very first things that you are taught is how to project the Great Light Rays. And who do you practice on?—Your loved ones, left behind! And that is why, sometimes, you will *feel* those who have departed. You will feel their Presence because it is a very easy thing, from the Planes of Bliss. In your Light body you do not have the density of the physical. And once you are shown the Laws of Projection, you are shown how to breathe, to exhale the quality that you wish to offer the individual. You exhale that into the Light Ray and then project it to the individual on Earth. Maybe you wish to send forth feelings of love and nourishment and support to assist the person you left behind and who is going through a hard time; or maybe you left children behind, and there are certain qualities in the Love Ray that you want to project to help them. It is because of this that sometimes individuals are certain, "I know that my father is with me. I feel him!" Well, it is not *him*—it is the Ray of his Love that he is projecting to you.

Angels building the great Cosmic Wall of Light

It is not the greatest wisdom to continue to accept there are yet discarnate energies in the world because that flies in the face of the tremendous work that the Archangel Michael, the Mighty Astria, Saint Germain and Beloved Victory performed for the freedom of the Earth from discarnate entities. To suggest that you believe that they are still here is a great dishonouring to the Great Archangel Michael and to the tremendous work that his Legions performed.

The greatest amount of discarnate entities that were in the atmosphere over one nation, that were cleared, was the nation Africa. There was a group of Angels that were detailed to the Second World War to do tremendous work there. But aside from those Angels, the largest group of Angels that gathered for the removal of discarnate entities were the Angels working over Africa. Then there were Legions of Angels dispatched to begin building the great Cosmic Wall of Light around the Three Americas so that the protection of the Three Americas could be built up.

It is a tragedy that the greater numbers of human beings do not realize how much protection is offered your nations and the Americas, by the Angelic Host. And if they knew this, perhaps your governments would be less threatened by the affairs in other individual countries. And I would just like to say that even though there are renegade nations, Dear Heart, you are all One. And what is taking place in Iraq and other nations in terms of war and terrorism, you can contemplate, "What part of the human race has not yet been healed when there is such suffering? What aspect of the Iraqi people, what aspect of the people of any regime in which there is lost will—in which people do not have their freedom—what is that reflecting in the degree of lost will that has not yet been healed in yourself?" It is easy to be quick in throwing judgement at these people, but when a *mass* of people come together to have this experience—although it is an experience they are choosing—you must also realize that these are courageous Souls to have this experience that is so limiting their lives. There is a greater picture to everything. Isn't there?

Karmic conditions are being consumed by Beloved Mary

Question: Is the Sacred Fire available in the Planes of Bliss for transmutation of former karma or discordant qualities?

Answer: Generally, no. But what does happen is that you have the great Dispensation of Beloved Mary, Mother of Jesus. And it is because of Her Dispensation that we really say to you—in ways you do not realize—She is Mother to the World, because for more than four hundred years now, Beloved Mary appears every single morning before the Lords and Ladies of Karma who are seated in the Spiritual Hierarchy in Saturn. And there she has to appear every morning. Can you imagine, four hundred years later and appearing at the same place and asking the same permission?

It is such a great Dispensation that the Lords of Karma will only grant it if she appears daily and requests it. In this Dispensation Beloved Mary requests that all incoming Souls preparing for embodiment be allowed to pass through Her Heart Flame, where Her Heart Flame can consume a great amount of discord or karmic conditions from previous life. So here is where the Sacred Fire comes in to help one returning to a new life on Earth. And to this day, Mary continues to project Her Presence before the Great Council at an anointed time. She appears at 7:07 every morning, in Saturn, and there She requests to again open Her Heart Flame for the next twenty-four hours.

This is how the karmic conditions are now being consumed for the many incoming Children of Light. It is being accomplished for all that are saying 'yes' to the Light. For those who just do not believe what they are being shown, for those who are caught in such a deep racial culture, for those who are caught in deep, extreme religions of the world—where no matter what you show them, as far as they are concerned, it is trickery, it is magic, they just can't believe it—then only eighteen percent of their karma can be removed by Beloved Mary. Those who are shown the truth go on to the great Mystery Schools in the Planes of Bliss and then will take a new embodiment on Earth. They come under an eighty percent purification of the discordant conditions of previous lives as they pass through Mary's Heart Flame prior to embodiment. Look at the children that are now coming forth. They are coming forth with great Light!

Unfortunately though, these children, who are coming forth as great Lights—and they have been coming through for many years—are more sensitive and many of the tragedies in the sixties, seventies and eighties, in which many Souls lost their way, in the Three Americas and other places in the world, were *those* Souls. The sixties and seventies was a time of great resistance to any form of obedience. It was a time of an expanded notion of love, of free states of love that was more recreational than of sound heart and mind. Many of these incoming Souls were caught up in this wave of rebellious love. In the past, there have always been many dangers when embodying on the Earth. There was not yet, in the seventies, the amount of awakened parents that are on the Earth today, to assist these young souls through the various cultural and societal changes that were taking place; so in the sixties, seventies and eighties it was very difficult for them. Although Mary would take much of their karma, they would find themselves born into a society with strong influences. And because their psychological and emotional bodies were more sensitive and less dense, the pressure that they were up against—the pressure of the influences of society—would weave itself within them and take over very quickly.

Question: What Dimension is the Planes of Bliss considered to be?

Answer: The Planes of Bliss are in the upper, upper reaches of the Third Dimension. When you hear me refer to the Realms of Light, I am referring to that upper part of the Earth's atmosphere where human discord cannot reach; that is where the Planes of Bliss, the Upper Realms of Light of the Third Dimension are.

Ascended Beings who created and own this System of Worlds also have the right to protect this World

The Fourth Dimension does not exist. Yes, there are discordant energies on Earth, and we include them all when we refer to the *sinister force*. We remind you that the sinister force was not created by God, by anything Cosmic, but is an accumulation of all human discord over centuries of time. Now, if you want to call them the *Greys*, if you want to call them the *Reptilians*, if you want to energize them a little bit more by giving them a classification and a label such as hate, selfishness or evil, so be it. This is all that human beings are doing, labeling and trying to identify different types of discord, but to us, all discord is simply a sinister force that interferes with the upward growth of humanity. There will be many who disagree with me, but that is fine. It is all the sinister force.

If you qualify the discordant energy that is in your world as 'any particular thing', then the energy will take on that manifestation. Then it will appear and you will say "See, it is real!" No, it is not real. *You* created it, and you qualified the energy. What is revealed to hundreds of thousands of human beings is often what they accept and agree upon as being real. This is why you hear me saying that you have such authority! When there are hundreds of thousands of you that agree upon something, it is your Life Stream that

195

creates it. I do not ever wish to suggest that the sinister force is a Cosmic activity; it is simply an accumulation of the worst kind of humanly created discordant energy. Indeed.

There are *constructive* entities, or energies, that are now assisting your world. Let's use the word 'Beings', because 'entities' have all sorts of connotations. Do they not? Are there destructive beings who are visiting your world from other Systems, from other Universes? Yes.

All Systems in *your* local Universe have now evolved to the *constructive* way of life. And if there are those beings that are partially destructive—yet there is evolution to their beings—and they are here, that means that they must be from outside of your local Universe. And are they permitted in? Yes. Because of free will, you cannot stop life in its desire. Yet the mass desire of whole groups of people is stronger to fulfill itself than the individual desire of a destructive individual. And if, in their evolution, they have the wisdom—they have created the science—that gives them the knowledge of how to work with Interstellar Space and move through Universal Systems, then they have the right to use that knowledge; they have the right to go anywhere in the Universe. But your Ascended Masters who own this System of Worlds also have the right to *protect* this System of Worlds, so they will only allow a certain amount of them in and they watch them all the time, and maintain the greater protection that is required.

CHAPTER SEVEN

Before I begin to share with you, I would like you to receive
a Harmonizing Presence as a blessing from the Seraphim
Angels, directly into your nerves, directly into your nervous
system. For there is that aspect of your physicality, of your
human body, that would receive whole new thresholds of
light if much of what has taken place in the nervous system
could be repaired or could be harmonized.

A Seraphim Angel Blessing

All you need to do, because you have Angel contact
here, is in your heart, perhaps, inwardly say, "I open to
receive the blessing and the harmonizing of my nerves,
my nerve system, from the precious Angels, the Seraphim,
and I am grateful for that service." Breathe slowly three
times while centering your attention in your heart and
whisper inwardly the prayer call three more times with
much sincerity and gratitude.

The Seraphim—those Legions—those Angels, who are
emissaries of Jesus the Christ, are the Christed Angels, and
sometimes they have been referred to as the Angels of the
Blue Lightning Flame. They will use either a Sound Ray
or a Light Ray, and under permission of your own higher
intelligence, intercept either the chakra system of your
body or intercept your life stream and the chakra ports
in your life stream above your head. Then they pass that

197

healing love—that harmonizing light—directly into your nerves, into your nerve system. The light inside your nerves can now build up so that you are able to receive greater thresholds of light directly into your brain and directly into your body, which will help your journey very much.

Anchoring the new paradigm—the Diamond Heart, the Indigo, the Violet Soul

Now I would like to turn your attention to a discourse on 'Anchoring the New Paradigm—the Diamond Heart, the Indigo, the Violet Soul'.

Indeed, the great awakening taking place within humanity at this time, the movement towards freeing humankind in the last century, out of its ancient limiting belief systems, and awakening humanity to its greater possibilities—rebirthing humanity to greater truths—has been the presence of Children of the Diamond Heart. They first arrived in the last century, and they are those who would begin to separate themselves from the conventional wisdom of the orthodox world and listen to a heartbeat, listen to an inner voice that is uniquely different than the world race-consciousness has lived by for centuries of time.

In the last century—especially the first fifty years of the last century—many of those who came, were pioneers who did not have the illumination to understand that they were Children of the Diamond Heart, evolved souls. Rather, they came into this world with a very, very specific function, a specific personality, in order to give to the world new technologies, new inventions—to intercept the world's thinkers with new ideas, new resolutions, and then prepare the way for the arrival of the Indigo Souls.

The Soul initiates levels of attainment

All on Earth are *Starseed*, and indeed, all humanity have come from the Sun at the centre of this universe, which I often refer to as the Great Central Sun. Starseed—the 'I AM' race of humanity on the Earth who have consciously placed themselves upon a ten million year evolution, understanding and studying of the natural laws of cause and effect, and naturally observing themselves as beings of light. In all of this, the soul—which magnificently weaves itself through the multidimensional being that you are, not only collects the experiences that you have, but the Soul initiates the levels that are before you, the steps of attainment that are before you. The Soul of your being, through the dialogue of your Higher Intelligence, initiates levels of attainment through your relationships, through your life concepts, through your understanding of the way the world works. For centuries of time the Soul had no access to the human self due to the density in the emotional body.

As the emotional body is healed and the Soul can access your outer self, your soul looks through your eyes and evaluates how you see the world, your Soul not only retains all the experience, but it initiates with your Spirit the interaction of events; the interaction of yourself with other human beings, and the staging of certain events, relationships, circumstances, in which you are called upon to make choices—you are called upon to respond, you are called upon to react. Depending on your understanding of the higher purpose of life—to love—and your ability to grow through the hierarchy of beingness, depends in part on what level, if you will, that you are moving through a masterful Soul evolution. In each Soul Evolution, the Soul desires to nurture into greater self expression, all the qualities of Divine Love.

The understanding of the Twelve plus one

The understanding of the *Twelve plus one* is critical now to you, because the next twelve years are intended to offer you the opportunity of a greater understanding and comprehension of your life, unveiling all the seeming mysteries and offering you those insights that were missing pieces to understand your life, yourself, the purpose of life, and the evolutions of life. One of the Soul Mastery evolutions is referred to as 'Children of the Diamond Heart', and within every soul evolution there are twelve steps, there are twelve qualities of Divin Love that must be groomed within oneself; with the understanding that each Soul Mastery level is an opportunity for *Beingness Realized*—to bring forth more of the full presence of creative self expression by expanding the qualities of divine love within oneself.

All these expressions, all these initiations, are to bring forth all the qualities of God-Being that are available within those initiations, if you will. All the qualities inherent within Divine Love, the twelve major qualities, united in balance, become the one great presence called Divine Love. The reflections of the twelve-plus exist on the Earth. In your calendar year you are reminded—twelve months in one year. There are twelve cycles in each Soul Evolution; each cycle is an initiation into one of the twelve aspects of Divine Love. Once those aspects are drawn forth into a conscious state of beingness, the twelve together form the growing presence of Divine Love in you.

As developing Beings of the Diamond Heart you begin to realize and remember that you are a Spiritual being

And so, you came to Earth again—beings of the Diamond Heart. And most of you who were born in that vibration have already passed through the Twelve Initiations into the Twelve Aspects of Divine Love and are well on your way moving through the next Soul Vibrations—the Indigo Soul or the Violet Soul. When you arrived in this World as Children of the Diamond Heart, you had enough spiritual presence and former attainment—you had enough deep memory within yourself, contributing to you being a person who would think for yourself—have your own values, be willing to stand out, even stand out in a crowd, if necessary. Definitely as Children of the Diamond Heart you had enough presence of love coming forth—weaving itself within your personality, within your multidimensional self—to very much make yourself your own person. Strong enough to be your own person that you could step beyond family beliefs, or the family ways in which the family does things, and even, if necessary, be referred to as different or a troubled member of the family! And chances are you are the most awakened member of the family, so to speak!

And so, as all of these things took place, you became your own person. You began to realize and remember that you are a spiritual being and you are seeking higher truth. You go through the challenges, the problems, the appearances and the growth. You go through the process of being de-hypnotized, in which all your experiences are seeking to remind you that all that is taking place in the world is a sub-reality; a sub-reality for so long—ten million years in the making—that all this *less than reality* itself became part of the atmosphere, registering in the human cells of humanity, and also into the Earth.

As Children of the Diamond Heart you do your best to understand why mystics say this world is an illusion, and to understand that human beings fell into a belief in two powers. You begin the journey—the healing, the awakening—to free yourself, and to look for the knowledge that will bring you back to the one truth. As you do this you move through rich relationships and circumstances; you move through ailments in your body; you move through things that happen in relationship that try to remind you of your *core perception*—generally perceptions long held against yourself and God—that you have been seeking to heal for many lifetimes

And as you do all of this healing and awakening, and finally reconcile yourself back to God, you realize the God of religion is quite a fictional God—you realize that God is the very essence of your being. You come to realize that there is a treasure house within and above you that you can source for all that you require into this life, and you develop the obedience and the willingness to daily do some form of inner spiritual work. After you pass through the initiations, you complete that which is the Diamond Heart, with a greater measure of the Qualities of Divine Love expressing and you pass into the Indigo Soul, to again measurably increase those qualities as the natural creative expression of your being on Earth.

The Indigo Soul—the Life Stream between your physical body and your Higher Self begins to expand

As you come into the Indigo Soul vibration, there comes a stark contrast in your lives as you observe two realities. You observe the limiting sub-reality that yet exists in your life, and yet, through your own inner knowing, you know that there is another reality that is a possibility, a reality that you can reach to. And you begin to observe that there are many just like you who are stepping out of their spiritual closets, if you will, and coming into community with each other for greater spiritual and self empowerment. As Indigo Souls, as you pass through the levels of Indigo Soul, that factor of resonance, which is your own inner knowing, inner feeling—grows strong within you, and the life stream between your physical body and your Higher Self begins to expand, delivering greater life force into your body.

You join with many others in recognition that there is an incoming Golden Age which most of humanity do not realize has arrived. In order to anchor this incoming Golden Age, first there must be a new matrix, a new paradigm, that comes onto the Earth; out of which you and those who are awakening might spread the word, and use that paradigm to create phenomena and miracles that will eventually awaken those who are not awake.

As an Indigo Soul you know that you have your own challenges, you know that the day must come in your lives where you must begin to demonstrate your own higher power; but it doesn't mean that you are not yet without appearances and challenges in your life. In fact, sometimes as the Indigo Soul, challenges and appearances can grow within yourself, within your body—ailments, lack, and all sorts of things can act up. And there is the temptation, as is the human; to judge that there are things wrong with you and you wonder what is going on.

Initiations of the Indigo Soul

The truth is, you have come close to the reality of your God Presence, and to God's love loving you and expressing through you; you are so close to that place of living this higher reality. Being an Indigo Soul is really about crossing a bridge for quite some time. It is about walking the bridge, the path; it is about leaving a world consciousness behind, one that has been made real by humankind. It is about finding your bridge and crossing that bridge—realizing there are greener pastures and higher truths and a much greater way of living life; where you begin to *demonstrate* your higher truth, on the other side of that bridge, a bridge to resurrection, leaving the crucifixion of the limited human life behind you.

As you work across the middle of that bridge and get close to the other side, quite often—because of human nature, because of the power of human attention—what is on the side of the bridge that you are leaving behind tries to follow you as trails of human energy that yet try to leech upon you and pull you back, and make you doubt if all of this even makes sense. And so for the Indigo Soul there is yet much doubt; and there is the human sub-reality—that has been so long in this world—that tries to hold you back.

Eventually you come to that place as an Indigo Soul where for the most part, most of the time, you are happy; most of the time you are joyful. You might find yourself having days where you relapse, where you fall back into limited and negative thinking, and where you have limiting experiences in your life. You have those reminders that come to you in the form of experience or in the form of counsel, that say, "Look, Dear Heart, you as an Indigo Soul, you are still having difficulty because you are using too much of your old limited human consciousness; you are using too much of your human energy, where at this time in your evolution you should be using more of your higher power and higher intelligence to get everything done in this life."

And so the Indigo Souls can go through some harsh reminders, especially if there are obstacles and difficulties in their life and they are trying to understand what is behind the curtain, what is in this energy. As their own human energy creates limitations in their lives, the Spirit Soul—the life that is in the Indigo Soul—is trying to send a message up to the surface, "There is an easier way of doing things. You are not using enough of your God Power. You are using too much human consciousness. Don't you know that you are already aligned? Don't struggle so much. Just come back into the arms of God. Just open the channel. Start expressing the higher frequency of Divine Love..."

So, there is this interaction that the Indigo Soul goes through, in which one's own life is sending a message up to the surface, "Look, you are going to have these challenges in your life until you lean more on me, the 'I' in the midst of you. Look, until you climb into your sovereignty and begin to use that authority of your life, use the power of your will, the power of your feeling and use the gift of your sight. Use the gift of mind, sight, body and feeling. Do not sacrifice any of these."

Use your mind to think and know what it is that you require, desire, and aspire to in life. Use your sight within your mind to see that which you desire, aspire and require. And as you use your sight and see that which you wish to bring forth or change or manifest in your world through visualization, then your *feelings* will come up and support you. And to manifest that, you learn to hold the vibration of manifestation within your physical temple. You can nourish and nurture the initial stages of that manifestation, so that the energy can freely go forth into the world as you channel more of the divine and higher frequencies of Divine Love. As that comes down through you, it takes a hold—it grabs your desires, your thoughts, everything in your sight; and that energy moves out into the world to produce those things, or to create the *opportunities* that will produce those things, in a much easier way. In this, only fear and doubt derail the energy of Divine Love to guide and fulfill you.

Thus, the Indigo Soul goes through these initiations. And then something nice begins to happen, and it comes between the seventh and ninth initiation level of the Indigo Soul. That's where you begin to acquire a majority of positive feelings in which, for the most part, you have many things right in your life: the relationship, the supply, the health in the body, and you begin to demonstrate some of this higher radiance of that wealth of spiritual beingness. It is beginning to manifest—not only *inwardly* as more peace, inwardly as the guidance and the counsel, the knowingness, the intuitions—but it manifests *outwardly* as being in fellowship with the right people in your life, and being at the right place to experience new opportunities.

There begins a whole new form of action, your energy seems to be revitalized, and the Indigo Soul begins to realize and has those epiphanies, "No matter what I am doing in the world—it matters not whether I am making dinner, it matters not if I am driving my automobile, or out at the workplace—there is something else that is happening every single moment—there is a new awareness, I am channeling a Higher Power, a Higher Intelligence. Greater light is coming through my eyes every day. My Heart Flame is delivering a Ray of Light out into the world and is doing work that I may not even know is happening at this time."

Relationships take on a whole new meaning, purpose and expression, and you begin to see the gifts in everything. You find your right relationship to the Heavenly Father/Mother and the heavenly realms, and your right relationship to the Earth. And in the relation of that which is above and that which is below, do you find your own individualized God Presence, and do you find that spiritual garden within yourself— you learn to till that garden, you learn to nurture and abide within that inner garden.

You realize that you are here to experience and express the very presence of God, and you realize that you are connected, that you are aligned, and that you have never ever had to struggle. Relax into this higher truth, relax into a renewed faith and trust that it is within you now. Your attitudes shift as you realize, "Why have I ever struggled, when all along I have been aligned to the God 'I AM' of my being? Perhaps I shall sit myself down and acknowledge this alignment, and invite this mighty God—the 'I AM'—to express more fully through my humanity and out into my world to do its perfect work."

The Way-Shower frequency...

Then, as you complete the initiation of being an Indigo Soul, your days become filled with deeper insights and epiphany; there is an excitement, a deeper awareness, there is a thrilling of life that you actually feel inside your physical body. You become aware of currents of energy coursing through your body, not only through the day but you are aware at night, while your body sleeps, that there is a whole threshold of light that is doing something else within you. And you realize that there is a preparation within you for the quality of the Way-Shower to come forth and express through you.

That quality, as it expresses, is a Soul Emergence of all your lifetimes that has moved into its completion; in which all the energy of your past lives—the *constructive* energy— begins to emerge from your Causal body, from your Higher Self, down into the electromagnetic fields of your feeling body; where these attributes, these achievements of past lives, are released into your feeling body. The Way-Shower frequency begins to show up within the vibration of your life, and more and more there are people who are drawn to you who are looking for the way, who are looking for direction in their life.

As you see and you notice and observe these people that are drawn to you for direction, for guidance, for counsel, you realize that the Way-Shower vibration has come forth within you, and you are going through the final initiations of the Indigo Soul—preparing to launch yourself into the initiation of the Violet Soul. As you go through those months and years, and you groom yourself, you make that transition into Violet Soul—you realize there is a *greater* Consciousness, a desire for greater creative self expression that is intercepting your *human* consciousness.

You realize that something is happening to your sight; you realize that there are moments during the day, when you are simply looking at things—or sometimes when your vision is relaxed—that there is something else that is catching your attention. You realize that you are beginning to see condensations of light, shards of light, movements of light out and around in the atmosphere; and these things begin to catch your attention as the Violet Soul initiates, and the qualities of Mother/Father God that exist within the Violet Soul, begin to fire the vibration of your sight up into a higher frequency of love and light.

The Violet Soul brings the Authority of the Violet Flame and the Violet Ray into your life

As you acknowledge this Higher Consciousness, this inner knowing that is growing within you—as the words 'I AM' ring truer and truer within your being, you realize that the emergence of the 'I AM' Consciousness is beginning to come forth within your being. You begin to honour those words and love those words, and desire to express the value and the preciousness of life. You begin to understand why those words 'I AM' are the most honourable words in all creation—they are the words that are given to you to express into manifestation all that you are becoming, all that you desire and all that you require!

In the beginning phases of the Violet Soul you use those words 'I AM' to consciously raise the light in your brain and to raise the light in your body. You use those words 'I AM' to speak higher statements of truth to correct every condition in your life. You use those words 'I AM' in front of statements of truth to initiate powerful forces of light to work through you, or with you, to correct conditions in the world. And indeed, the Way-Shower and the emergence of the 'I AM' Mystical Consciousness comes forth within you and you begin to accustom yourself to miracles; miracles are beginning to unfold. You are connecting and beginning to express *The Greater Powers of this Universe!*

Levels of the Violet Soul—the Rainbow Man, the Rainbow Woman

Then there comes the emergence of the Rainbow Cosmic Consciousness; there is the re-emergence as you move through the fourth through the seventh levels of the Violet Soul—The Rainbow Man, the Rainbow Woman, the Cosmic Consciousness of the Seven Rays, the Rainbow Rays begin to emerge and express through you. Do you know, Dear Heart, that the Mayans prophesized that between the years 2003 and 2009, the Rainbow Man would arrive on the Earth? This is a natural evolution to the Violet Soul, and indeed, the Violet Soul is the initiation of the Seven Rays of development—the Seven Rays of the Universe—that pertain to the Seventh Golden Age that your Earth is moving into.

The Violet Soul brings forth the authority of the Violet Flame and the Violet Ray into your life. And because of the purification—the Laws of Transmutation, the Laws of Transfiguration and because *alchemy* is a very natural role of the Violet Flame and the Violet Ray, great change begins to naturally take place within you. As the Rainbow Mystic Consciousness begins to express through you, the light that comes from your eyes reveals a new world of miracles, and your awakened thoughts, feelings and words make the sub-reality and limitations of this world stand down.

Just as Jesus the Christ spoke *His* words, in which no density of the world could stand the light and the truth behind *His* words, as the consciousness of the Rainbow Being comes forth within *you* and prepares the final weaving, the final purification of your human form— bringing forth greater thresholds of light that harness your multi-dimensional self into a whole new higher state of being, a higher state of living—*your* words become a command to life. As you use the words of life, as you use the invocations of life—and empower those words through the power of your Soul, your Spirit—words become pure Cups of Life. You become that force of light—the light of God that never, never, fails.

During all these passages, all of these initiations— through Diamond Heart, through Indigo, through Violet Soul—life, the world, is your stage, because you are those Starseed awakened and healed sufficiently; you are those Starseed who have made effort to live right lives in the majority of your lifetimes. You are those Starseed who in ancient civilizations have been the thrust of everything good that would improve the world for a while, until finally the sinister force collapsed those great civilizations that you as Starseed created.

The only reason that those civilizations collapsed, was because you—as Starseed who built those former ancient great civilizations, did not have the power of the Indigo Ray on the Earth; you did not have the power and the presence of the Violet Ray of Purification on the Earth. You had not yet developed those God Rays because they were not yet the authority governing the Earth, and because human beings' attention was so enjoying the fruits of the great civilizations that you built for them—once again those civilizations that you as Children of the Diamond Heart created, collapsed because of the attention that the human held upon discord, and the failure to give obedience to the one law—Love! That will never happen again!

Grooming yourself beyond Violet Soul into Radiant Rose Soul

In the past, before the year 1901, there have been a few times in which a human being could evolve through the twelve evolutions of a Soul Mastery into another whole level in a very short time; could go from Diamond Heart into Indigo—very rare, but it has been done. Because your Earth is now under the Authority of the Violet Ray, and because of the Mother of All Dispensations being given to humanity, because humanity has responded, now it is possible for a group of human beings to do on the Earth what has never been done before—to move through two or more great evolutions of the Soul; to mature itself from Diamond Heart to Indigo to Violet Soul, and then to the next level, the final state of the evolved Soul on Earth, the Radiant Rose Soul, all in one lifetime. Few human beings have ever achieved this final achievement of the Soul—the Radiant Rose Soul—in the unascended state. Jesus the Christ is one of those few. He went beyond the Violet Soul into the Radiant Rose Soul.

You have come to invent the future

Lets for a moment discuss this new paradigm. Due to the fourteen million plus people on the Earth today who know and who have accepted the reality of God inside and above as a Higher Self Presence, and those who have not yet awakened to this higher truth—because of the race consciousness of their culture and beliefs, their societies and their nations, they are not yet able to awaken to this higher truth, but they are living constructive lives and they are probably Diamond Heart Souls—that are coming forth now, hundreds of thousands of human beings who have taken their place in anchoring a new paradigm, a new civilization on Earth.

You are not only here for yourself, Dear Heart, because chances are that each of you in former lifetimes have made sufficient effort to raise yourself back into God Consciousness—you are here because of the need of humanity; you have *delayed* the journey and have been willing to continue to come and evolve and grow through the human theatre, so that more of humanity may have the same opportunity that is before each of you.

So I say to you, you are those awakened Starseed who have come to the Earth to invent the future. You have come to anchor a new paradigm onto the Earth and to show humankind a new way of living life. You have come to invent, you have come to bring forth new inventions, new engineering, new technologies, new sciences, new music, new art, new foods and new medicines. You have come to show humanity that human beings can gain a greater knowledge; and using that knowledge, human beings can use the Elements of the Earth and create for themselves life-force giving products, a food chain with a higher life-force, that will contribute to restoring physical bodies to their original Divine Blueprint.

You have come to invent the future, and these next years are about each of you finding your place in this. Some of you have already begun; others are well on their way. You are intended to explore, "What is my piece in this? In what way do I show up as being amongst those who have come to invent the future?" The inventors of the future are here. There are more than seven hundred thousand who are now living it in form, their careers and their lives. Yet, there are more than thirteen million who have to find their piece in the next several years.

All the help is here to assist you in doing this. And I will say something here that I have repeated often—*you are the authority for your life*—no one else, Dear Hearts, but you. You are the authority for your life! You do not need a psychic, you do not need a priest, you do not need a channel—you need *you*! You are the authority for your life stream! Mother/Father God has given you of their life. Your Higher Self is your treasure source of divine love, it is the living gift and treasury of their love and their love for you is endless; it will never stop. They have loved you so greatly, that they have given themselves, as your Higher Self, your 'I AM' Presence. It is the Greatest Power in the Universe that is the nature of your Higher Self you are now, Dear Hearts—to express through your human lives and out into the world what will anchor the new paradigm and invent the future.

You are building a new Etheric Light Grid onto the Earth

Some think the new paradigm is here. I would beg to differ. In a way it is here, but it is in the upper atmosphere of the Earth, beyond the reach of human creation. And what is happening is that millions of human beings are knowingly and unknowingly *channeling* the Cosmic Knowledge, the Cosmic Energy, the Cosmic Light and the Cosmic Love, that is up there in that new paradigm, onto the Earth. Hundreds of thousands of human beings are streaming that light down through themselves, and that is why I say that there is a time in the evolution of your soul where you realize, "Beyond the every day activities of my life, there is something else that is happening all the time—my life is delivering a Ray of Light out into the world, my eyes and heart are streaming light out into the world. So maybe I shouldn't walk around with my head down. Maybe I should keep my head up, so that light can go out and make contact, even if it is for three seconds..."

This is your world, and you are here to weave a greater light, a greater love, that has been absent for so long, out into the Earth, so that a new paradigm can anchor into that Cosmic Energetic Grid that you, through your light and your love, is building on the Earth. Take the time each day to make sure you are filled up with God's love so that when you are out in the world you are releasing Rays of Light that are connecting to other human beings; as such you are building the Etheric Light Grid onto the Earth so that this new paradigm can anchor itself and then spread all throughout the human emotional and mental body; so that humanity, when they are ready, can take an instantaneous leap in consciousness, because all has been laid out in preparation for them.

And so, it is really important to be in fellowship; to be in spiritual fellowship with your spiritual community, to connect, to be communicating with each other. It is important for you to ask yourself, "What is my piece? What is the part that I play in this jewel of inventing the future? What have I come to do?" Your future is intended to be *so* different, especially for you, because the future has nothing to do with anything that has taken place in your past. Your present is changing so rapidly, you can hardly keep up with it! Everything that you are here to do, everything that is the purpose of your life, is what is to yet take place in your life and in your future.

Service to Godself 'I AM', Service to Humanity and the Earth, and Service to the Spiritual Hierarchy of Light

I would like you to consider and accept that perhaps there is a Threefold Magical Purpose to your Life—to be of service; to be of service to the God within you that gives you life every day, the evolution of your being. Secondly, it is to be in service to humanity and the Earth, and to give that light to humanity. And third, to be in service to the Spiritual Hierarchy in the great Octaves of Light; where Angels, Ascended Masters, and great Beings of Light live, where you might become an open door for their love to flow through you, to reach more of humanity. And if you sign up for the Higher Threefold Purpose of your Life, to give justice back to your own Source of Life, to serve the light of God inside you, to serve humanity, to serve the Earth, and finally to serve the Spiritual Hierarchy, by inviting it to be so, then you invite the unseen Forces of Light and Divine Love to work through you. And this is where day to day life becomes so much easier than it has ever been before. You find your freedom and become a force of freedom for others.

You know, I would like you to take a deep breath into many of the things that are taking place in your life, because life wants everything to become easier, for life loves to flourish. And if you could just say to yourself many times, "That which has been difficult, that which has been struggle, is now behind me. I am through the roughest part. I have come through the more difficult experiences and I can see the light ahead of me. I can feel the light inside of me. Everything is becoming easier now."

Qualify your every day, and then your Life experience can show you that there is an easier way of doing things

Realize there is a thing that happens with Indigo Souls—especially between the seventh and eleventh evolution of Indigo Soul. Your life desires that you start using the power of qualification; that you start each day, after you have been filled with God's love, to qualify how things are going to take place in your day. Because your life desires that you have that epiphany, that awareness, a self-realization where a light awakens in your mind—an insight, an *aha!* And you will have that *aha* if you will begin to qualify your day, every day and then your life experience can show you that there is an easier way of doing things.

You are the inner orchestra and the conductor of your life. Begin to qualify what is going to take place in your life, and then you leave that alone; you do not allow wondering; you do not allow doubt; you do not even allow yourself to think about it again—as far as you are concerned, your attitude is, "Those things are handled, they are qualified, now let's just let the day unfold..." Qualifying is a gift of life that is given each of you. It is predicting how your day is going to unfold as you desire it to.

Some of you who have been on this journey with me for several years will remember that I love to encourage you to leave the W's alone—the *inside you* will take care of the W's. You know the W's—they are, the where, the when, the how, the what, the who and the why. You know the dialogue, "Oh, yes, I would love to do that, but, *where* am I going to get the money from? I would love to do that, but *how* am I going to get the time?" It is the dialogue; it is the human dialogue of the altered ego.

Give yourselves the time to be in touch with the dream inside you

I encourage you to take all the time in your life to aspire, desire and require. If you do not give yourselves the time to be in touch with the dream inside you—so that you know what it is that you desire and require and aspire to in life—then how can you qualify your day; and how can the inner orchestra of your inner resources, that is the facet of your being, go to work to make those things happen?

I would love you to be in that place, Dear Hearts, where, if somebody came up to you—a friend came up whom you hadn't seen for a while and that one said, "So, what are you doing with your life?" Well, you respond and for the next three or four minutes there is this outpouring from you, "This is what I am doing, and this is what I am going to be doing." There is a knowing within you, a sharing of all that you are being and doing. And the other person just shakes their head, "Wow, you really know yourself, don't you? You really know what you want. I envy you."

Give yourself the time. Honour yourself. Be willing to know what it is that you desire, what it is that you require, and what it is you aspire to in life. Write a journal. Be very familiar with this; so that if anybody asked you, it would be right there. You would know exactly what it is. And then, when it comes to every day, once you have done your inner work in the morning, you fill up; it simply means that in the morning you take that five to seven minutes and remind yourself that you are aligned, and just invite God to come forth fully inside your mind, your body and your world, and to govern everything. And just let yourself be filled.

Then start doing this magical thing—start qualifying how everything is going to take place that day. Look at what is on your plate that day. You can do this on your way to work; you can do it while you are driving your automobile. In fact, it has been shown that while part of you is busy doing something, such as going about your errands, *this* is a good time to qualify your day. It would probably be best that you be alone. But yes, qualify your day, and that's simply stating how your day is going to take place, "Today I am going to have an awesome day. Today I am going to stay in my Heart, and my Heart is going to govern and guide me. Today my Presence will go forth before me, miles ahead of me, just lining everything up; everything is going to be perfect before I even get there. My appointments will be on time today. These interviews that I am having today, they are all going to work out perfectly. These people will recognize the assets and the attributes that I have to offer. People are going to be saying *yes* to me. My manuscripts will be accepted today," as an example. Just apply it to everything in your life, roll it out, just qualify how everything is going to unfold for you, such as, "I only have fifteen minutes to get the car to the mechanic shop, but I am going to do it, I am going to get the car in; the car will get finished in time and I am going to be on my way!"

And you know, people get caught up with 'how'. How? Because when you do your part as director of your life—the different aspects of your inner resources show up. The world is your stage; it is your canvas waiting for you to create upon, waiting for you to think, waiting for you to qualify, to create. When you start doing this, all these facets of your being will naturally play their part well—your Spirit, your Soul, your Flame, the Goddess within you, your God, your inner mind, intuitions, instinct, passion, vision and knowingness will all come together for you. All these facets of your being will naturally release that intelligence that will go ahead of you to open all opportunities and doors.

You might say, "Well, can I actually qualify? Can I actually say how a person is going to respond to me?" Yes, as long as it is constructive. If you are a writer, and you are trying to get your book published, you can say to yourself, "Today I am going to be magnetized to the right publisher and this publisher is going to love this manuscript and they are going to buy it." Yes, you can do that, as long as you are constructive, absolutely so. Because the truth is, you are doing this all the time; you are doing it quietly in that dialogue inside you in which you 'wonder' how you are going to make ends meet, it is this limiting dialogue that you have with yourself, that qualifies your day in a way that is very painful and less than fulfilling. Yes, your day must come together with your will and determination and unwavering mind. Like everything, practice makes perfect.

Do not feel there is any limiting condition in your body that you have to accept

So this is something to desire to happen, that you as Indigo Souls qualify every day the way you would like it to be. Do not accept that there is any power or force outside yourself that could limit you; do not feel there is any condition in your body that you have to accept. Dear Hearts, there are precious people who are dying; there are good folks who are dying now, because they have accepted life-threatening diseases into their bodies. When the truth is, there is enough that has been invented, in the new world of those who have come to invent the future —life-threatening disease can be turned around if you have the right attitude, the spiritual truth and the right products doing the right thing in your bodies. And that is the light of God expressing through the elements of this world.

The light of God is expressing through new doctors and new scientists who are delivering wonderful products; products that were here ten million years ago, that will elevate the power within your electrons, that will speed them up, that will cause energetic activity in the brain to work in a whole new way that will allow your organs to strengthen and rejuvenate; that will allow the damage in your cells to be corrected. It is all here. No one has to die of cancer. No one has to die of aids, if they have the right attitude and the right help that is out there. But people need this information, and it is out there. Not only information, but wonderful new holistic and medical products and inventions that can save lives, are coming forth. And I say this to you because this is a sample of those hundreds of thousands of people who are already out there who are here to invent the future and show the world another way of doing things, evolving life, *being* life.

You have had ten million years to *be*. Beingness offers, in its mighty initiation, *becoming*. Becoming is the great vibration that is taking place within the Indigo Souls. The only way you will become something that you are not yet, is by applying yourself; by doing the inner work, changing your attitudes, opening yourselves up, and inviting the Glory of your God Being inside you to fulfill itself. Take an active step to freeing yourself and offering freedom to others. Claim your own inner happiness and love your life free!

CHAPTER $\mathcal{E}$IGHT

Archangel Michael—who is the Great Archangel who also participates in the Creation of Angels themselves—has offered to everyone, specific Angels, to work with them. I encourage you to participate in the meditation which will follow by being the receivers of the beautiful blessing we wish to bring through, and opening to the Angels that can descend, defend, and protect your lives. In the meditation, we will be calling in the presence of Archangel Michael and his Legions of Angels.

Warrior Angels and the Angels of the Cosmic Blue Flame Sword

There are many different kinds of angels that work with this great Archangel and those who have been perhaps most commonly known to many of the students in the earlier years, are the great Warrior Angels who would sweep through the Earth and begin to undo discordant human energies.

Then there are Angels of the Cosmic Blue Flame Sword. They are the Angels that carry the sword, and where an opportunity is given, will actually anchor, if you will, a beautiful etheric lighted Sword of the Cosmic Blue Flame in an individual's feeling body; where one can learn, through practice, to take up this sword and cut away from oneself any discordant energies. In any environment you can take up this sword—however etheric, yet real—and through the authority of Archangel Michael, release that Cosmic Blue Flame to dispel negative energies anywhere—peoples' homes, the work place...

Angels of Immortal Love and Power

There is another group of Archangel Michael's Angels, that are my favorite, and they are the Angels of Immortal Love and Power. These are the Angels that can be called in to work with you in your own private life. These are the Angels that will descend into your homes. They will stay with you. These Angels of Immortal Love and Immortal Power are those who will take up assignments, if you will, and provide service in your life, including protection of loved ones, protection of children and the protection of home.

These are Angels that are also capable of sourcing miracle powers. It would take days and days and days to explain all the different miracle powers of the Sacred Fire that these Angels can source. These Angels source *The Greatest Power in the Universe*, the Sacred Fire of God's Heart. These are the wonderful Angels that you can call in prayer to protect your thoughts so that your mind is protected. These Angels of Immortal Love and Power are the Angels you can call into your projects, inspirations and dreams.

Many human beings who have experienced failure in their projects do not yet understand that behind that failure are the lower vibrational energies of the world; which can be one's own or from outside in the world, whether it be one's own doubt or simply the sinister force or the negative energy that is in this world.

One area—and this is an area I think you might really be interested in, when working with these Angels—is that the Angels of Immortal Love and Power can be called in to any project, any business, the beginning of a new business or the beginning of a project. Anything that you want to bring forth into fruition, it is with these Angels that you work. Let's say that you have a wonderful idea or that you have a determination to heal a relationship or bring forth a new career or a new business project; all of these things are just examples of where, if you call upon Archangel Michael's Angels of Immortal Love and Immortal Power, they are capable of sourcing all the Miracle Powers of the Sacred Fire—not just the Blue Flame, but all the Seven Rays and their significant Flames—the greatest powers in the universe, to keep your projects protected and make them successful. They are Omniscient Angels and they can source. They *will* source the greater powers into your lives when loved and called into action by you. In the future you have a world in which your lives will unfold in beautiful ways; the world is going to become an outer activity in which you can demonstrate the *greater* in your life. That greater work must be protected, for the world is yet filled with much chaotic energy.

So this is a splendid group of Angels, specifically when you have a new idea, you have a project, you have something that you wish to do, to achieve—you have art that you wish to take to market, you have a relationship that you wish to heal, you have a new idea that requires more information, that requires resources or that requires the bringing together of certain people who have certain talents for a project. Again, this is just a sample of the areas that these magnificent Angels can work in, when you call them forth.

Beyond 'coincidence' is usually an Angel

Until the Cosmic Law permits differently, Angels will always remain invisible; and yet the result of working with these Angels one-on-one, inviting them in, is magnificent. Remember, Angels can hear your thoughts. They can listen to your thoughts and are also capable of *placing* thoughts in your mind. And remember, secondly, precious Hearts— beyond coincidence is usually an Angel!

And so, these steps are intended to make this which seems unreal, more real for you. I desire to emphasize here that especially if an idea was protected the moment it was *conceived*—if it was given protection *then*, and qualified to be protected all the way to manifestation—the degree of success that you would have in your projects would just spiral. So this is something I would really like you to remember—the moment that you have a wonderful idea, immediately call upon Archangel Michael's Angels of Immortal Love and Power to come in and protect that idea and to assist you in taking that idea, fully protected, all the way into manifestation.

Now remember, these Angels are omniscient. They will know what is necessary to bring forth the idea into fruition; they will know where the resources are and they will know what kind of people you will need to participate. They will know where the doors of opportunity are and how to open those doors for you. So this is a really wonderful, resourceful group of Angels with whom you might like to make best friends. Once you start working with these things and you make the calls every day for them to come in and work with you, what you will begin to see is that things flow a little bit easier, the right people are responding; you will see this degree of synchronicity and alchemy appearing; things will just come together beautifully. "Alright, what is it that I require?" You call in the Angels of Immortal Love and Power to come into your project, and then they come to be of service to you! Be sure to offer your love and gratitude to them for their service; and remember, Angels love to be of service.

A Meditation and Invocation

This Transformation Meditation is dedicated to working with Archangel Michael, working with his Angels and what he offers everyone at this time. And what I would like you to do is to open the power of your imagination. Imagine the beautiful Blue Flame Angels; imagine those Angels with you...

Take a moment to acknowledge your divinity. Let us begin the Invocation keeping it in the first person, an Invocation to opening our lives—to opening the door of our lives to Archangel Michael and his beloved Angels that he offers to humankind at this hour. *Affirming inwardly and quietly, from your mind into your heart, where the Angels will receive this message:*

"Through my own beloved Great God Self and under the authority of Archangel Michael, which he is to the Earth, I call forth to Archangel Michael to bring to me those Angels that will most assist me in my full enlightenment, my complete return and remembrance and experience of love, those Angels that will remain with me through the journey that eventually leads to its complete fulfillment and the Ascension of the world."

A call to the Angels of Archangel Michael for the disconnection from any discordant energy...

"I now call forth to me, from Archangel Michael, his Warrior Angels, and I call upon one of Michael's Warrior Angels to stand before me with the Sword of Cosmic Blue

225

Flame. I call upon this beloved Angel—which I greet with my heart of love—to raise its Sword of Blue Lightning, and I call upon this Angel to sever any energy connecting with me that is not Love's Perfect Presence, and any energy that is discordant that I may have ever sent forth in this life or any other life. I ask that any discordant lines of force coming in or going out from me be severed with one mighty stroke; that this Warrior Angel and its Cosmic Blue Flame purify the energy of that line of force that is in the world, and take that energy out and return it to the Universal Storehouse of Energy."

...Imagine a beautiful Warrior Angel before you, raising that sword with blue lightning coming out of the end of it, and drawing a Cosmic Blue Flame around you, disconnecting you from any discordant energy. Continue now to decree:

"I call upon Archangel Michael's Warrior Angels to cut me free of any negative lines of force, or depleting lines of force that may exist between me and any other human being. I ask that any lines of force, any energy lines between me and anyone else, that is not constructive, be severed and purified. I call upon this Angel now to lift its sword, strike its sword, and sever those energy patterns now, and dissolve them into the Violet Flame and the Cosmic Blue Flame. Take a deep breath. 'I AM' grateful."

Imagine in your consciousness now that the atmosphere of your consciousness is becoming endless light, and in your mind's eye, as you allow yourself to see light all about you, allow yourself to imagine many beautiful Angels coming close to you. These are the Sacred Angels with the Cosmic Blue Flame of Archangel Michael, ready to stand at your service and respond to your call. Imagine hundreds of them coming to you, walking out of the light towards you. Take a moment to visualize.

226

A call for the Planet and Her atmosphere...

In a few moments we are about to make the call for the Angels of Immortal Love and Power—and that each person might truly receive this assistance; I am asking that we provide a service for our planet.

As you allow yourself to see those beautiful Angels, I ask that you would join me now in making the following call, quietly from your mind into your Heart, out to the Angels "My Beloved Great God Self, Supreme Presence 'I AM', I call upon your power and Archangel Michael and his uncountable Legions of Warrior Angels and the Angels of the Cosmic Blue Flame to roam through the atmosphere of Earth. Come, Legions upon Legions upon Legions of Archangel Michael's Angels. Flood the atmosphere of Earth and fill the Earth's atmosphere with your Cosmic Blue Flames and dissolve and consume all negative thoughtforms, all discordantly qualified energy. Raise your Swords of Sacred Fire, give the One Mighty Stroke, and dissolve those conditions in the atmosphere, and set everyone free. Mighty Angels of the Light of Archangel Michael, we thank you for this service."

A call for your city, your country...wherever you live...

The second call is for the area in which you live. "Mighty Angels of Archangel Michael and Your Angels of the Cosmic Blue Flame, descend, descend, descend, into the atmosphere over...... (fill in your city name)...descend precious Angels, raise your Cosmic Swords of Blue Lightning and give the One Mighty Stroke and release your Blue Lightning and Cosmic Fire Flame and dissolve all negative energies, all impure energies in the atmosphere and in the powers of nature and the elementals. Strike your Cosmic Blue Flames into the Earth—into the gas belts of the Earth, into the tensions building up in the Earth, and cleanse and purify this area of all negative and lower vibrational energies.

"Precious Angels, stay, stay in the atmosphere of .... Stay with us, precious Angels, and free the powers of nature, free the weather conditions of all negativity, and set everyone free and force the awakening of every human being in this area and all outlying areas. And I ask my own Great God Self to give Archangel Michael and His Angels whatever they need to set everyone free. I thank you."

Now remember, Precious Hearts, your imagination is a powerful faculty of the Inner God Sight. Open your imagination and imagine tens of thousands of Angels descending over the whole lower area where you live, the outlying areas, and the other cities surrounding your area. Imagine tens of thousands of beautiful Angels unleashing lavish light of the Cosmic Blue Flames into the atmosphere and the Earth. Imagine, Blue Flames likened to forest fires ten thousand feet tall from the surface of the planet, up into the atmosphere, down into the Earth, cleansing and purifying. Imagine these Sacred Blue Flames wrapping around every human being, enveloping them, silencing all discord, purifying all the discord, setting humankind free; setting the powers of nature and the forces of the elements and all Earthly Kingdoms free of all impurities. Let it be. Let it be. Let it be. Ask that this be sustained every moment, every day.

A call for the Angels to assist you

Now let's make the call for *you*. Take a deep breath, and let's continue. "My Beloved Great God Self, Beloved Archangel Michael, I ask that you would send forth into my life one or more of your Angels of Immortal Love and Immortal Power. Oh, Michael, Precious Angels, I open the doors of my life to you. Come, Precious Angels, descend, descend, descend into my life. Come and stay with me, Michael, that I, too, may serve the light.

"Angels of Immortal Love and Immortal Power, come, descend, descend, descend, into my home, my automobile; descend into my thoughts, my body, my feelings. Descend into my workplace. Descend into my projects. Descend into my business. Descend into my relationships, my intimate relationship. Descend into my family. Precious Angels, I welcome you.

"Angels of Immortal Love and Immortal Power, I call forth your protection around my life stream and around the life streams of my loved ones, my family and my friends. I call forth your protection and purity into my home, my career, my projects; and I call forth your protection of ideas coming forth from my higher mind: protection of my dreams, my aspirations and my goals.

"Angels of Immortal Love and Power, come. I welcome you into my life, to be with me every moment of every day, so that tomorrow, next week, and next month, as I consider new ideas and new projects, I can call forth your presence of love, protection, purification and perfection to flow into all my thoughts, my feelings, my dreams, my relationships, my projects; and hold them immaculately protected all the way into perfect manifestation and fulfillment; that my life on Earth will reveal the light of my Great God Self. I welcome you, Precious Angels, with all of my Heart. God bless you, Archangel Michael, for the release of these Angels into my life."

Now allow your imagination to have fun. See the Angels descending. See the Angels descending into your home in your imagination. See the Angels flying down, descending and being with your loved ones, your partner. See the Angels descending into your workplace, your projects…

Have fun with this. See the Angels actually flying down and descending, just like Super Woman, Super Man! See them descending one after the other, there is no limit. And know they come and they will stay with you.

Know that you do not have to rush to assign all of them projects *now*. You can assign them projects over the next days, weeks, months, and years, and ask them to stay with each project until each one is fulfilled perfectly. They are here to help you fully awaken, to help you to bring forth your divinity, to fulfill your higher purpose.

Welcome them, welcome them. Let no doubt cross your mind that they are not with you to help you to bring forth the perfection of your God 'I AM' into your world. The light needs you. The world needs your light. And the Angels are here to help you protect and bring forth your light into the world. Send all your love, gratitude and blessings to your Great God Self, then on to Michael and to the Angels. And bless everyone.

CHAPTER *Nine*

I would like to bring to your attention that many of humanity are moving into a whole new experience of attainment, the kind of attainment that will bring forth a higher evolution of mind, consciousness and the very heart of humanity; the unveiling of present mysteries that will allow a new civilization to unfold in the next twelve years much more magnificently than the evolution of humanity in the space time of the Industrial Revolution through to 2006.

The civilizing of humanity, the evolution of Divine Man and Divine Woman

Just imagine the unfoldment of a new civilization, a civilized humanity and an evolution of Divine Man and Divine Woman, the unveiling of the Universal Mysteries, human beings by the millions applying Universal Laws of Divine Love, applying that law in bringing forth their own great inner light on the Earth, that inner light impacting the rest of humanity in the most constructive way possible.

Truly we have now entered an era in which attainment is a higher purpose to be conscious of, to be thinking about, and to contemplate at this time. Each of you by your own efforts—by the homework that you are doing and the desire to awaken yourselves—is in a much greater position to use your consciousness, to call forth all that you wish to attain. Each of you are in a position now to have for yourself the spiritual experiences of God Source, to feel an inner golden glow as a tangible reality, to feel the essence and the reality of your own Heart Flame.

More of humanity today are acknowledging that the *Father Within* that the Master Jesus spoke of is an actual Living Eternal Flame—unseen by human eyes—that is resident, that is living inside, at the very centre of the heart area. And within that flame are the qualities of the Godhead, ready to announce themselves, ready to express within the human self, the greater qualities of God. Through this Great God Flame, each is given the gift of consciousness.

I urge each of you, in this busy world that you find yourself in, to realize there is yet much that you must bring forth, much that you have chosen to bring forth in your life. There are yet new phases in your life that are coming, that you have set up yourself, even before coming back to the Earth in this embodiment. And to best facilitate you bringing forth and achieving your dreams and aspirations in this life, in this lifetime, can each of you, when you accept that you have this living flame that is literally holding the God Presence within, desire to communicate with that Inner Presence.

It is so relevant that you do have the time, ten minutes, or whatever it is each day, to give your whole attention to the bringing forth of your spiritual Presence. This is one of *The Greatest Powers in the Universe*. To bring this magnificent presence forth not as a thought, but as the very essence of your being that you feel inside you—as the *reality* of you—that begins to influence, transform, transmute and begins the metamorphosis of the human form into greater perfection. Each one can now use their consciousness and the power of prayer and meditation to call forth an expansion of the God Presence within, to call forth the assistance of any Ascended Master.

Summer and autumn—the attending of your garden of manifestation and the harvest

August is always that time of the year in which there is a strong energizing presence within the human spirit on the Earth that attends to the garden of manifestation that you wish to bring forth. In the summer all the kingdoms of Earth are in support of bringing forth the new energies of manifestation. In much the same way, the autumn harvest, serves a human being as a time that offers a great energizing Presence that seeks to energize your thoughts, your dreams, what you wish to manifest; to energize those things into a fulfillment of experience and manifestation.

To support the process to harvest in autumn the garden of your dreams, your aspirations and your goals for yourself, I encourage you to let not one day pass that you do not feel your spiritual Presence; that you call forth into full expression in you, the Flame of Divine Love. And know that you have the ability—through the power of invocation and will—to harness these greater powers and call forth the Flame of Divine Love into all your activities that you are involved in at this time. Through this Mighty Inner Flame you open the door to *The Greatest Power in the Universe*, Divine Love; and Its source, the great Sacred Fire Love and Power of the Infinite 'I AM' Presence, as it expresses throughout creation through the Angelic and Ascended Host, and now through you.

Start working, days, weeks, months ahead of time, with your future manifestations. Start working with your dreams and aspirations—energetically and qualitatively—from a point of consciousness that harnesses your higher power. Allow the days and weeks to be qualified, expanded, perfected, and protected, by the Flame of Divine Love and the Company of Heaven that you call forth into all your activities that you are to participate in at this time. Use this energy, this actual Presence of Divine Love. Use the power of your God Source and the Ascended Host and the Angelic Host, to expand—by your prayer call—the Flame of Divine Love, into everything.

Precious Hearts, go to the God of your Being, say, "I acknowledge all of the gifts that I have, all the activities in my life, my abilities, my talents, everything that I seem to have been given that is my way of showing up and that which naturally expresses through me, I offer all of that to be an Open Door in which you, the light of my being, touch humanity."

More of humanity must be touched at this time. More, must the student body of spiritual groups that are growing throughout the world, touch the heart of humanity and make a difference. The God of your being, and the Ascended Host, are seeking pathways to every human heart who is thirsting to experience the reality of their being; to experience God, to unveil the mysteries. What an opportunity that is! Don't miss this opportunity to seize the power. Call upon the Flame of Divine Love and charge it into every one of your activities; and offer every activity that you are involved with, back to God as an opportunity to express Its perfection into your life.

If you could see what the Ascended Masters are doing at this moment for the Earth!

I say to you, Precious Hearts, if you could see from the inner standpoint, the Ascended Ones who are walking the Earth, who are in such service to humanity at this hour, if you could see how Beloved Ascended Jesus Christ descends from the higher Octaves of Light and walks through places of the three Americas and throughout the world, where He anchors His Flame of Cosmic Divine Love for the constant purification of the Earth. If you could see how Michael and his Legions of Angels continue to sweep into the atmosphere every evening to cleanse some of the discordant creations that humankind still generate onto this Earth. If you could see some of the Legions of Angels that descend into the Sacred Forests of this Earth that are being pillaged at this time, you would be amazed. If you could see some of the work of Angels who descend to heal some of the gaping holes in this Earth created by human beings and what they take from this Earth, you would love those Angels! Of course all of the Ascended Host are invisible in their work on Earth until the Cosmic Hour strikes, that compels humanity to acknowledge their existence and assistance that is being given.

If you could see and know the intervention that is happening at a Cosmic Level to this Planet, you would say, "My God, how is it possible that beings from other systems and Ascended Beings and Angels from higher stratospheres, that so love this Planet, can intervene and bring Cosmic powers to save this Planet." Yet the numbers of humanity that know and care about this Planet are so small, but growing, yes, absolutely. Every single day the numbers of humanity that know and care are growing.

There is a new kid on the block

It seems appropriate to say—it was only back in 1937 that Ascended Beings in the higher realms of light yet held the question as to whether humankind would make it, that is, survive. The reputation humanity had in the higher realms of Earth, the reputation it had in other Star systems, was that humanity had made Planet Earth a dark star. We considered that humanity had really done a job of almost destroying itself. But now that has changed! There is a new kid on the block! And that new kid on the block is a civilized human being who is finally fulfilling its destiny, developing an inner light and letting that light create a new peaceful civilization on the Earth. That new kid on the block is a more peaceful, creative and caring human being who is finally fulfilling its destiny, becoming more conscious of the light, desiring the light and letting that light create an uplifting presence on the Earth. Humans are discovering they are self conscious intelligent beings that can become even greater than they are at present.

A new relationship with life, with each other is unfolding. An uplifting time is coming in which humans are going to create a new era of attainment—and the greater knowledge, greater love, greater wisdom they will creatively express—is going to teach them how to weave and evolve with all the kingdoms of the Planet to extend creation, to bring forth creation; rather than taking from this Planet and creating what was never good in the long run. Humanity in the next twelve years will learn how to harness Universal Energy. Humanity is going to learn how to synthesize itself with all the kingdoms of the Earth, to bring forth wonderful new inventions, technologies, and wonderful new elements; no longer harmful to humankind or to the Earth, but helpful, that which does not destroy, but that which extends life.

You, and millions of individuals like you, are given an opportunity to be living channels; not only of the Great God Presence, but to quicken your path with the help of the Ascended Masters and the Angels who desire to bring forth into outer expression the great Inner Light that is inside you as quickly as possible. And so, yes, as you withdraw your allegiance from that which no longer serves you, and as you seek to find your own sovereignty and no longer give power to that which is less-than in the world; know that the Angels and the Ascended Masters are here to assist you.

Your call to them can quicken your own experiences, perfecting your own world; allowing you to be a channel, in which greater beings of light who have attained, might do work through each of you to touch the rest of humanity—to purify from this Earth, forever, everything that is destroying life, so that finally there is no longer anything discordant left on this Planet; and this Planet becomes the shining jewel that she is intended to be—the showcase of God individualized, in harmony with the powers of nature and the forces of the elements, bringing forth life flourishing creation.

Perhaps the visions of Nostradamus and the prophets, can be those dreams that begin a new cycle for humanity

Therefore, I would like to invoke now the Presence of the Supreme Creator and the Presence of your own Great God Selves, and the Presence of the Angelic Host and the Ascended Host who have but one desire, and that is the Divine Plan to save humanity. It does not mean just a plan to save a few million, rather it is a plan to save every single soul, whether in embodiment on the Earth or disembodied at this time.

The Divine Plan is fulfilling itself, and it is working. But yet, even at this hour, as we are moving through a cycle of transition and transformation there is much chaos on the Earth. If we were to move forward with the ascension of the world, which is its destiny, much of humanity would not make that ascension. Therefore, may your lives be so lived that not one human soul, embodied or disembodied, misses the opportunity that will unfold in this new cycle.

Perhaps the dreams and the visions of Nostradamus and the great prophets, can be those dreams that begin a new ten thousand year cycle; not only of peace, equally into a Planet of exquisite perfection—the true Garden of Eden.

Therefore I ask you to open your hearts and be willing to receive the greater assistance that is being offered each of you. You may or may not, depending on your own current course of study, be aware of those things that I am going to call forth; but all that I am about to call forth, I am going to ask that it come forth through the expansion of your own inner light. Therefore, you are safe to receive, because your own inner light is the greatest guardian of your human self and will never allow you to receive more than you are able to receive. Therefore, I encourage you to feel absolutely safe, open and receptive, become a Crystal Cup, ready to be filled and soak up this beautiful, beautiful love of which the Ascended and Angelic Host are ready to pour forth an avalanche, that you may take that love and express it to the world.

As we are all one, I call forth these blessings to go out to all who are reading these words and opening their hearts to receive.

Invocation to *The Greatest Power in the Universe*

As best as you are able, for the first two or three minutes, hold your focus upon the Mighty Presence of life within you. It helps to visualize a Golden Flame inside the chest area, surrounded with a golden sun's halo. Just fasten your attention for two or three minutes, still yourself with a feeling of gratitude and then hold yourself open and receptive to the following blessings of Eternal Love. Let's begin with a deep breath and decree:

"Mighty Presence of life, I speak to you within the human heart of every one, and the Eternal Flame that lives within each. I greet you as the Great God 'I AM', the Mighty Presence of Life, the greatest love in the universe, the greatest power in the universe—the Threefold Activity of Love, Wisdom and Power in Perfect Action. I greet you and bless you for eternity for this transcendent service called forth.

"Through the life stream that each one receives every moment in their life, do I call upon the Mighty Presence of each, to open the Cosmic Doorway to allow the great Ascension Blessings to come forth; to expand the Spiritual Integrity, Presence and Flame, that each is carrying in their lives. And I am eternally grateful."

The Golden Healing Hands of the Ascended Jesus Christ

"Mighty Presence of Life, in the Name, Love, Wisdom, and Power which Thou art, I call upon the Ascended Jesus Christ. I call upon the Ascended Jesus Christ to pour forth His Luminous Presence, His Cosmic Christ Healing and His Eternal Love as a Mighty Current of Healing energy, through the minds, bodies, beings, and worlds, of each one. I ask that the Beloved Presence bless for eternity all those who are turning towards the Light. And I ask that the Golden Healing Hands of the Ascended Jesus Christ descend and be placed upon the spinal columns of each person, straightening the spinal columns, and filling the spines with Golden Liquid Light of Eternal Courage and Strength."

The Buddha and His Emerald Green Ray

"I call upon the descent of the Seraphim Angels—the Christed Angels—to descend and expand their mighty Christ Flame in each one. I call upon the descent of the Emerald Ray. As I reach out my life and my love to the Buddha, I call upon the Buddha, through His Emerald Green Ray to expand the Buddha Presence within the Heart Flame of each one; bringing forth a transcendent peace and happiness that is the feeling of right desire, and all that the Buddha offers. I ask that the Buddha project those qualities He radiates to life, that He awaken those qualities within each one. We love and bless the Precious Buddha."

Mary, the Mother of the World, and the Angels of the Rose Pink Ray of Divine Love, Mercy, and Forgiveness...

"I call forth the descent of the Angels of the Rose Pink Ray, and I call upon the Angels of Love, Mercy, and Forgiveness, to descend and to fill each one with the Rose Pink Rays of Divine Love, Mercy, and Forgiveness. I ask that each receive the greatest showering of love, mercy, and forgiveness. And I ask the Angels prepare the way for the descent of the Mother of the World, as I call upon Beloved Precious Mary, Mother of Jesus, to descend in the arms of the Angels, upon the Rose Pink Ray, to each of us.

"We ask that Precious Mary descend and be with each Life Stream for a few moments. And I ask that Precious Mary pour forth Her Heart Flame with Her Healing Love, and place that around each one's physical heart and brain, and bring forth a perfect healing in the physical heart and physical brain. I ask that wounds of hate, wounds of grief, and wounds of suffering and loss, be healed with Mary's Healing Presence. And I ask that Precious Mary—through the Angels of Love, Mercy, and Forgiveness—bring forth that Rose Pink Ray and pass it through each one's life stream. I ask that all the mistakes of each one in every embodiment be brought into perfect balance through the will of Mary and the Angels of Love, Mercy, and Forgiveness."

Archangel Michael and His Angels of the Cosmic Blue
Flame of Immortal Love and Immortal Power

"I call forth the Presence of Archangel Michael and His Angels of the Cosmic Blue Flame of Immortal Love and Immortal Power. I call upon Precious Michael and His Angels to raise their Mighty Sword of Freedom and set a ring of Cosmic Blue Fire around each one, and cut free and loosen everyone free of any lines of force that are discordant that may be coming in or going out to other human beings or from themselves. I ask that Michael, through His Mighty Sword of Freedom protect each one in a wall of Sacred Blue Flames that cuts each one free of discordant energy. And I ask Michael and His Angels of Immortal Love and Power to build a permanent wall of Cosmic Blue Flames around us—a mighty pillar rising up twelve feet high, permanently sustained by the Higher Self of each one, that each one may be disconnected from the discordant energies of the world and free to express the perfection of the Great God Self within. We love and bless Michael for His transcendent service, and His Precious Angels."

The God and Goddess of Purity and Their
Angels of Eternal Purity

"I call forth the Presence of two Ascended Beings so forgotten by humanity. I call upon the Living Presence of the God and Goddess of Purity and Their Angels of Eternal Purity. I welcome you and I call you forth in the Name, Love, Wisdom, and Power, which Thou art; to descend and be with each Life Stream, Beloved God and Goddess of Purity. And blaze forth your Sacred Blue Flame of Cosmic Christ Purity through the minds, bodies, beings, and worlds, of every one. Anchor your Flame of Eternal Purity within each one as a constant expanding and purifying Presence, to set the minds, bodies, beings, and worlds, free of every impure thought, feeling and quality. We thank and bless the God and Goddess of Purity for this transcendent service."

The Queen of Light, and Her Angels from the Great Heavens

"I call forth one who is so loved throughout the Cosmos for all that she has attained, for all that she has given. In the name of the Divine Mother, I call upon the Queen of Light and Her angels from the great heavens above. Precious Queen of Light, descend, descend, descend. Come and let each feel your love and your freedom. Touch the minds of each one, and set their minds free; set their consciousness free of the concepts that limit and diminish the human spirit and its light.

"O, Queen of Light, set all minds free with the power that you have. Set the consciousness free so there may be the knowing and the feeling of the Oneness of all Life. O, Queen of Light, expand Your Light into the minds and brains of each one. Place your blazing White Fire inside the minds and brains of each one. Hold it, expand it, and cause it to be eternally sustained, to assist each one in the days and weeks that follow. We love and bless you for eternity, Beloved Queen of Light."

Saint Germain, Chohan of the Seventh Ray, the Violet Ray, The Seventh Seal

"Beloved Saint Germain, Chohan and Lord of the Seventh Ray, The Violet Ray, The Seventh Seal, I greet you. Mighty Saint Germain, I bless you for your transcendent service to humanity for the past seventy thousand years, and I call upon your transcendent service to each one. Saint Germain, you have stated clearly that you will respond to every call. You have challenged the Students of Light on Earth, and I meet your challenge, Beloved Saint Germain, and I call out to you in my heart.

"Beloved Saint Germain, Mighty Chohan, we love and bless you for eternity for your transcendent service as Father of the Seventh Golden Age that is being ushered onto the Planet. We give you all credit, together with Jesus and the Ascended Host, Thou who has saved America and the world.

"Beloved Saint Germain, as you stand with each Life Stream with Your Precious Violet Ray and Your Violet Flame, Your Seventh Ray that You behold, I ask that You would extend Your Heart Flame of Freedom and Liberty and all that you mean to life as the Violet Heart Presence around everyone. Beloved Saint Germain, send forth your Heart Flame and place your Heart Flame of your Violet Flame Love to Life—the *greatest* purifying power in the universe—and place your Violet Flame within the mind's eye at the centre of the forehead of each one. Anchor your Violet Flame within each person's forehead to awaken the mind's eye, to awaken the Sevenfold Flame of Creation within the brow of each one.

"O, Beloved Saint Germain, you know these Children of Light who are on the Earth at this time and those who are waiting embodiment. Assist each one in fulfilling the Akashic Record of their life, the highest achievement in this lifetime. Place a wall of your Violet Flame Love around each one, and let not the sinister forces and the shadows and discord of the world touch these precious hearts again.

"O, Beloved Saint Germain, we know you as Joseph, father of Jesus. We know you as Shakespeare, Christopher Columbus and we know you as Merlin. We know you as the great and mighty Guru who came to India seventy thousand years ago. We know you as an Ascended Master who has served humanity for seventy thousand years. Be with every human heart. Fill each one with your love, with your Healing Presence to Life. We know that you hold a dream that not one human soul will be lost. Anchor that dream within everyone.

"Saint Germain, fill each one—their minds, their bodies, their hearts—with what only you can possibly know is the most perfect thing for each one to receive at this time, that will allow the human discord in their lives to stand aside and allow the perfection to come forth, with nothing stopping their light ever again. Your name means Freedom. Your name, Saint Germain, means Liberty and Justice—Democracy for All. Therefore, fill each Life Stream with your Living Flame, that each one in this life will fulfill the Call to Life as quickly as is possible. And I ask in the name of the Higher Self, the God 'I AM' Presence of each one, for this transcendent service. I ask that God and the Higher Selves of humanity will bless Saint Germain for eternity for this transcendent service that He offers."

I ask that each one now join me, silently in your prayer, to call upon your God Life to bless those who have come forth—to bless them for eternity for the transcendent service that has been offered by each. And I ask that all we have received continue to expand every hour, every week, into the future; and all we have called forth be sustained, that every time we remember this Invocation in the days and months to follow, instantly its effects will double.

We bless and we say, "God Bless for Eternity the Great God Presence 'I AM' and the Company of Heaven. God bless you for eternity, and may our lives on the Earth now become a blessing for humanity and the Earth, the Powers of Nature, the Kingdoms, the Forces of the Elements. May our lives come into right relationship with the Earth and be a blessing to all Life. God bless life. God bless *The Greatest Power in the Universe!* God bless the Sacred Heart Flame of God that abides within each one."

I AM Akasha, I AM Asun and we thank you!

CHAPTER *T*EN

I Am Akasha and I greet you out of the Radiant Rose of my Love. It is wonderful to have this opportunity to bring to you the message, the love, and the radiation of the Planetary Guardian from Venus—the Beloved, the Mighty Sanat Kumara.

Today there are greater numbers of human beings who are hearing of this Great Being. His authority is far reaching in this System of Worlds, past, present and future.

The Authority of Sanat Kumara came forth four million years before the first of the 'I AM' Starseed arrived

Those who have the Authority as Planetary Guardians who are called the Logos, are those Cosmic Beings of Light who have gained the Ascension, who have come forth from the Great Central Sun—as you have—and have gained their Ascension in other Systems of Worlds. And they have risen up the great spiritual hierarchy to such a degree—beyond even the Ascended Masters' level—that They achieve great positions of authority over the development of Systems of Worlds. They become such Mighty Cosmic Outpourings of Light, They become instrumental in the future creations of *new* Systems of Worlds. Such is our Mighty and Beloved Sanat Kumara from Venus, Son of the Goddess of Venus who governs that Planet.

The Mighty Sanat Kumara and many others of the Logos (this is a Great Council, in the Thirteenth Octave of the Universe) are Individuals of great authority who do assume *responsibility* for this world, this System of Worlds. And that responsibility is timely and intervention does come forth at different seasons of humankind's evolution.

The Authority of Sanat Kumara came forth eighteen million years ago. Four million years before the first 'I AM Starseed' took embodiment on the Earth fourteen million years ago. In this way, He participated with the Seven Thrones who created this System of Worlds—the Seven Mighty Elohim. The Seven Mighty Elohim are the Great Creator Beings who come forth from the Heart of Creation to participate in the creation of new planetary Systems of Worlds.

The Authority and the Will of the Mighty Sanat Kumara is Evolution Itself

And in the creation of the powers of nature and the forces of the elements, and all the Kingdoms that have come forth, and in the creation of the physical embodiment for the 'I AM' Starseed to embody as human beings, did the Planetary Logos place His Divine Authority and Divine Will within the projected Unfed Flame from the Mighty 'I AM' Presence of all of you. The Unfed Flame is the Great Love Flame of God, individualized.

The authority and the will of the mighty Sanat Kumara is evolution itself, and it is under this authority that He places within the Unfed Flame of every human being—and beings on your sister Planets—the desire for evolution; the desire *To Be*, the upward reach, the desire for growth, the desire for transformation—indeed, the desire for change through upliftment. That desire comes from the Great God Flame of the mighty Sanat Kumara that He placed within your own Sacred Heart Flame as you came forth, preparing you for your first embodiment on the Earth.

A Logos will take on a physical embodiment in order to become the Authority over a physical planet

As many of the Logos do, once a planet and System of Worlds is ready for embodiments, many of the Logos will come into physical embodiment. And even though ascended and free already, they will take on a physical embodiment in order to become the authority over the physical planet of that System of Worlds.

There has been much discussion around whether an ascended being comes back into an unascended life. It is most extraordinary, and it does not generally happen. It does not happen for the Ascended Masters. It would only occur at a much higher hierarchy; in which a Logos, or a Being of great Cosmic Authority, in laying out the Divine Plan for the evolution of a species, will come in when the Cosmic Hour allows, and take on a physical life. The Logos will take on a life form so the Planetary Logos, and the Divine Plan for a new world, might become an authority in physical reality.

Sanat Kumara took up His first embodiment on the Planet Venus and became the Cosmic Christ to Venus

It is for this reason that even though Sanat Kumara was a part of the creation of this System of Worlds, when it was his opportunity to become the authority for physicality in this world that he took up his first physical embodiment on the Planet Venus. And through the evolutions of those embodiments did he become the Cosmic Christ to Venus a very, very, long time ago. And Precious Hearts, when the Earth most required it He came to the Earth in a *number* of human embodiments. There is many a legend in your world about that.

The Son of Brahma

The Beloved Sanat Kumara carried within His Pure God Flame the seed that brought forth the evolutions of the *religions* of this world. Behind all that has ever come forth, whether it be the authority of His brother who is a Logos known to you as Mighty Sananda, or in His Ascended state, Beloved Master Jesus, or whether it be the Logos of the Violet Flame, Beloved Saint Germain—all of these, according to Divine Plan, will take on physical lives at certain times.

In the ancient days of religions, you have perhaps, in your memory, heard the phrase *Son of Brahma.* The being that is referred to here, in a great religion that came forth in India, was indeed Sanat Kumara's first life in physical embodiment on the Earth. Beloved Sanat Kumara was, and will forever be, the Son of Brahma.

Sanat Kumara has been the Authority over all Divine Plans that your Earth has been progressing through

Because his authority is so great, he actually represents the will of the 'I AM' Seed of the Great Mighty 'I AM' Presence from the Great Central Sun, which is the Creator of all individualizations of Godsource; It has produced your own life on Earth, your own Mighty 'I AM' Presence.

As He is the authority for evolution, Beloved Sanat Kumara has been the authority and the author of all Divine Plans that your Earth has been progressing through. Because the Cosmic Hour allows it, your Earth is under the greatest evolution and change in the quickest amount of time that has ever been recorded in this world. This is why

250

Sanat Kumara comes to you and to many of the students at this time, to remind you the changes that are coming forth on this Earth are inspired by His own Unfed Flame—and the Love Flame within you, that remembers the Divine Plan and the natural evolution of life and this Planet.

And because His Unfed Flame became one with your own Heart Flame before you took embodiment, within your own Unfed Flame, the Patterns of Divine Plan, the Patterns of Grand Design, the Patterns of Evolution, and the need and necessity for change on this Planet, exists within each and every human being. It is at a level of awareness in which indeed, Dear Hearts, the density of the outer self is often an obstruction to that awareness.

The Divine necessity for change

You are Beloved Children of the Light, Beings of Godsource. You have been working with your own Great God Presence; and all of you, in varying degrees, are lessening the interference between the Earthly self and your Divine Self, your Beloved 'I AM' Presence. It is for this reason that you are also awakening through the fields of sensitivity, intuitions, and awareness. Each of you are gaining a greater awareness today, and your world is becoming a testimony of the evolution and the change that has been seen in the last one hundred years—this change and quickening that you have heard me speak of that will continue to come forth in the next twelve years.

Again, the author of this great change and a new Renaissance period which has begun is the Beloved Mighty Sanat Kumara, and I bring this sacred remembrance to you so that you might feel a closer relationship with this great God Being. The awareness and the desire for change—the desire for evolution—is very strong in your world. The forces of darkness that yet find pawns within this world will

251

soon find that the day of reckoning is upon them; because Sanat Kumara again is *amplifying* that Divine Design, that Divine Will, and the Divine Necessity for change. And He is amplifying that through the Children of Light in the world today. Is that not magnificent?

Mozart, Chopin, Alice Bailey, Madame Blavatsky, Edgar Cayce...all over-lighted by Sanat Kumara

Beloved of the Heart, you might like to know that Sanat Kumara has over-lighted many human beings on the Earth. Especially when higher purpose was so important, because your higher purpose has the opportunity to impact many thousands, if not millions, of lives on Earth. It is for this reason that Sanat Kumara was the direct over-lighting Presence of Master Mozart, Master Chopin, and perhaps more current—well, let's put this in some order—yes, Mozart, Chopin, Alice Bailey, Madame Blavatsky, and that one which has been known to you as Edgar Cayce; all of these individuals were over-lighted by Sanat Kumara in the same way that the Lord Maitreya over-lighted Master Jesus in His life.

I have asked it, and I believe that Sanat Kumara will offer each of you precious students and all of you who are reading (listening to) this in future time for a way in which he can over-light you. He will give you an understanding of how this happens, so that His over-lighting Presence— the projection of His Luminous Presence can cause His Golden Sunshine to rest above you and upon you. You know, Precious Heart, whenever the eye is caused to see the Light of Sanat Kumara, the only words one can utter about His light is Pure Golden Sunshine. I have requested that He create a way to help you, and know His Presence of Divine Love can be projected above you and upon you; and as you call Him forth, this blessing can go forth out into your world to help each of you fulfill the higher purpose of your life and the Divine Plan.

If you have read about the life of Mozart, the life of Chopin, the life of Alice Bailey, Madame Blavatsky and Edgar Cayce, and if you looked behind the curtain of their life and did some research, you would find that these five individuals did have their own human challenges, indeed. And yet, were these challenges so great that the Mighty Sanat Kumara could not over-light those five in such a magnificent way that the higher purpose of their lives was fulfilled? Every one of those lives was absolutely fulfilled, Dear Heart!

So you see, in your evolution, in your journey, in your own Ascension Path, in your journey to your own Self Mastery, even though there is that which you have not mastered in your life, it does not stand in the way of living and fulfilling your higher purpose. Just as Mozart, and Chopin, Alice Bailey and Madame Blavatsky and even Edgar Cayce had difficulties in their own lives, yet great was the success of the *higher purpose* of their lives. For the Mighty Planetary Logos does not fail at anything, Dear Heart. This Mighty Being has over-lighted many others too, who have impacted the upward spiral of the Human Race.

A challenge for your Christed Selves and the Ascended Masters—how will your physical bodies sustain the Vibration of the Violet Soul?

I would just like to take a few more moments to share with you, if I might, the Soul's evolution. Through recent events of Cosmic Intervention that have taken place, many of you now are moving upward from the Indigo Vibration and into the Violet Soul. You have moved through a time, my Dear Hearts, in which tremendous inner work has been accomplished within each of you; inner work that has not yet found its way up to the surface and out into manifestation.

Many things have happened deep inside you, in the feeling side of life, in the soul, and even to some extent to the flesh body with the cells of the body being so expanded and much work being accomplished. It is for this reason that it is very important to take care of yourself. It is very important to honour yourself. It is very important to nurture yourself. It is very important—I am going to stress this so that every one of you hears the importance of this— it is very important that you are getting your rest. Whatever amount of rest that the physical body and the brain seem to require at this time, please give that rest to your physical garment. Not only the rest that is found in the sleep state, but the rest that can be experienced when meditating each day with the Ascended Master's Consciousness and the great Illumining Silence—the great Inner Voice that comes out of the silence of your own Heart Flame. I recommend some time each day that you lie down quietly and be very still for fifteen minutes and ask an Ascended Master to fill you with His or Her Ascended Master's Consciousness while you enter the inner silence. This is very important.

In the coming days you will find yourself making, and arbitrating, some wonderful new decisions for yourself; decisions that affect your immediate and long-term life. You will find that you will be charged with making more decisions, and it is very important that you have the light—the clarity of light—in the mind, in the brain and the feeling side of life. It is very important that your body receives the nurturing rest that allows it to move into a higher light frequency. Many of you have been raised or will soon expand into the Violet Soul. This brings with it a greater opportunity for creative self expression and mighty initiations, but it also presents a challenge for your Christed Selves and the Ascended Masters, and that is,

"How will your physical bodies sustain the vibration of the Violet Soul?"

The Goddess of Venus, offers Her Cosmic Love Supreme to assist the physical body to assimilate the Violet Soul

A great Dispensation from the Great Central Sun has allowed the Cosmic Mother of Venus to come to the Earth and to release a rhythmic pulsation that would release Her Cosmic Love Supreme; its intent to become a part of your lives and especially help you in the physical consciousness—the physical bodies. This great gift of Cosmic Love Supreme continues to flow in from the Goddess of Venus and can be offered you if you ask for it. If you will lie down—even when you go into the sleep, and call upon the Goddess of Venus to fill you with Her Cosmic Love Supreme to do everything that is required to strengthen, to purify, and to raise, the energy of your atomic body and your body's consciousness, She will send this Ray of Her Divine Love to you; so that more quickly your body can assimilate the full light vibration of the Violet Soul. This will help you at this time. This is a great gift that Sanat Kumara's Mother offers you.

Already we can see something that is taking place. We see there are aspects of the Violet Soul that are holding itself back; because the body is not yet carrying the frequency of light that it requires to carry in order to express more of the Violet Soul vibration. And this is what the Mighty Saint Germain knew was going to happen. And although you may be passing through the Twelve Initiations of the Violet Soul—which encompasses the experience of Divine Love in the face of provocation, yet there are aspects of the Violet Soul vibration that your own Higher Mental Body Christ Self is holding back, because the physical body has

255

not yet assimilated enough of the Cosmic Love Supreme—the Cosmic Light Supreme that the Goddess of Venus has offered, to help your bodies raise into a higher light frequency. Remember, the gift of the Violet Soul for each of you is the desire, passion, talent and ability for greater self expression.

Balance in rest, good foods, and fresh air for the Violet Soul body

Now, if the body does not have its rest—if you don't have balance in nutritionally good foods, balance of the right water element in your body, and balance of different kinds of exercise—balance in being still and being outdoors and getting fresh air, the body has difficulty in attaining a higher light vibration that expresses the Violet Soul. These are little things, but little things that, if they go unaddressed, can become *more than* a little thing, yes? And so I am to remind you, Dear Heart, a great effort from the Angelic and Ascended Host is underway to help your body consciousness to make a tremendous frequency shift so that it can carry higher light vibration—meaning the Violet Soul of you can come forth in its Full Encompassing Presence.

There is a deliberate *holdback*, if you will, at the present moment. Remember, the Violet Soul brings naturally a greater wholeness of you forth into self expression. It's a wonderful gift and you don't have to beg for it. It brings more of your Ascended Self—that aspect of you that didn't come into this world, into expression. Or, what you have also heard me say—it brings more of your greater life into expression. However, in order for this to take place, the sparkling inner world of inner sunshine that the Violet Soul carries must have the higher vibration in the physical body and must have the means to enter into the cellular structure of the body. This is why these things have been brought to your attention.

I seek to encourage you to assess the balance in your life. Your light has gained its freedom; your Presence is so close to you now. Your intuitions, your sensitivity will serve you well. And every one of you, when there is peace in the mind, can ask the light within your heart very simple questions, and begin to have the answers to those questions. Especially now that awakening humanity are in the third phase of Self Mastery; in which life seeks to be a constant and conscious reflection, asking yourself, "What is it that I most require in this moment? What is it that is taking place in the next thirty-six hours, forty-eight hours? What is it that my body requires; my energy requires? Is there any type of food; is there any particular environment to be in?" Just ask those questions gently and you will have the answer.

And then if you will just remind yourselves that we are asking you to keep up your prayer call to the Goddess of Venus, the Sacred Mother of Venus. Ask Her to direct Her Cosmic Love Supreme especially into your physical body, so that the consciousness, the flesh structure, and the very cells and atoms of which your bodies are composed, may go through a greater raising activity, allowing the Violet Soul expression through your physical body with much ease and grace.

The Violet Soul compels wonderful activity in the physical body

There are many joyful experiences coming for you as all of you evolve beyond the Indigo Soul and into the Violet Soul. It has compelled each of you to open to a greater understanding of the Natural Laws of Manifestation, an understanding of yourselves, your minds and your feelings.

It has compelled certain healing and purification, so that now as you enter into the next soul vibration, the Violet Soul, much of what has been accomplished in the mental and feeling side of life can now become achievements that are more creative, more physical, more tangible, more material, more real and actualized in outer expression.

It is for this reason, that just as the Indigo Soul compelled much healing, much personal development, much understanding of metaphysics; *the Violet Soul* compels the *physical* body to quicken the vibration of its energy. It compels the raising of the physical body into a higher energy vibration so that the accomplishments made in the mind and feeling—and your spiritual Vision, your Field of Dreams, and your spiritual Road Map for the years ahead—has a wonderful physical vehicle in which physical, tangible manifestation may come forth into your outer lives, making you much happier than ever before!

I hope you understand also, the essence of what I am saying to you; that just as the Indigo Soul compelled wonderful activity and correction in the mind and feeling—which is yet to be really experienced by you—the Violet Soul compels wonderful activity in the physical body and outer expression of your creative life. And when that activity in the physical body is allowed, then my Dear Hearts, the crowning accomplishment and victory of effort made in your mental body and feeling body is experienced in the physical. So I hope that you will take my meaning into consideration and apply it to your daily lives.

Bless you, Dear Heart, I Am Akasha and our Beloved Sanat Kumara is now ready to share with you.

Sanat Kumara from Venus speaks...

Beloved students, I, Sanat Kumara, come to you this hour and release into your own lives My own Heart Flame's

Sacred Fire Desire for your freedom; and all that will bring you forth into great and happy moments, so quickly, so tangibly, in the wonderful years that are yours, which are ahead of you. I greet you!

I bring you greetings from My Mother and I bring you greetings from my Brothers and Sisters—the Lords of the Flame from Venus. I am so grateful that you lend your ear to me; that I may continue to open a place where your feeling side of life can expand the acceptance of our reality and our closeness that can come to you in the gifts that we wish to bring you from Venus. We thank you.

Venus—the Guardians of the Earth and those who would embody on the Earth

Longer than you know, Beloved of the Light, has been our place as Guardians of the Earth. Millions of years before the Starseed began the great exodus from the Great Central Sun towards the Earth, did the Starseed of our own world, our own Planet, make the exit from the Great Central Sun to our home Planet, Venus. We embodied upon our world, and evolved with the assistance of the Great Host of Light into the Fifth and Greater Dimensions and experiences of light. Once the Starseed of *Earth* began its exodus from the Great Central Sun, *we* were placed as the Guardians of the Earth and those who would embody on the Earth.

There is much reference in the modern metaphysics and I am grateful for that reference—to those who have accepted me and those who know of my own exile to the Earth long ago to assist mankind and the Earth's evolution. Yet, long before *I* came to the Earth, has my world—has My Mother, and our Planet been Guardian over the Earth and the people of Earth. It has always been our role to guard the Earth. We have guarded you; we have loved you and we have called to you for centuries of time.

For millions of years we have sent forth the call from our Great Temples of Light. I have stood in the great atmosphere of your own Earth and I, for decades upon decades, have called you. And those of you, who are awakening today, are those upon the first ranks who heard our call and reached up to that light, which sought, to move through the density and the discord of the Earth's atmosphere and into your precious life streams.

I hope you will accept all of us from Venus as your Guardians of Love Divine. For, Dear Hearts, if you will accept that we have always been Guardians of your Earth, and as you continue to grow in acceptance of my reality, can the greater gifts be released into your outer life. We have waited several million years for this. Although those who own your world placed us in temporary Guardianship of the Starseed of Earth and this physical Planet, yet, we too, have had the experience of obedience to the Cosmic Law. It has not allowed us to interfere with the activities of humankind, unless those activities brought the Planet *Itself* into great peril, or brought the mass life streams of those embodied on your Planet into peril.

Fortunately, the love, the mercy, and the forgiveness of life itself, created cycles in which the *potential* for extinction and termination of mankind has allowed my Brothers and Sisters and myself to not only command and project our own Heart's Flame to the Earth for the greater protection that is required, but also to come to the Earth as Guardians—it has allowed the evolution of the Earth to continue to what it is today.

I have opened a Dispensation to all the Children of Light

I wish to provide each of you a greater assistance. There is a remarkable path and journey that is ahead of you— the life of Higher Purpose and Divine Plan. And indeed, as I held my light over such life streams as Edgar Cayce, Mozart, and others, did I do this by placing the Golden Sunshine of my love above and around those individuals. In the Ascended Masters' terminology we call the Golden Sunshine Halo, *The Luminous Presence*.

I have opened a Dispensation to all the Children of Light, which if you will ask me to place upon thy crowns the Luminous Presence of My Love, then this shall be a Golden Sun's Presence above and around you. Then this will be a Luminous Presence of my love that has been qualified to go forth out into your life ahead of you in future time—to be that Great Central Sun's Magnet's Presence that magnetizes to you all that is required for the fulfillment of your higher purpose and the Divine Plan fulfilled. It will go forth out from you, days and weeks ahead, to provide for you the protection. And it will provide the purification for streams of electronic energy to come to you upon which your higher purpose can unfold.

I offer you this gift of my Luminous Presence—the Golden Sunshine of my love, to which many students of the past have loved to refer. But, you must use *your* authority and ask for it. Call upon my Luminous Presence to be anchored above and around your forms as a permanent sustained action of my love that goes before you, opening the way for you to live and to realize the higher purpose and the Divine Plan of your life.

Dear Hearts, it will do much more than this if you will *unite* this, with another activity I offer you. And these two activities will in future time, when enough effort has been made by you, give us the opportunity, with others of the Ascended Realms, to step out of the ethers and to stand visible and tangible before you, and prepare you for your final hour of ascension. It will allow us to release our own Heart's Flame of our Sacred Fire Love through your outer selves, removing the last of the limited consciousness that you might enjoy the ascension the original divine way; and that you might cause the resurrection of your physical bodies up the Great Life Stream into the Electronic Presence of your Great God Selves—completing your long, long journeys in this third dimensional reality of Earth.

And this second activity has to do with your *Electronic Circle*. Around you is an electronic circle—an electronic force field, a band of electronic energy—that is expanding out from you as a result of your prayers, your calls, and your meditations. I ask you to use your authority and call upon me, because I have a certain jurisdiction here. Call upon the Sacred Fire Love of Sanat Kumara's own Unfed Flame; to pour the Heart Flame of My Sacred Fire Love directly into your Electronic Force Field that surrounds your physical bodies. And I will do this.

This is one of those great decrees and calls that you make once a day until your ascension. This will allow my love—the Sacred Fire of my Heart—to pour into the Electronic Force Field around your bodies, to burn out the denser atomic energy that is smothering it—allowing the Electronic Force Field around your physical body to bring the Eternal Design of your higher purpose and the Divine Plan of your life fulfilled. This way, all the energy around your forms, as it expands out into the world, can be electrified with our love. This shall open the way for your own Unfed Flame to go forth at your command and to do all things for you.

These two things, Dear Heart: my Luminous Presence anchored permanently above and around your form and my Sacred Fire Love of My Unfed Flame placed as a permanent outpouring into the Electronic Force Field around your physical body—will truly open the way for the liberation of your highest purpose and the Divine Plan of your life fulfilled. It will lead you most certainly on the Path of Ascension in this lifetime, and it will eventually compel one of us to stand before you to prepare you, and to prepare your earthly garments—as we have prepared many who have come before you for the hour of your ascension.

I, Sanat Kumara, offer you a Miracle Mantle of My own Heart's Flame Sacred Fire Mastery of Love Divine

I come with many gifts and I wish to help you in a manner that is the final taking of the control of the power of attention. Over centuries and centuries and centuries we have waited while the pressure of human creation and all the problems that it creates has commanded your attention. We have waited patiently, knowing that as you gave your attention to the problems of the world that it was a trap. As you surrendered your attention and those faculties to the problems of the world and as you addressed those problems with fear, no sooner had you addressed them, another problem stepped forth. Such, indeed, is the nature of human creation and its demand upon the attention of a life stream on Earth.

I wish to offer a Miracle Mantle of My own Heart's Flame Sacred Fire *Mastery* of Love Divine to each of you that is the Sacred Fire Life's Control of all discordant energy; energy that has come under the human law of human creation. I can offer it into your life; I can offer it into the environment that you live in. I can release the command and the projection of my own Heart Flame that can take control of all discordant creation and all the energy of your forms that has yet come under the influence of negative qualities and free that energy up so that each of you can take your final command of the power of your attention and begin to live lives of greater freedom.

It is a great truth Mighty Ones of the Light that all life returns to its starting point. We have been very blessed upon Venus to be Guardians of your world. It has created the greatest blessing for my own family and our people of Venus. For centuries of time we have projected the command of the Sacred Fire Love to the people of Earth, and the atmosphere and the great Kingdoms that are your Earth's natural expression. We have loved you; we have loved your world. We do not hesitate to offer our love. Command our love; receive our love that will set your lives free, because it is in your greatest interest. We are commanded by the Great Beings in the Great Central Sun to do so, and we know that love must come back, millions upon millions of times greater, to us.

Of modern history in the last two million years, for seventy-five thousand years I have been a constant presence in your world and in the higher dimensions of your planet—unloved, forgotten and denied by most human beings. I only have returned to Venus when My Mother, the Goddess of Venus, has called me—that is the only time I have left your Planet. It is because of being forgotten, that the release of my own Heart's Flame from my own Sanctuaries of Light in Heights of Creation has been limited to what I can truly offer. And so we have waited.

Akasha, the Great Cosmic Angel of the Eleventh Dimension

My Dear Heart, your Beloved Akasha is much more than you are allowing yourself to remember or realize—she is a great Cosmic Angel and Ascended Master of the Eleventh Dimensional Reality. And it was in the early years that She reminded the students that She had come from the Eleventh Dimension—where Her original home is—under service and Divine Contract to the Divine Mother 'I AM' Presence of the Great Central Sun, to answer a Call of Service to the Third Dimension of Earth.

264

And I say to you, Dear Heart, that it is through Beloved Akasha and all that She has offered you, that we are grateful to Her that She has joined the Mighty Saint Germain and She has joined the Ascended Jesus Christ, the Master Kuthumi who is your World Teacher and others, in teaching you the necessity of the Command to Life that She has offered you into your awareness, to desire within you new patterns and a new willingness to turn your attention to your Presence and to us, and command the release of what will eventually set your life free.

Cosmic permission of the Great Divine Director who is responsible for all Souls in this Solar System

It is just for a while that you have reached up and called to *us*, and I wish you would think that it has not been so long and not such an arduous task. For seventy-five thousand years *I* have been calling to *you*, to awaken out of the chaos on Earth. I have projected my own Heart Flame under the cosmic permission of the Being known to us as the Great Divine Director who is responsible for all souls of all Planets in this Solar System. I have received permission to send forth my call into the centre of the human heart— the Super Electron, the First Act of Creation, the Super Spark of Love, out of which the Individualized Life Flame is formed in the physical heart.

Long ago, I sent forth my call, love and light, into that mighty spark of love that has been in every physical heart you have used in physical embodiments. Every human being has received this call and this Command to Life that I have offered. But very few of the numbers of those embodied on the Earth—and those out of embodiment at this time—have responded or been sensitive enough to become aware of a voice that was calling to them in the darkness and chaos of this world. Except for you; you and those precious Children of the Light throughout the world who are just like you; those who have felt a calling in their heart, those who have heard the message, "Come home. Come home! Rise and come home into the true God Divinity that is your birthright."

There is just the one Mighty Flame that each of you are in physical embodiment

You have heard this call to come home and you have heard it lifetime after lifetime. And as such you have arranged your lifetimes healing, reclaiming and allowing yourself that mission of earthly lifetimes until there was only one extension of you, one expression of you, one great projection of thy Mighty Flame of Life—thy Mighty 'I AM' Presence of you—on Earth.

There are many mysteries in the ancient occult of your world that are reference to former times of the great 'I AM' Presence having *many* life streams going on at once on the Earth. All of these things are true in many of the past lives and former centuries of civilization. Great has been your evolution, Children of Light. And I wish to raise you in your awareness of this. Today there are no longer twelve individualized outer flames of you in expression on Earth—there is just the one Mighty Flame that each of you are in physical embodiment. And this in itself has been a great activity of accomplishment and victory.

And now, Dear Hearts of Light, what stands before you is your final crowning victory over all that is of this world. The light of day has not yet revealed how all this victory yet shall be attained by each of you, but it is upon the great *Line of Certainty*—that governs certain activities of the Earth from the upper Realms of Light of your own Earth's atmosphere, that we know that each of you will gain your freedom, in the present lifetime that you are now in these physical embodiments. And I offer this to you from my sister the Goddess of Faith. And may you use this mighty statement of truth and gain your great victory in this life! May the Flame of Faith find its expression in your outer lives.

In former civilizations there were manifestations of the Sacred Fire in the Sacred Temples on this Earth

I have been with you many times. Forgotten in your current consciousness are those former civilizations in great ages even before the seventy-five thousand year period that I have been with you. We were with you in the Third, the Fourth, the Fifth, and the Sixth Golden Ages. We came to you during that time when Beloved Akasha & Asun were your parents and guardians, in Delphi, in the land that is today the lands of Greece. We were there and we were in other civilizations, and we brought forth, actual, *physical*, tangible manifestations of the Sacred Fire.

We built temples on your Earth that are much like your great cathedrals today. And in every one of those temples we anchored the Eternal God Flame of Life. And throughout those thousands of years of those former civilizations, as long as our mighty Eternal Flames of Light were ever lit in the Eternal Altars of those Temples of Light, the people of Earth lived wonderful lives. All was in a state of resurrection; all was in a state of grace and peace. And the people of Earth flourished and civilizations grew. Humanity loved their Creator.

Every individual must learn to draw the Unfed Flame, the Mighty Flame of God Life, into their own life

And then, my Dear Heart, came what always comes— the withdrawal of our Sacred Flames. When there is that which is temporarily given to you to assist you and to demonstrate the purpose of life, did those who own your System command that we withdraw the Cosmic Eternal Flames, which we brought to the Earth.

The Flames were tangible; you have seen them. And there is no part of your soul that does not know the truth that each of you has seen the Mighty Unfed Flame of God Individualized. For you, My Dear Hearts, were there in those former times of wonderful manifestations. You saw the actual Actualization of a Mighty Universal Unfed Flame from the Godhead. You saw them in sanctuaries throughout the world.

And then the command came for us to withdraw those Mighty Unfed Flames; for it is the Great Cosmic Law of Life that every individual must learn to draw the Unfed Flame, the Mighty Flame of Life, into their own life form through the acknowledgement and adoration of their own Mighty 'I AM' Presence.

The return of the Mighty Flame of Life over the atmosphere above Earth

Many have been confused and wondered, "If such great civilizations have been on the Earth, then why have such heights of evolution not been sustained if they were so great?" It is because every one of those civilizations was sustained by the Lords of the Flames from Venus. We brought *Our* Sacred Fire Love to the Earth. We created Miracle Mantles of Our Sacred Fire Love Control to all life and human creation. And thus the peoples were maintained in a place of peace and love, and the people did bring forth their own great evolution. But again I say to you, these things are only given temporarily, and they are given to show individuals that they themselves must create

268

these Mighty Flames of Life from the Great God Presence within. And this is what must happen now.

Your own Ascended Masters—your own advanced brothers and sisters who have ascended out of Earth's history, have now placed the Mighty Flames of Life, Individualized or in a Threefold Action, in various activities over the atmosphere of Earth. These God Flames of your own Earth's Ascended Masters are now the closest they have ever been to Earth. And they are waiting to anchor these into physical, tangible manifestation in your third dimensional realities. This is what life has always waited for, dear Children of Light, and each of you have a wonderful opportunity. It is the command; it is the way of perfection.

Some of you journeyed for a time to Venus...you know how to build the Flame of 'God, Goddess, All That Is'

Some of you have had opportunity in the Fifth Golden Age—you had a great opportunity to enter into our School of Light. And some of you came for a time to Venus, where you experienced our Realms of Perfection—Twenty-eight Realms of absolute love and perfection. You experienced our great Kingdoms of Life. You knew for a time such happiness, that you loved and loved and loved, because it made you remember the love and the happiness that all of you experienced in the Great Central Sun before you left your Heavenly Mother and Father.

And so it is that you have memory of these things. You do know that the way of perfection, the way of true love and happiness—the way this world is overcome, is the command, through your own Beloved Inner God Presence, that it anchor, build and expand the Mighty Flame of Divine Love; first within your physical bodies, then within your homes, your workplaces, your activities. For that, My Dear

Sons and Daughters of Life, is the Flame of God, Goddess, All That Is.

It is the Flame of Omniscience, Omnipresence, and the Omnipotence of the Godhead in a Threefold Action that is a compelling radiation that is Love's Miracle Mastery of Peace and Perfection to Life and the consuming of all discordant creation. It becomes a Radiation of Love and Life that it is the great lifting and resurrection which allows you to rise up into the true use of your own Higher Intelligence, your Higher Mental Bodies, or as your Beloved Akasha refers to it—your own Christed Self.

We have brought these great gifts to the Earth time and again. Three of your religions of the world—from the Far East to the Middle East—do have reference in their ancient scrolls of that One who came forth from the Voice of the Silence. It is a reference to my Presence joining certain of the Great Masters of old, such as the Lord Melchizedek and the Lord Metatron, in our Service to Life in past ages.

I, Sanat Kumara, Am here on your Earth with the Seven Lords of the Flame of Venus, and the Mighty Victory

So many gifts and blessings have been given and all that has been given under the Command of Life has been withdrawn, so that human beings would create those Mighty Flames of Life of their own free will. Tragically, as we removed our own Sacred Fire Love from the Earth, humanity fell back into that place of not commanding life. It is then that we took up our great role in the projection of the Flames from our own world. And ultimately, due to the great peril and potential extinction of the race, did I finally choose the exiling of my Life Stream on the Earth until the actual ascension of mankind and the Earth begins.

I understand that there are reports that I am no longer on your Earth. This has been confusing. Yes? Even your

Beloved Akasha has addressed that the Mighty Sanat Kumara, as I am addressed, has left the Earth for a while. But always I have returned; for I am now under command, in my vows, to remain here to work with all ascended and unascended humankind to assist the restoration of Divine Destiny, the great awakening out of the duality, and to restore the Oneness of Perfection to Life to all life on this Planet.

So let us get clear. Although I must return home from time to time, I am here to stay until the Ascension of the Planet. It is for this reason, and the fact that seven of the Lords of the Flame from Venus—of the twenty-eight Lords to our world—have been temporarily relocated to *your* world, that I come with great assistance. And I also come to your world with the presence of my cousin, the Mighty Victory; who is of my family, the Kumara's, who are also the Guardians of our own Planet, Venus. And it is for this reason, my Dear Hearts, that we are all closer to you now than anyone on Earth realizes; for our Ascended *physical presence* walks on your Earth, yet invisible to humanity until the Cosmic Hour commands otherwise. And where the Cosmic Law permits, we do whatever we can to help humanity at this time.

Do not *ask* Me—*Command* Me!

With this now, My Dear Hearts, let it be known that unlimited assistance can be given to you; in which the true sunshine of Love's Eternal Flame can come into yourselves and out into your worlds, to give you the absolute freedom and control and victory over all limitations in this world. We too, offer you, *The Greatest Power in the Universe* for your use.

However, for this to take place, the Great Cosmic Law demands that for us to release such a Miracle Mantle of

Love's Mastery Control, the people of Earth must willingly, through their attention, open the door to us. And the only way you can open the door to us, is to turn your attention inward in acknowledgement of that Mighty Love Flame within your own heart centre, and command that Flame to take its toll within your human form, opening the way for your Christ Self to take its dominion in your Earthly lives. And then, turn your attention upward in great adoration of that Mighty Presence of Life—your Ascended Self—that waits for your ascension; as It releases Its own Ascended Heart's Flame of God in, through, and around your human forms.

Then you turn your attention to any of the Ascended and Angelic Host, and give the Command to Life. Command me—do not *ask* me—*command* me to release my own Heart's Flame of my own Miracle Mantle of Sacred Fire Love, Control and Mastery, into all the energy in your mind, body, feelings, and world, for the absolute purification of all discordant creation into the divine, so that your own great 'I AM' God being may produce its Presence of Divine Love and Light within each of you. And that you may awaken from the last sleepiness and become those who walk upon the Earth such a blazing Sun's Presence of Light, Love and Wisdom—such a Power of Perfection, that the hordes of fear and darkness dare not even look in your direction!

The world delights in itself

I alone, Am quite sufficient in taking the whole student body that exists today, who love the Light, and free every one of you of discordant human creation! But I cannot do that without you taking command of your attention. To this, I have watched your worlds. I knew that I would have this opportunity to address you, and I am grateful. For this reason I have asked my brothers to watch, to look into your lives, to see how each of us might help you. If I am to help you, I am going to ask you to remember something—"The world delights in itself." The world as is presently known as duality consciousness or human creation—delights in captivating and capturing your attention, convincing you that there are those things that must be handled before you turn your attention within and upwards and open the door to God, your own 'I AM' Presence and to us.

These are the last trappings of the world; for as long as you will find it important to handle problems before you open the door to the Great Solvent of all problems, will you find more problems coming through. And this is just one of those little things that is a rascal in your world. Dear Hearts, you can tame this rascal. Make it a choice to the best of your ability that you will not give your attention to the problems of this world. You will not give your attention to anything in the world until you have taken *control* of your attention, *command* of your attention, focused it within: first upon your Presence, second upon any of the Ascended Host, third with the command that our own Heart's Flame of Our Miracle Mantle of Sacred Fire Love Mastery and Control take complete control of all discordant human creation inside you and your world so you may have your *certain* freedom, that you may have your resurrection, and that you may have your ascension and victory over everything in this world. But not only for the divine fulfillment of that which brought you to the world, but also and equally important, if not greater—that the Divine Plan for the World—the Divine Plan for your Planet, must be fulfilled.

Be a blessing to the World, the Planet, and Her Kingdoms by sending your own Light Ray forth

It is a significant thing to come to you in service to the Light of God that never fails. Let your life be a blessing to this world. Make a vow that you will do *your* part—just as we do *our* part—in loving your world free of discordant human creation. Come to your Presence, and through your Presence to me. I do not *need* your love, but the Cosmic Law demands that you generate love from out of your own Heart Flame and send that love as a projection, as a command, to that which you wish to have universal assistance from. And so whether it is your call to your own Beloved Lord of Life, your own Master Jesus or that which is the destined Sacred Mother of the Earth, your Blessed Mary, Mother of Jesus, whomever you turn your attention to, realize that this is how you open the door—place your attention first upon God and then upon any of the Ascended Host and then send your love and gratitude.

For example: "From out of my own Heart Flame, Beloved Jesus, I love you; and I command that my own Heart Flame send forth a Love Ray of its own to greet and enfold you. And I thank you for your transcendent service to the mankind of this Earth and her Kingdoms." Such is an easy and a simple way of generating, sending, and projecting your love through the Command to Life. If you will do so with as much feeling and love as you can, I assure you that there is not one Ascended Master in this System of Worlds—or Ascended Being from any other System of Worlds who you project that love to—who on the instant that Love Ray leaves your heart, will not receive that Love Ray and send back to you thousands of times greater love; enfolding you in a way that the Master's love knows how it can best serve you in your outer life experience.

It is the easiest thing to do, but requires a little training and a setting up of new patterns and habits of just fixing the attention upon your Presence and the Ascended Host; sending your love and then giving the command that your own great 'I AM' Presence enfold you in its own Love Flame...and that the Love Flame in your own Sacred Heart Centre take its toll through its expansion through your outer self. And you command your Great God Presence to make you the Individualized Flame on Earth; in which that Flame releases the Divine Consciousness that you are, into your awareness, and with that release, brings you into a resurrected place where you *are* the Individualized Flame of Life. Not only are you a being that has a Mighty Flame within for you to love and expand, but you *become* that Individualized Flame of Life, endowed with the powers over the five elements; upon which those elements will joyfully respond to your command *on the instant*.

These gifts are mighty. They are as free as the air that you breathe, and require only the establishment of new daily activities, setting aside the determined time and space to do your calls with a sincere heart and mind. Then throughout the rest of the day, whenever you have a moment or two, turn your attention to God, your Presence and to us in prayer. Command that we release our Heart's Flame of Our Sacred Fire Love's Miracle Mantle Mastery to Life—in, through, and around you for the end of all limiting creation; that your Divine Plan, your Higher Purpose, your Divine Fulfillment, may come forth in the future of days. And the more you make that call—remembering to first generate the love to the Master that you are calling—will we respond and send back, thousands of times greater, the love of our own Heart's Flame to you!

✳

CHAPTER *E*LEVEN

Bless you, I Am Asun. Dear Hearts, I wish to explain something to you. You know I can come and be very joyful and very jovial with you; we have received your acceptance, and my Beloved Akasha has established a connection with the will of your feeling side of life. So we can be very joyful and we can be very animated with the light and the energy we wish to offer you, in your acceptance of our presence.

But when one comes forth who holds a spiritual position of authority in the Greater Realms of Light, such as a Cosmic Being that this Mighty Sanat Kumara, Lord of the Flame of Venus is, when He comes forth and wishes to offer you not only a message of importance from His Heart's Flame, and He desires to extend His Presence upon a projected Ray of Light, so His Ray of Light can come into your feeling body as a blessing and carry His love and message to you, then the Messenger, Usa, has to hold firm to a very still and calm place to allow that to come forth so the message and love can come through without any disruption. It is not that the great masters are so serious and somber, although their message is of great importance; it is a great delight for the Master to be with you! When the Ascended Masters visit your Earth Plane they often will take on a physical appearance that conforms to your world and enjoy many of the things that are here. All throughout the Cosmos, all love the balance of life. And I assure you that the great Ascended Masters, and especially Mighty Sanat Kumara, love balance. His favourite thing is to enter into the Sacred Sites of the Earth where great musical sounds are played by some of your Earth's Ascended Masters. Quite often He will appear in a physical form and will come into many of your events down here on this Earth. He has been to many of the fine live plays, how shall we say, musicals and He loves opera. He has been to many of the fine operas, and He loves some of the new music that is coming forth, and has a special love for Spanish guitar and ballads.

So you see, this great Cosmic Being has been in our world here for a long time. And quite often He will adjust His vibration and appear in a physical form—or what *appears*, I should say, to be a physical form—and will walk into wonderful places and enjoy many of the things that are here in this world. He is a lover of music—this is one of His passions to life. So I don't want you to feel that He is a Cosmic Being that is beyond your ability to connect with Him just because the transmission seems to be so serious, for these Ascended Masters also take time off to enjoy the wonderful manifestations that come through human beings' artistry of life. Yes?

It is just *wonderful* what is coming to Earth!

Great times are coming on Earth. And although certain adversity and chaos is coming too—as you enfold yourself and gather yourself in all these wonderful gifts that are the Miracle Mantle of Love's Sacred Mastery, then, Dear Hearts, those difficult things will not touch you. Remember, there is now in place the collapse of the last archetype energies of an older paradigm, and those who represent these energies. There is no archetype of *all that has been* without their ambassadors in this world. Yes? So, as pillars of human discord will fall, those who are most responsible for these things will fail as well. In their place, are wonderful new manifestations of technology and invention and those who are the freedom mediators, wonderful visionary people coming into place with new ideas and designs, wonderful new ways of doing business, which is much more uplifting for the evolution of humanity. It is truly exciting what is coming!

Many of you who are evolving through the Indigo and the Violet Soul now—expect a greater desire for creative expression of your life; expect new thoughts and feelings and new passions that will well up in you. I urge you to not disregard these new creative impulses as you experience them—allow them to come forth. Don't just set them aside, bring them into your heart, and discover the new that wants to happen in your life. As you get in touch with the creative that desires to express a more fuller you, bring that into your Heart Flame and let the Heart Flame direct it into manifestation. Indeed.

Many of great Cosmic Authority are presently tending to World events

It is wonderful to share with you the radiance of our Beloved Sanat Kumara, the former Planetary Logos. I enfold you in His Heart's Flame—His great Heart Flame's Command to Life, that being Cosmic Love Supreme. You know, Dear Hearts, this Great Being has gained His evolution as a result of service. That is, His service to humanity. Sanat Kumara along with the Great Divine Director, the Ascended Master Victory from Venus and many others of great authority are presently tending to world events. They are working very closely with that which is termed the *Twin Flame Ascended Couples* who have extraordinary power to release Cosmic Light Rays and Activities into your world, and your System of Worlds, to produce what needs to take place for the upliftment of humanity and the Earth. Every being, including you, has a Twin Flame, created from the same God Flame from out of the Heart of the Infinite 'I AM' Presence Creator. When Twin (Flame) couples have both completed the Earthly journeys achieving their ascension, they are a powerful force to assist humanity.

From these Ascended Beings, there is a great outpouring of Cosmic energies being given to assist the Earth at this time; and within that outpouring is the Ascended Master answer that always carries a loving radiation that seeks to permeate human consciousness. But not only human consciousness; it seeks to permeate the human will, the human feeling side of life. It has within it the Ascended Masters' strength, the Ascended Masters' courage, for human beings to rise up and do what the world requires at this time for its current evolution of greater light, love, peace, harmony and the evolutions of harmless technologies.

Projecting the likenesses of Ascended Masters into World events

The All-Seeing Eye of Cyclopea always reveals what is the future as far as you wish to read the future into all fields of possibility, probability and certainty, so it is not to say that the Ascended Masters are not aware of human conditions that prevail. The All-Seeing Eye will show the Ascended Masters all possibilities of human thought patterns that are gathering a momentum in your world, and it will show them all the potential outcomes. And it is within these outcomes that all the Ascended Masters work, to try to assist humanity at this time. Indeed, I wonder what might happen if you project the likeness of many of the Ascended Masters that you have pictures of now, and project their likeness right into the White House, to project the Ascended Master Jesus as standing right in the centre of Baghdad—to project the image of an Ascended Master Presence standing in the offices of the President of North Korea, as an example?

Do you know that the radiance of these great Masters projected by you could alter potential probable outcomes so that they become more constructive? You know, you are all part of the *greater* aspect of all life, and it is not possible to focus your attention upon an Ascended Master—even without calling to that one—and not activate their assistance to you or where you project their presence to. Even if you do not call to Master Jesus, even if you do not call to the Mighty Sanat Kumara, just hold an image of this Great Master of Light standing in the Oval Office. These great Masters of Light have the power to command such a force of light out of their Heart's Flame and out the mind's eye, it just causes the individual who is receiving that light to receive what will consume the shadows that are lurking within the individual that is causing them to act in a certain way. Yes?

And it is not just the leaders of your nations, but to those that you wish to offer assistance to. And when offering assistance—especially to those who have come and are *seeking* help from you—it is very important that you seal yourselves in the light; it is very important that you insulate yourselves. Now what the Beloved Sanat Kumara has offered you, to pour forth His Sacred Fire Love into your electronic force fields around your bodies, do you know what that will do for you, Dear Hearts? That will actually insulate and protect you. When you are calling forth a Tube of Light from your Presence, in and around you, it will eventually insulate—up to a thousand feet out from you—your Electronic Force Field so that you have nothing interfering with you, that you have nothing interfering with your plans. Isn't that wonderful?

There is not anything that you cannot apply this to. You can project an image of an Ascended Master Presence into *any condition* in your lives. If you wish to change a thing, you project an image of an Ascended Master Presence, and see that one standing in a blazing outpouring of Sacred Fire Gold, Violet and Blue Flames. Then you not only purify this condition, but you allow that which is the original intent of what you really wanted to manifest, or what you wish to assist in the world, to prevail. I hope you will love to use this. Indeed.

Calling your Presence to come forth into *action*

You know, Dear Heart, Akasha and I have spoken with each other recently regarding addressing your Presence. As we look at the different worded expressions, and we look at your feeling side of life, we see how much your feeling side of life is accepting what is being offered you—we feel all of you would benefit if you use the words, "My Beloved Great God Presence come forth into *action*." When you are consciously connecting with your Great God Presence, if you would do this for a few months, if you would just focus on calling your Presence to come forth into *action* through you, I think you will love the difference it makes in your life. Say, "Come forth into action," and really exert as much energy and enthusiasm that you can in that decree, and then target that statement wherever you wish. There is much that has been given in our dispensation *Soul Journey*. There is so much that the Master Saint Germain has given in His *'I AM' Activity* and there is much that is given in *other* Activities that, my goodness, if you heard us wrong, you might think there is no time but to do your decrees, prayers and your mantras!

It is not a good idea to do your prayer decrees for a couple of hours to the point you become tired

Well, the thing is this, Dear Heart, it is not a good idea to do your prayer decrees for a couple of hours to the point you become tired. When you do that, the energy of your decrees bottoms out and since it is the last energy that you exert in your decrees or prayers that should be dynamic; you can see the reason for this. Rather than doing your decrees for a couple of hours, it is best to sit down for twenty minutes and give forth some real powerful decrees as sincerely as you can. Really bring your whole self into it and just give a good release of your energy into this sacred prayer time. Then you have time to meditate, contemplate and be in the inner stillness for a while.

The Mighty Sanat Kumara has shared with you and He has given you the goods as straight as possibly can be given. "Why do I not have more perfection of my Great God Presence, and why do I not have greater expressions?" Isn't that what he said? I love the way he used that word *expressions*. We have not used it too much in our language, but I understand what He means. Well, the answer is that the vibration of the outer self is not matching the vibration of light within the Heart Flame. So, "Mighty Presence of Life, come forth into *action* and release your Sacred Fire Love! Release your Violet Purifying Flame through this outer self; and hold that Violet Flame Love in me, purifying this outer self, until it's vibration matches the light of your Golden Flame within my heart! See that it is done! Quick as a flash at lightning speed!" My Beloved Presence, "I love you, I bless you and I thank you". So, it is better to fire off a few good, happy decrees, charged with your full energy.

You are directors! Isn't that fun? You get to direct it all! Sanat Kumara has given you a wonderful decree. The language of words can often satisfy the palate of the intellect, because sometimes the mind can be a little rascal. So we can understand this. "Oh, yes, I understand. If my Great God Presence is going to manifest, directly out of the Universal, that which I desire in my life, then the energy of this body must match the light in my Heart Flame! All right, well, what a very useful technique!" Yes, words projected are intended to become *Receptacles of Light*.

Now let us take you back to the words of the Master Jesus, " 'I AM' the Resurrection and the Life of my mind and body." Now remember, this statement the Master Jesus gave has all the elements of the Master Powers of your Great God Self; it has the Sound Ray; it has the Light Rays; and it has the Sacred Fire Love. You are leaving it up to your Presence to decide which of those and what colour or what intensity to use because you are saying " 'I AM'—God in Action—the Resurrection and the Life of..." And you fill in the space with wherever you are going to direct that to, yes? Again I say, You are directors! Isn't that fun? You get to direct it all! You are finally taking your place in life. You have the opportunity to lay down your sword of struggle.

Dear Hearts, I have heard a few of you, say recently to each other "Well, I'm struggling with ...blankety-blank-blank..." Well, the two of you need a good remembering. And the rest of you, if you think that you haven't used the word *struggle* recently, forget it! I urge you! Stop saying, "I am struggling." That is the worst way to use the words 'I AM'. Don't you think so? Watch your worded expressions more. It is all right, you are all forgiven for having an *oops!* moment, that is, if you forgive yourselves.

" 'I AM' the Resurrection and the Life..." and now you can complete this mighty statement with what you wish to decree into your life. When you use that wonderful statement " 'I AM' the Resurrection and the Life" you are leaving it up to the authority of your Great God Presence; you are using the authority that the Mighty Sanat Kumara has invited you to remember. It is your authority to *call* on as many higher powers as you wish. It is the authority of the Greater to *give* those higher powers to you when you ask and decree: " 'I AM' the Resurrection and the Life of my mind and body. 'I AM' the Resurrection and the Life of eternal health, beauty, youth, and perfection, expressing through this outer self. 'I AM' the Resurrection and the Life of every cell of my body. 'I AM' the Resurrection and the Life of eternal youth expressing through this outer self, each and every moment. 'I AM' the Resurrection and the Life of the organs, the bones, the muscles and the joints of this body."

Speak you decrees with enthusiam for about twenty minutes, then meditate and then go about your day. You have released all the energy and the will required for manifestation. Keep reminding yourself, "These are not just worded expressions, these are light expressions that have been charged and given by great beings of light. They have all authority in them to release what this outer self requires for the light of my outer self to match the light within my Heart Flame. As certain as I continue to do this, then the Great God Presence has nothing in this outer self that can possibly interfere with the fulfillment of these decrees."

Slam-dunk!

There still can be a little confusion, a bit of scratching the head, "Well, how can a little thing possibly be an obstacle to my Great God Presence?" The answer is free will and the authority that you have, you have not yet recognized. Whatever you have allowed to accept or register within your outer self, your God 'I AM' Presence, as far as *It* is concerned, accepts this as your will. Remember the great saying, "God is no respecter of persons." I don't think you even truly understand this statement. What does it mean, "God is no respecter of persons"? It means God is giving life force and doesn't stop giving, whether you *use* or *misuse* the life energy!

God's Life Force is passing through all of you. It is given freely and is not withheld if used destructively. It knows that if you use Its life energy wrongly, that it is just going to come back very swiftly and slam-dunk you. Karma! Don't you think? And you know it! You know it, don't you, darlings? You absolutely know that this has happened! Indeed. *Slam-dunk*...isn't that a fun word? We heard one of the precious awakened souls in Canada use this term. And I thought it was very fun, indeed!

We love words that have impact. We love words that make a great point and are filled with feeling. You don't have to have a whole conversation although conversation is good too. A glass of wine, great company, good food and conversation can be wonderful, yes? Absolutely, Dear Heart!

So what I am getting on about here, is, that you will have greater success in your life if you just say, "Now my great God Presence, come forth into action! You express your perfection through these words! You express your power through these words! You express your Sacred Fire Love through these words." I now affirm, " 'I AM' the Resurrection and the Life of all the energy of my home. 'I AM' the Resurrection and the Life of my career. 'I AM' the Resurrection and the Life of my higher purpose. 'I AM' the Resurrection and the Life of my Divine Purpose Fulfilled! Make it so! Make it so!" And you will find that the feeling body releases that energy and just sends your call quickly up to your Great God Presence, and gives it the opportunity to release into your outer life what you require.

Mount Rushmore

All right! Enough of that! What else do I wish to share? What else is on my mind? It is this. There are great Cosmic activities in your world. There are Sacred Sites in your world; and those Sacred Sites are protected by the Ascended Masters' Sacred Fire Love and Power. They also carry the Electronic Pattern of the Perfect Intent of what has been placed there for the future evolution of the human race and the world. There is a force field around these places that radiates Divine Intent.

You have a place in America, where the faces of past Presidents have been carved out of the rock—Mount Rushmore. Indeed. It is a *Sacred Site* where a tremendous pattern of light is held—America in its beginning when the 'I AM' Race came to America.

Stonehenge

There is Stonehenge. There is, in Stonehenge, the actual *design, the Divine Blueprint* of the human race, the 'I AM' Race—all the way to its beginnings—and records of the journey of duality, and the journey back into the journey of one and of Perfection. Hidden there is the Divine Plan for the Ascension of the 'I AM' Race; the Ascension of the Third-Dimensional reality up into the Fifth Octave of Life.

The Grand Design—the grand scheme of that whole journey—is hidden within and underneath Stonehenge, those strange looking stones that are standing there. The Grand Design is within and underneath. What is left there of the stones is certainly less then the original physical manifestations of those rock formations. It is significantly less then what was actually there when they were placed to protect the records of the Grand Design of the human race and its evolution and ascension. But all of that is held within Sacred Chambers, within and underneath Stonehenge. It is the Sanat Kumara, the great Guardian to the Earth who placed it there.

The Ark of the Covenant, an Oath, a Promise, will again be revealed

What else?—The Grand Design of the Ark of the Covenant that ensures that the human race gets to where it's going. That Ark of the Covenant is sealed, and it is hermetically sealed, but within it holds the Grand Design of the promise, that at the end of the day, the end of the journey, all of life would come back to the One—All that wants to come back into the One. The protection of this Ark is the work of the Mighty Sanat Kumara. It is the word of God, the Infinite 'I AM' Presence. It is an Oath, a Promise. Many an Ascended Master has reminded the Children of the Earth about this great promise of the Creator. Beloved Akasha will soon reveal this Oath and Covenant again.

The Threefold Flames...and old ideas of wars...

You know there are great activities that are unfolding in your Earth Plane. One of them is the Threefold Flames that are in your Earth's atmosphere. This activity came under the manifestation of Mighty Saint Germain. It was his authority that allowed the Ascended Masters to place, up in the atmosphere above the human discord, those Threefold Flames; of which there are now over one hundred and seventy positioned in different areas of the world.

There is a great outpouring of light that is coming from these Unfed Flames of God. These are powerful influences from the Light of God that never fails! The Great Sanat Kumara has asked Saint Germain to amplify within the human heart, the *desire* for evolution—the desire to peacefully revolutionize the political convention of this world, the ideas of nationalism, sovereignty, old ideas of war, within a rapid transition. And it is for this reason that even those organizations that gather in newly formed leagues—such as the Arab League, the United Nations, NORAD, NATO—will come under an uplifting influence, if you will, of tremendous activities of Light from these Threefold Flames that the Ascended Masters have placed in the upper atmosphere.

The first Threefold Flame came forth in 1936 was anchored over Chicago; and then more were anchored in different places in the three Americas over the past seventy years. Now, they are showing up over Europe—first in France, then over England, Germany and Switzerland; over the Asian Sea, over Australia, New Zealand, and some are showing up over the atmosphere over Africa. The Flames continue to expand, placed there by the Ascended Masters.

To give you, perhaps, a proper understanding of their Cosmic assistance—if these Threefold Flames did not exist in the upper atmosphere, you would have seen complete disintegration during the Cold War of the forces of NATO; and you would have seen that Cold War break out into something uncontrolled. You would have seen the disintegration of the United Nations, as has been the disintegration of Leagues of Nations that preceded it.

And so, many do often wonder, "Well, we have all these things, these activities. Are they really happening?" And all that we can say to you is that if these Cosmic activities did not exist, and if you did not have Great Beings such as the Planetary Logos stepping in and communicating with your Earth's Ascended Masters, there would not have been a shift in human consciousness that was required to influence humanity in an uplifting way. Especially since the end of the Cold War you have seen a shifting in human consciousness; a shifting of consciousness that is taking place within the seats of government, in which—it is almost unbelievable, in human terms—that in nations such as France and Germany and other countries of the world, the idea of war is an aberration. So you can see, there is a real shifting taking place in human consciousness.

The simplicity in all of it...

My point, Dear Heart, is that because of the Cosmic Activity of your Earth's Ascended Masters, this has given the Planetary Logos an opportunity to come in and use those Cosmic activities and come along and say, "Now, we've got to progress things further and a lot quicker." And, you know, whether it be for the world, or whether it be for yourself, evolution oftentimes requires change, doesn't it?

Change from what has been, into something new, requires transformation. So you can think of him as the featured Ascended Master to help you if you want change in your life. Who do you call?—The Mighty Sanat Kumara! He is a great one, because the will for change, the will for transformation—evolution—comes from Him. As He stated, it came from His own personal Flame in the creation of the 'I AM' Race. So, you call upon Him to give you the assistance in any changes that you desire to make in your own life; and to guarantee that your life is fulfilled in this lifetime. If you want a guarantee that your higher purpose and the Divine Plan of your life is fulfilled in this lifetime, He can assist you greatly.

Don't go and say, "In the next year..." because then time and space is not going to be friendly for you—you're going to place pressure on yourself. Don't feel you have to live your higher purpose all in one year. It will create pressure and challenge for you. That is not what you need, another challenge! So you say to your Great God Presence, "It is very important to me that I fulfill my higher purpose and the Divine Plan of my life in this lifetime, and I give you all authority to make it so. Bring into my life what is required, and take out of my life what could be an obstacle." Don't you love the simplicity in all that?

The degree to which Akasha can continue to assist you...

I do not know if this has dawned on you yet—because I have not looked into your feeling body on this—however, Akasha and I have spoken to each other about this matter. The degree, to which Akasha can continue to assist you, Dear Hearts, will eventually depend upon your own willingness to speak to your own great God Presence to be your Master Teacher in all things.

And when you command your own Great God Presence within and above you to teach you on everything, and to use every available means to teach you, to lift you, through all the journey that is ahead—to guide you and to mentor you, then your Mighty 'I AM' Presence must use every available channel—including us—to get the point through. Understand? I am sure you do! And so, it is very important for you to remember to go to your Presence and say, "Now teach me, and guide me in all things. Use every available channel to make it so."

You are here to make an impact

Next. There are great outpourings of light coming in from the great Heavens above, the Cosmic assistance is here. There are all sorts of possibilities that may yet come forth, however we do know, Children of Light, that regardless of what unfolds in time to come that there is an attitude upstairs, as far as the Ascended Masters are concerned "Well, as far as the human can go, down here on the Earth Plane, anything could happen." But of course, what is watched is the heart of humanity. What is watched is the totality of the desire for peace. What is watched is the measure of love, strength, and courage that is building within human beings. And based upon this, the All-Seeing Eye does give the Ascended Masters various outcomes with which to work.

The most important thing for all of you is to know that you can carry on in your lives; that you can be that positive impact in your own life, and you can be an impact in the greater world. You do not need to take on anything that is going on in the world; you can insulate your personal world by calling upon your great God Presence and the Ascended Masters to keep flooding the electronic force field outside of your bodies with their Sacred Fire Love, Purity and Power. That will insulate all your energy. You do not know, Dear Hearts, how far your electronic force field extends. Well, eventually, it will expand as far as you want it to. But for now, be satisfied that you can get your electronic force field to five hundred or a thousand feet out from you. And certainly, if you are in an aircraft or you are out in a city or in a mall and your electronic force field outside of your bodies are insulated with the Ascended Masters Sacred Fire Love—my goodness, you could walk through shadows of death and nothing could touch you!

So you see, it is going to be very important not to be bothered by anything out there in the world, rather to know that you can make an impact. You are here to make an impact. You are here to continuously call forth everything that is going to bring you your freedom. Let us go back to those words "I call forth into action." Akasha and I are asking specifically that you will try working with those words over the next couple of months, because we see that it will do something in your feeling body. "My Beloved Great God Presence, come forth into action through this outer self! Come forth into action in my higher purpose!

Come forth into action in bringing me to that place where I am living my greater life fulfilled! Come forth into action in my projects and my goals!"

And you know the greatest thing to give your Presence the opportunity to do, is allow It to glorify Itself through you. And what does your Presence do when It is glorified? It produces what in your life?—Perfection. That is what It loves to do, to produce Christ Love and Perfection in you. And that is why you want to give your Presence the opportunity to glorify Itself!

You are happy now that two-thirds of you stayed up in the Higher Realms of Light; you would have no aspect of yourself to rescue you down here! It is all right, that was the Divine Plan anyway. Always remember that when we are speaking of your great God Presence—or your Mighty 'I AM', or your Christ Self, we are simply only speaking of the real and greater and total you! We are speaking of your Grand Cosmic Self, that is *The Greatest Power in the Universe*, individualized of our Beloved Creator. We are speaking of the *Greater* you. We are speaking of your own Master Self, that two-thirds of you, fortunately, that was not foolish enough to come down here on the Earth! I am just having fun with you, Dear Hearts. You are glad perhaps that two-thirds of yourself stayed up there in realms of light; so you would have a higher aspect of yourself to call upon to fill you with the greatest love of all, Divine Love. One day you will fully embody your Grand Cosmic Self. It is your Destiny.

So it is to remind yourself, "When I am speaking to my great God Presence, when I am speaking to my Divine Self, I am not speaking to any force outside of me. I am speaking to our Divine Mother/Father's Individualization that is my Divine Self." By now you understand that the Heavenly Mother/Father, the Great Mighty 'I AM' Presence, the Great Central Sun, governs Its physical universe through its individualizations; and through the unascended one and the ascended, It experiences Itself in all levels of the universe. This includes inner levels of the universe that sustain physical manifestation. And you here are in that which is the lower realm of physical manifestation, and when you get back together with your Grand Cosmic Self, you interface and intersect with all levels of dimensional reality, inner and outer. Understand? Good!

If you are going to do nothing, do it well!

Question: You know Asun, when you talk about *come forth into action*, it brings anxiety up in me, I feel guilty, because all I want to do is lie down and rest.

Answer: Our Beloved Daughter has spoken very well, that presently, and at other times, in light of my sharing *come forth into action*, what our Beloved Daughter is saying is that there are times, like right now, when all that one really feels to do is just to lay the body down. Indeed! And I believe we have got this covered; I am speaking of when you are entering into your prayer calls. Don't get yourself too tired, and perhaps use the phrase "Come forth into action" and give forth some ten or fifteen minutes of real energizing calls. But, we have also said at other times that you have got to honour yourselves. There are some times that one should tune in and ask, "What does it really feel like that I most require at this time? Does it feel like I require a nap? Does it feel like I need a rest? Does it feel like I just desire to be in the arms of my Presence and call upon my Presence to take care of everything?" Each of you moves through natural phases and cycles, so honour them.

You do not always know what is going on at the inner levels of your being. And Dear Hearts, this metamorphosis that we have spoken of over the last couple of years, the metamorphosis that is going on in your bodies, can make your body itself require more rest. The initiations—the soul initiations which demand that your experience world, the world of manifestation, the world of relationship be used to move you along your life initiations—it, too, can be a little tiring at times. And so, never feel guilty about anything, first of all!

And it is fine. It is fine. If that is what the body needs, it is to just lie and rest, and it is good. But if you are going to nurture yourself, nurture yourself well. Do it good; do it all the way. In other words, put on some wonderful music and ask yourself, "Now, what is going to support me? It seems that all I really require to do is nothing right now. Well, how well can I do nothing? Well, can I just climb into bed and get all sorts of fluffy pillows and teddies and put on some music and just be." If you are going to do nothing, do it well! Understand? Indeed! "You know, God, I call upon you to take the momentum of all my calls, and just bring them forth, because that's about all I can do today."

In other words, you transform what you are feeling into a nurturing of self. There is no point in doing what we have asked you to do, if it is going to fire up a resistance in you! Or, "I am doing this only because Asun said I should?" No, no, no, Dear Heart. We are saying that when you are doing your calls, you will find it helpful, perhaps, if you do it this way; making sure you don't do too many calls that you get tired and be sure to be dynamic, add a little bit of punch, because then you are putting your energy into your calls. And there are other times, there are days, in which all you can do is to just put your palm tenderly over your Heart Flame, and say, "You know, God, I call upon you to take the momentum of all my calls, and just bring them forth. That is about all I can do today and thank you." Indeed.

But Dear Heart, then you must also do what you can to keep yourself in a place of harmony, too. Because if you are in that state in which you just want to rest, then you are also in a place of great sensitivity. And in that state of sensitivity, you might just say to yourself, "Now, I must take extra care not to be in a place of reaction, but just to rest in my own energy, and not be too concerned about anything because this is a day for *me*." Understand? Wonderful!

All things considered, the future for me is a holiday

Can you look at the future years in your life as a wonderful holiday, a time of great fulfillment? It does not mean that you are not going to be doing things, but you are open to look at experiences differently. You see, human consciousness is always 'brooking'. To brook something means you are connected to it, means you are a part of. You know, you have a brook, you have a... Do you know what I mean? Oh, you don't know; you are going to make me explain it! Well, you see, you have a little brook. What is a little brook, first of all—a little stream. Well, a stream is passing through something that has been cut out, yes? And so the water is brooking both sides, is it not? And so, because it is brooking both sides, it is taking on the *qualities* of both sides. So when we say do not brook with what is in your past, we mean, "Do not connect with it." Understand? Oh, very good!

Where was I going now with this? What am I talking about? Oh, yes, your journeys. Through the use of words and understandings, you are often brooking the past and compelling it to be part of the future. And so, oftentimes, it is just to shift some ideas, especially because ideas for change and new ideas often originate from the Heart of Sanat Kumara himself, such as "How can I look at the future? Whether the future be my career, my home, or my higher purpose or whether my future be relationships with others or a significant other, whatever it be. Whatever it is, can I look at all of this in a certain manner as if it all was a holiday? The next years are a holiday for me. This is the journey. For a long enough time the journey has been very difficult; sometimes happy and sometimes difficult. But for me, if *concept* is yet going to linger in my human consciousness, what concept can I give my future that can be a happier influence as to the outcome? Perhaps it is to look at my future, and all things considered..."

All things considered, that is a phrase I am using now Dear Hearts; all things considered, this is Asun's lasso, it includes everything. "All things considered, the future for me is a holiday, a time of great fulfillment. It is a time of perfect balance, a time of great joy. It is a time where my experiences will be wonderful!" You know, Dear Hearts, sometimes you take a holiday, and you will go hippity-hop, out of Canada. You will perhaps go to Africa and you will see the great Victoria Falls. Or you will go hop-hop-hop, and you will travel to Switzerland and you will see some of the wonderful things there. And hop-hop-hop over to Asia, and you will see some of the joyous manifestations there. And hop-hop-hop, over to Egypt, and you will see the Pyramids and other things. Yes? And you come home, and even though you have been on vacation, your awareness has expanded, right? It is like you had been off to school. So you come back and you are more learned! Is it not so? But you were on vacation, were you not? Indeed!

So you see, you can formulate the idea that vacation can be a discovering experience, a discovering experience that is very pleasant. "Oh, yes! I was in St. Peter's, and I saw all Michelangelo's work, I saw all his paintings. Oh, it was magnificent! Just filled my soul!" Yes? And so you see, a holiday can conjure up the joy of new experiences. It is not about just having fun! Well, it is *all* fun—it could be sitting in a canoe fishing, and maybe the fish is going to give you an experience, a learning experience; especially if he pulls you off the boat because he is bigger than you!

And so you see, it is to think of the future likened to a holiday. "I am going to take in a lot. My soul is going to soar and grow. All life will be a great inspiration. And no more discord! I will move insulated in this world, no longer taking on the tragedies that human beings still create. I welcome the future. It is filled with change. It is even a place where my body will transform and look exactly as I want it to. It is a place where I carry joy and peace in my feelings…"

The intellect only knows the past. The Heart knows the future you want

In the journey ahead there are going to be times that you will meet up with individuals who are nervous or discordant, and more and more you are going to desire to be the Peace Commanding Presence within yourself. Peace Commanding Presence, Dear Heart, is a tremendous quality within you. Desire to be the Peace Commanding Presence that just floods over everyone, that just floods over everything in your world. And treat the future as a great holiday that gives you the opportunity to live your higher purpose, to make an impact; a great impact, not only on your own life but an impact on the entire world around you.

Remind yourself that the intellect only knows the past. The heart knows the future that you want. "I will not let my future be held hostage by the path of association that my intellect knows regarding former experiences. I open my future. I open my heart to the future. My future is about my heart. It is about my great God Presence. It is about my Golden Heart's Flame. My future is about embodying *The Greatest Power in the Universe*, embodying my Grand

Cosmic Self, the 'I AM' that 'I AM'. It is about my spiritual being, and fulfilling my higher purpose. My future is about fulfillment because my God 'I AM' within me is in action in my life; and if It is fulfilled...my goodness, *I* am going to be fulfilled!"

A 'runner' is an experience or a person that brings you into a situation

A 'runner' is an experience or a person that brings you into a situation that you think you are not ready for. "Love, Dear Heart, Love!" Relationship would be a wonderfully good thing for the likes of some of you. Understand? Indeed! Because it can be a good thing! Especially when you dedicate all things to love, all things to your *own* evolution and freedom and the freedom of others, when you are sharing the path with another, and love all things with that *other* person's evolution.

There are wonders of human sharing. Humans have got themselves all tied up around the intimacy with the physical body. But there is much greater intimacy—the deep sharing of thought and the deep sharing of feeling, that can truly cause souls to come together and just soar, that create very loving experiences in this life. And it is sometimes just nice to have a companion. You have all sorts of concepts out there as to why you shouldn't, but I think it is just a far good thing to have a companion in life. What do you think?

We are not *shoulding* on you. All of you in your own heart know that there is a time for all things. "A time for all seasons, a time for all reasons." And then of course sometimes it is time for experience, but you are perhaps a little hardened in that area, and you have not opened to the idea that it is timely for a certain experience in your life. So then your higher mental body comes and speaks to us or someone else, and along comes a *runner* to you. And a runner is an experience, or a person, that brings you into a situation that you think you are not ready for and then comes the resistance. It is interesting to watch your resistance come up, for we see that sometimes you are resisting what actually resonates very well with you. Interesting indeed it is.

Do not restrict your Life. Let it.

And so, this journey ahead can be a wonderful journey for you if you choose it so! Already a number of you have shifted and you have made some moves, new locations, or you are preparing for future work, future relationships, and new phases in your lives. Do not associate with old ideas as they limit you, "Well, you know I am thirty, forty, sixty years in the body, so I can't do this." Oh, junk those kinds of thoughts, Dear Heart! The God in you is in action now in your lives. It is the knower; it is the giver; it is the doer. Don't restrict your life. Let it. Trust your life.

Oftentimes there is something that wants to come into your life, Dear Hearts, but you are just not in good charity to yourself. Sometimes it would be better to just say to yourself, "I am going to let it come to me. Rather than struggling for that financial freedom, rather than struggling for that individual, or whatever it is, I am just going to let it come to me."

You all have something in your worlds that is in a resistance, and sometimes there is too much human struggle to try to change the experience you do not want in your life. So when there is something in your life, where you really would like to have a different experience, but you have got your human in there, and you are trying to fix it—you are struggling with your manifestation—it is better to say, " 'I AM' the Great

Central Sun's Magnet's Presence, magnetizing this person in my life, magnetizing all the money I should ever require." Or, " 'I AM' the Great Central Sun's Magnet's Presence, magnetizing to me the opportunities, magnetizing to me the resources, magnetizing to me that perfect lover..." Or whatever it should be. Then let it be. Have faith in your life.

And then just say to yourself, after that wonderful decree—affirming—you say, " 'I AM' the Great Central Sun's Magnet's Presence, magnetizing the perfect gift into my life!" That's powerful! Assertive! Then you can shift and go into the feminine, the heart, and you can say, "And I am just going to allow that gift to come forth. I am just going to allow that money, or whatever it is that I require, to come forth." Know what it is that you desire. Be assertive. Exert the energy. Intention! Then surrender, to allow the God in you to move into action. Stay out of doubt, don't worry, no struggle, trust your life and be happy.

The experience of *wanting*

Often, the things that you are desiring—often the thing that you want in your life—your great God Presence wants it for you too! But you started struggling, you started *wanting* it so much, and what is the universe giving you?— it is giving you the experience of *wanting*. The Universe is an interesting friend. It's giving you the experience of wanting. Rather than giving you the *thing* you want, it is giving you the experience of wanting.

Because you've got yourself into a fix—you've got yourself into a right pickle by holding this vibration of just wanting something—what experience are you having every day?—You are having the experience of wanting, or struggling with something that is in your life. And because that is what has taken hold of your feeling body, your feeling body and the universe must give you the experience of continued wanting and struggling. Remember, "What I feel, I make real!"

Question: What is the difference between *want* and *desire?*

Answer: Well, ideally, there is no difference; except when you are wanting something and you will not leave it alone, it turns into a feeling of struggle. I am just using it in a different way, ideally it is the same. But what happens is, that when you want something and it has become a problem—you want your financial freedom, but my goodness, you have ended up with just the opposite—you want to be free of it, right? And so what happens is, days and months pass, and you find the situation prevailing and it is not changing. So when you have a *want* to be free and there is struggle vibration because of what is *not* taking place, then the universe, your God life, gives you the continued experience of wanting, rather than the desire fulfilled.

However, oftentimes the desire for your financial freedom is a desire from *God* in you that is acting. But *you* have come along and said, "What am I going to do?" You have brought in all this human limited energy, "What can I do? What am I doing wrong? What can I do differently?" And so, judgement against self comes in—that you don't have financial freedom because you are some dummy, you are not doing it right; or you have gone and misused life energy, and you are being punished. All sorts of human concepts and all of it is not true!

Anything good and constructive that I could possibly desire—this is God in me, desiring

The judgments on yourself are so harsh, Dear Heart. And oftentimes they hold hostage the very thing that you are struggling with. So, what are you going to do? You are going to remind yourself that, "Anything good and constructive that I could possibly desire, is God in me, desiring. So maybe I shouldn't hang on to it so desperately. Maybe I should realize that this is what God wants for me. And maybe I just need to decree that I already *am* my Heart Flame's Magnet Presence magnetizing all good to me."

Your Unfed Flame, your Heart Flame, is the Great Central Sun's Magnet within your body. It is given you to magnetize the direction of your thought and feeling into your life. And so, put it into the affirmative. "It is time that I bare everything. All the energy in this condition that is not working—that I bare it clean. So regarding this subject, this condition, I call forth the Violet Consuming Flame to consume all the energy of it. Take it all up, so that I can start with a clean slate. Then, I shall sit…"

You do not have to decree for ten days to do it, Dear Hearts! Just call it in! "I desire all the energy on this subject; I desire it clean, scrubbed up!" And then, "Mighty 'I AM' Presence, 'I AM' the Great Central Sun. My Unfed Flame is the Great Central Sun's Magnet's Presence, magnetizing this money and supply into my hands, magnetizing this individual into my life, magnetizing the fulfillment of this project now made manifest" or whatever it is that you wish, that you have struggled with! And then say to yourself, "If I am desiring this, then it is God in me that is desiring! And God does not fail at anything! And so what I am going to do now is just surrender, and just allow that to come to me." Hands off! Time to go party! Time to go put your attention on something else. Time to go paint or whatever it is!

Now, I, Asun, do not wish to say anything more. There is a time for everything, yes? Indeed. I am grateful for this time I have had with you. All right. Let us close our sharing with a Benediction.

Asun's Benediction

"Mighty Presence of Life, Thou hast hidden Thy Splendour within my heart long enough. Come forth into action and release your light, your love, your wisdom, your power and your perfection, through this outer self. Great forces of light, join with me, and release into my life all the Sacred Fire Love that just loves to heal, loves to lift, loves to correct.

"I call, in the name, love, wisdom, power and authority of my own Great God Self, to the Mighty Sanat Kumara. I bless Him for His transcendent service. I invite His Sacred Fire Love into my being and world; and all that He knows that I require to fulfill my higher purpose, to make a difference in this world, and to be of service to the Divine Plan.

"I call upon the Mighty Sanat Kumara to speak, through the hearts of humanity, the Divine Plan of the Divine Evolution for the human race. I call upon Sanat Kumara to use His authority as the Planetary Logos to speak through every human heart; to guide every human being on Earth into right action, to protect all that is good and constructive, and to remove from this world all that is destructive. I bless you, Great Being of Light!"

Beloved Akasha and I enfold you in the Light of God that knows no failure. We seal you in our own Heart's Flame. God Bless you, Dear Hearts, and Namaste.

CHAPTER *Twelve*

I Am Akasha and I greet you out of the Diamond Heart of my Love and I enfold you in the Love of God that knows no failure. I bring you glad tidings this day. I bring you the Rose Pink Ray of the Divine Mother and the Lady Ascended Masters. I offer you the Light and the Love and the Victory of the Ascended Host who wait for only an open Heart, an open door within each of you. May the great Ascended Host come forth as a Mighty Light within you that lifts you up and out of the confusion and the destruction of this world and up and out of the clutches of that which yet wants to destroy this world. I bring you greetings from the Ascended Host. God bless you, Dear Hearts.

Resurrection Day

November 22, 2003, was Resurrection Day for the people of Earth and your Planet, initiating a Dispensation of Resurrection for your world! This is a beginning of a new cycle for humanity and the Earth that has been delayed for some time. Since 1994, many of our discourses and the light that we have offered have been to prepare the many awakening souls on Earth for this new cycle. We began our own service to humanity when the Light gave my Twin Flame, Asun, and I the Dispensation to come to the Earth again.

We began our work as Emissaries of the Master Jesus. And because of our Love for Him and His beloved Mother, Precious Mary, and of the great Ray that would be the authority for the incoming Golden Age, the Violet Ray, have we sought to contribute to the desire of the Ascended Host to assist in this new Resurrection Cycle that would be the beginning of a Raising Activity for the peoples of Earth. Part of the plan within this new cycle is that tens of thousands would become free of the social and racial consciousness that most human beings yet feel hypnotized under, gain their sovereignty, learn of the great Presence of Life that is within, and continue the great journey of awakening and healing each other and this planet and—the perfecting of life, with the attention held upon the Great God Presence within and above.

I wish to share with you what the Cosmic Law has recently given us permission to do. And with it I hope to give you an understanding. After my sharing I will receive and transmit the words and the blessings of Mighty Victory from Venus and His gifts to the world.

The first three years of every decade of this last century a sinister force has always tried to control humanity

For centuries—longer than you care to remember—there has been an evil, a treachery and a sinister force in this world that continuously, age after age, has turned humanity away from the light and into the darkness. From 1939 to 1953 the Mighty Archangel Michael, and a great being, forgotten by humankind, Beloved Mighty Astria, entered into the Fourth Dimension and into the Psychic Realms and into your own Earth's atmosphere; and began to fight the battle for humankind between the forces of darkness and light.

In those years, every dark magician and discarnate energy that was using the sinister force was removed from the Earth's atmosphere. In the following years that led up to the early 1970's, all poltergeists, and all discarnate entities were removed from the Earth's atmosphere and the Fourth Dimension, the Psychic Realm. A Decree was given by the spiritual hierarchy, from that time forward, everyone who leaves the body through *the change called death*, regardless of the life they lived, would not be able to remain as a discarnate entity here to bother the rest of embodied humankind.

This set the stage for a great cleansing, a great clearing of discordant energies on Earth. It was an opportunity for those who have had sufficient light within them, to use that light to awaken to greater purpose, to begin to think for themselves and look for some meaning to life, more harmonious, more real and sane, than the mass of humankind were following. Yet, in the first three years of every decade of this last century, a sinister force, has always tried to control humanity; as it did in the first three years of this decade. Now that force has failed.

This Resurrection Day was intended to take place forty years before 2003! What happened at that time?

This Resurrection Day is the beginning of a great Cycle of several thousand years to come, in which the light coming to the Earth now will be a *constant*—not an emergence, not a convergence, not a wave that then rolls back allowing humanity to integrate—but a constant outpouring of light that is the resurrection of humanity and the Earth, the powers of nature, and the forces of the elements!

This Cosmic Activity, my Dear Hearts, was intended to take place forty years before 2003! And you might ask yourselves, "What happened at that time?" the assassination of an American president!

The sinister force has always known that the great Perfecting Activity of the Light of God that never fails is the right use of the power of *attention*. It knows that if your attention is held on that which is good, that which is of the light—if your attention can be turned inward and upward—it is only a matter of time and space to break free of the chains of discordant human creation; and have a life in which you can begin the great Freeing Activity and create greater evolution, love, joy and fulfillment.

It is for this reason that the sinister force struck on this day in 1963 and captivated the attention of the masses of the people in the assassination of an American president. This successfully once again delayed the Divine Plans of the Ascended Host to continue to raise life on the Earth; that life could become free of the nightmare, the selfishness and the hatred that certain human beings created in this world.

In the middle of two wars, two Armageddons, a way was found to release the Light back to humankind

The Divine Plans to raise this Earth and humanity and to help human beings realize that long before *the experience of being human* they were spiritual beings, light beings—have been delayed for millions of years, Dear Hearts. There have been many plans to save humanity; and so many of these plans have been set aside because not enough of the attention of humanity was upon light, was upon love, was upon goodness, was upon God.

The great Cosmic Law did not allow us to interfere because the *free will* governing your Earth was yet in place. If human beings' choice was to turn away from the light and believe in a man-made, invented God, there was no power in the universe that would allow any of us to interfere. So all we could do is watch—watch human beings come under the controlling Presence of a miserable group of selfish human beings who have controlled your world longer than you want to know.

However, in the last century, the Ascended Host had some successes in appearing visibly before some students who had enough light within them. A way was found in the middle of two world wars, two Armageddon's, a way was found to bring the light of truth back to humankind. And that way was the Presence of the Ascended Master Saint Germain, who came to the Great Cosmic Being who governs your system of worlds, and stated, "I have found two souls strong enough to *restore* the knowledge that Jesus offered that was covered over in the year 325AD!" And indeed, those two souls were found; and the beginning of the return of the Sacred and Higher Knowledge began to flourish on the Earth, Dear Hearts. Many Students of Life in the twentieth century turned towards the light; realizing that the God found in most of the religions was a very limiting understanding of God.

Now the number of human beings who are awakening on Earth has grown by the millions. Many human beings who have come to realize that God in your reality is your own Beloved Higher Self 'I AM'; that is the Individualization of 'Mother/Father God' at the centre of the universe and that the Mighty Presence of God, the Father Consciousness spoken of by Jesus, exists within your human forms as an invisible, yet real, mighty Flame of Life within you. And as this group of awakened human beings grew in number throughout this last seventy years, every means was being used to begin the great resurrection of humankind.

Master Jesus' role and Plan for the Resurrection cycle

My Dear Hearts, the Ascended Jesus Christ did not make any mistakes—all that was played out in His ministry was played out so that there would be a future of human beings who would live as He lived, begin to walk on Earth and demonstrate the same Higher Powers and Presence of God that He demonstrated in his own life!

The greatest prophet, the greatest demonstration of the higher and natural powers of life came to this world two thousand years ago—the Master Jesus. He spoke the words "The courageous and the illumined shall inherit the Earth." The Bible suggests that He said "The meek will inherit the Earth" however that is not a correct interpretation.

Master Jesus knew that the fulfillment of His ministry would be through those humans who would be so raised by their love for life, their love for God. He knew that these humans—with their love for expression, their love for creation, their love for perfection and beauty—would be those who would go through a great raising activity. And if the raising was sufficient to take the mass of humanity out of a desire for war and into a desire for peace, then this would bring a new cycle of re-birth on Earth. It would create a new cycle lasting thousands of years that would be identified and go down in the history of humankind as *The Great Resurrection Cycle!* The years 2003 to 2012 will be critical to this whole new Cycle of Resurrection.

It is your destiny to become Sovereign Creator Beings of Divine Love

On November 22, 2003, the Resurrection that Master Jesus lived and hoped for, began. And it means that now there comes a *constant* Light from Heavenly Sources that is pouring to the Earth; Light from many different sources,

Light from your own Great God Presence, Light from the Angels, Light from the Ascended Host, Light from great Temples of Light and Realms of Light that exist in the higher stratospheres of your Earth. This Light shall be as constant as the Light you experience in your daytime, when you experience the sunlight of your physical sun.

The Light will be in a constant flow and comes with a raising quality to it. It will bring with it an illumination process that will allow each of you to understand yourselves as Creator Beings and allow you to become free of every limitation. It will allow you to move into the most magical and loving experience of human life—that it is your destiny, to become Sovereign Creator Beings, Great Beings of God with full understanding, comprehension, and manipulation of the natural Laws of Manifestation; producing joy and happiness, youth, health, and perfection, in yourselves, your personal worlds, and the world Itself!

Nothing can stop what has begun November 22, 2003!—It was Resurrection Day for Humanity and the Earth! Within the essence of this Resurrection is that the great Flame of Life within each of you, and every desire you have to be free, will be amplified and fulfilled. For this, my Dear Heart, is one of the greatest of all desires— absolute freedom. One cannot have a desire for absolute freedom without having within their soul the recognition of the necessity to use the gift of life in the most loving and constructive way.

You are Souls who have prepared centuries of time for this cycle of Resurrection—and now it is to find your unique expression of who you are

Unlike the great resurrection of Master Jesus' Ministry, the next several years offer individuals, just like yourself, greater opportunities to go out into the world and flourish in your own dynamic passions, your purpose—whatever is the Divine Plan for your life. A New Era of awakening is upon the Earth; this new Seventh Golden Age is for you. You are souls that have prepared centuries of time for life on Earth after 2003. Now is time to get in touch with the unique expression of who you are and what you have come to do!

It is to find your passion and your creativity, your inner talent and genius and to live it! It is to say *yes* to your life and give permission that your life be fulfilled and of service! It is to have recognition within your soul and your heart that you have a *greater* life than the intellect could possibly imagine on this Earth that is waiting for you to realize and experience. And that really, Dear Hearts, begins by saying *yes* to that greater life, and to do everything you can to complete the final healing of lost will, and desire the awareness that God is the very life of your being.

In the great Realms of Light there is no difference between the worded expressions 'God', 'Life', 'Love', 'Self', 'Light', and 'Perfection'. To us those words all mean the same thing, and they are in essence who you truly are. They are the true nature of your being. They represent the mighty Flame of Life that exists within each of you. And if there are experiences in your life that are less than the qualities of what those words speak of, it is only because you qualified your outer life—due to beliefs and the feelings that have been held within—with discord and limitation. May I remind you, Dear Heart, that Resurrection Day has taken place on Earth by Mighty Cosmic Forces of Light that love humanity. Your thoughts, your feelings and your worded expressions are going to become more amplified and illumined now. Therefore what you say, think and feel, will find manifestation in your life much quicker than before. You are the authority in your life, you are a sovereign being, and your future will reveal this great truth to you.

Life and the energy it provides loves to be qualified and commanded. I know this flies in the face of those who seem to be victimized every day, yet the great truth is—life must be commanded as to how you want it to act in your lives. And in order for life to be commanded you must rise and accept your sovereignty that you have come from the light, you are born of God. This sovereignty in your light—and your desire to use the life you are given, constructively—will give you the unlimited life that awaits you.

The future, how magnificent! Ahh, the music, the dance, the arts, the Song of Life, the great evolution in technology and invention that is coming forth will transform the world. Your world has changed much since 1963 in all facets and in all aspects of life, has it not? You will hardly recognize your world with the great advancements that are coming. You will hardly recognize the kind of technology you will use in your outer life, every day! Such is the great, great evolution that is coming! Humankind is ready!

A *Global Village Community* is growing amongst humanity, there are many who have come and served

You are all working together in this plan to uplift humanity, more than you know and your consciousness is united, Dear Hearts. There is a *Village Community* amongst humanity—there is a *Global Village* that is growing—and there are so many who have come and served. The wonderful John Fitzgerald Kennedy, the glamorous Princess Diana who gave of her Life so that the emotional body of humankind could heal! Why, Dear Heart, why do you think the Angels and the Ascended Masters such as Master Jesus, why do you think they wanted the great reunion of humanity to take place? So that when they, under Cosmic Law, are given permission to release the light into the feeling side of humanity, that not one human being is left out!

The tragedy of the Kennedy assassination changed the use of television. And television and technology has created a global village community of humanity. The tragic death of your Princess Diana, my Dear Hearts, that tragic death brought about the attention—there it is again—the *attention* of the world on what once again was an absolute insane act, the loss of her life. And, Dear Heart, that in turn united many of humanity in the feeling side of life. You are *one!*

You are so one in consciousness and nature that the next few years are going to reflect this truth to you. The ability to think a thought form, the ability to send a thought form to a loved one who may be thousands of miles away will become greatly enhanced so that that loved one picks up the thought and telephones you and says, "I received your message." There will be moments of epiphany, when you just realize, "Oh, my goodness, just a moment ago I was thinking about this and look what has happened!"

You see, epiphanies cannot just be of the mind and the feelings; they require a *body consciousness* to be experienced. Your bodies are Temples of the Most High Living God, and the Most High Living God is the light within you and that will come forth more into your experience. Transformation is coming forth inside every one of you just like a determined teenager. And you know what a determined teenager can be, Dear Hearts! That is what the light is doing within the hearts of humanity!

Due to humankinds readiness for cosmic intervention, these next years are magical. Magical! You can stretch boundaries of consciousness and experience. You can have a life that is absolutely greater than anything that has ever been your experience, but you have to allow *wonder and magic* back into your life. You have to allow trust, faith and confidence back into your life. You have to reach up to the stars and dream. Get rid of *buts!* "But, but, how? How do I do this?" Reach up and dare to dream!

All you have ever had to do to create reality and experience is think it, see it in your mind, feel it, and hold it in your heart and be ready to take action

Your Heavenly Father gave you His mind, His power and consciousness; the ability to think and to execute a profound decision for your life—the Gift of the Holy Father! And the Holy Mother gave you the Gift of Desire, Feeling and Heart. The Father energy, the electronic, the Mother's energy, the electromagnetic; so that you could think, you could have a thought and the Divine Feminine aspect seals and clothes that thought in the Desire Side of Life, so that your heart could hold that manifestation and radiate it out into the world of form and experience.

I say to you, my Dear Hearts that is all you have ever had to do to create reality and experience — think it, see it in your mind, feel it, and hold it in your heart and be ready to take action. Let it be a vibration of energy and consciousness working together, so real to you, and let the God of your being *naturally* manifest it. Or as my Beloved Asun can say so eloquently, "Let God do the detailing." But God does not know what to detail, if *you* do not make a choice. You must use your God given will!

Too often, my Dear Hearts, I still hear you use the phrase, "Well, we'll see what's coming. Well, we'll see what's down the road." Oh, yes? You are still letting the universe make decisions for you? You are still letting *whatever* make the decisions for you? You are a Sun's Presence of Light to your life. Nothing can show up in your life without you thinking it, believing it, seeing it, accepting it, feeling it and acting upon it. This is a Universal Law, and no one can escape it.

A Message from a Tall Master from Venus—the Mighty Victory

It is with a truly humble heart that I, Akasha, prepare to deliver a message transmitted by one who is one of the Tall Masters from Venus. He is one of the Lords of the Flame of Venus. He is cousin to that Great Being who exiled Himself thousands of years ago to rescue the Earth from an impending disaster, Sanat Kumara. For years and years His Planet has played a guardian role for the people of Earth and Earth itself. He is the Mighty Victory who has known nothing but centuries of victory in every single accomplishment; in everything He has ever tried. He has never experienced anything but victory! And I say to you, Dear Heart, this is a Great Being of Light to have on your side! I thank you. Here is His Message.

Beloved of Akasha & Asun's Family of Light! I AM Victory! I am truly grateful to greet you out of the Garden of My Eternal Heart, and I thank you for your presence here today. You have no idea of the joy and the great communion that is taking place within your own Earth's Ascended Masters and my own family in Venus, the Kumara's. For that small portion of humanity who are now reaching up and loving their own God Presence; and giving recognition of an Ascended Host who stand ready to deliver you from every limitation that has ever been in this world. It brings great joy to our hearts.

I enfold each of you and I offer you the Cosmic Purity, the Cosmic Power, the Cosmic Victory and the Cosmic Love that is the Sacred Fire Love Supreme of my Planet Venus.

The Sacred Fire purification of the *people* of Earth and the *structure* of the Earth, the Planet

Although your science cannot see it yet, our Planet is not really any longer a Planet. It is in the throes of a great transformation and ascension itself into a sun not unlike your physical sun. And when our Planet graduates into a sun, it will be moved into another system, where, like your physical sun, it will be a Sun's Presence to a whole new system of worlds. But we cannot move our Planet until our commitment to the people of Earth is complete.

The Supreme Goddess of Venus—and my family, the Kumara's—have decreed that we will not leave Earth at this time. We will always be available to every being who reaches up to us until the sinister force has been removed from your Planet, and the destructive use of human beings' free will, under Cosmic Law is removed!

So, my Dear Hearts, we are here to stay, not only myself, also the other Lords of the Flame of Venus, and my cousin, the Beloved Sanat Kumara. When we offer you the Garden of Our Heart, it is because, Dear Heart, our Realm of Light in Venus is a state of absolute luminosity and perfection. And it is the destiny of *all* the density in your world that is to become so raised through the Sacred Mystical Fire, that your human forms, as well as all forms of substance, shall become purified, transformed and shall radiate a great luminosity of light. But this cannot be accomplished, Dear Children of the Light, until there is the Sacred Fire purification of the *people* of Earth and the *structure* of the Earth, the Planet.

Saint Germain—the Violet Ray from the Great Central Sun

It was when Saint Germain came to the Earth that we from Venus could come closer to you. Saint Germain—that Cosmic Being of the Violet Ray from God, came in several physical embodiments to the Earth, and then gained His Ascension as the Mighty Saint Germain—is now the authority of the Violet Ray from the Great Central Sun. And when His Violet Ray became the authority for the Earth in 1928, this opened the door for many of us who have had to stand by and watch the discord on Earth, come closer to humanity. This gave us the opportunity to come closer and closer, and wherever there has been light in a human heart, to stand behind those hearts and do everything that would soon bring them their freedom.

The great and natural activity of life is the Perfecting Activity of the Sacred Fire. And as your Akasha said to you, there is but one thing that is the Perfecting Activity— and it is your ability to hold your attention often enough upon that great, Glorious God Presence within you and that Glorious Ascended Self that stands above you that is your own Great God Presence 'I AM', not somebody else's, not some organization's, not some religion's, but your *own* Great Glorious God 'I AM' Presence!

The Sacred Fire of Venus is anchored in the Earth

Humanity owes a debt of gratitude to the Mighty Saint Germain—who was Joseph in a previous embodiment, father of Jesus the Christ—for returning the great knowledge 'I AM' to the world. And when Saint Germain traveled to my Planet not so long ago and asked me to join him in the freedom—first of America, then the Three Americas, then the world—I said I would join him in this wonderful plan

318

for humankind. We were given permission—and we did anchor in your physical Earth a Flame—the Cosmic Purity, the Cosmic Power, the Cosmic Victory and the Cosmic Love that is the Sacred Fire Love Supreme of Venus.

We anchored the Sacred Fire in the structure of Earth for the time when there would be those humans who would discover our existence; so that as we, the Lords of the Flame of Venus, who have remained with your Planet, any time that any of you would turn your attention to the light, we could help you. So that when you turned your attention to your God Presence and then to any of us, and asked us to enfold you—your personal life, your loved ones, your nation and your world—in our Cosmic Purity, Power, Victory and Love of Our Sacred Fire of Our Planet Venus, then this would give us the permission and the authority to do so, to help you. And we could do this quickly because we already *anchored* these Cosmic Higher Powers into your world!

The greatest, liberating thing to do in life is to fix your attention upon your Presence. This is the great Oracle of Life. This is the great means in which you—by placing your attention upon your Presence, in prayers, in meditation—invite your Presence to fulfill Itself in you, as you and through you. As long as you have the understanding that your Presence you are reaching up to is your real self, your true self, that aspect of you that is made in the image and likeness of God/Goddess All That Is, will come forth according to your desire and will. And as you do this, my Dear Hearts, this is what allows the perfection of God through the release of mighty streams of energy down your life stream, inside of you and out into your world as the perfection, the divine plans, and the Divine Desires that your own Beloved Presence has for you, come forth into manifestation. But you must remember that it is your true God self.

The Mighty Saint Germain and his own Students to Life—your own Beloved Akasha & Asun and various other spiritual groups that we wish to honour as well, have served you as your humble servants in helping you to remember that you have this beautiful Presence within you and above you; and that your attention held upon this Presence is the means to bring the perfection into your outer life.

Yet, Beloved Earth Flames, We offer you *our* Sacred Fire. And why do we offer you our Sacred Fire Love from Venus? We offer this to you because we know that you have centuries of lifetimes that have tremendous momentums of humanly discordant qualified energy. It is this humanly qualified energy that maintains limiting appearances in your world; including for those of you who have found the light, the seeming momentum of the aging of the physical body.

Reach up to your Presence, and then reach up to us and call our Cosmic Love, Cosmic Purity, Cosmic Power and Cosmic Victory into yourselves for the absolute purification and the restoration of everything in your life, including your body. Call it into your nations, your loved ones, your homes and into the activities of your life. Just make this call three times a day. Then you give us the authority to release our Cosmic Powers.

If you want your freedom and your ultimate Ascension *only* through your own Great God Presence

'Appearances' have momentum only by the use of human power. My Dear Hearts, stop using *human* power and start using the power of your own Great God Presence, and reach up to us; because, you see, it is not practical with the busy lives you are living—nor do you have the training that is required—to hold a Cosmic concentration of your attention upon your Presence.

If you do not want Beloved Jesus or Archangel Michael, if you do not want the Legions of Angels that God, the Mighty 'I AM' Infinite Presence in the Great Central Sun is sending to the Earth—if you do not want any of us to help you, but you want your freedom and your ultimate ascension *only* through your own Great God Presence— then you would have to train yourself to hold a Cosmic concentration of your attention held upon your Presence for at least a hundred and eighty minutes at a time, unbroken. And the last human being to achieve this, My Dear Hearts, was the Blessed Mother of Jesus the Christ. This She had to accomplish while her husband Joseph— Saint Germain—passed the seed of Jesus' body from His mind's eye into Her mind's eye. It is in this way that Blessed Mary received the seed of Jesus' form.

I do not believe, Beloved of the Light, that you are yet trained in mind to focus for one hundred and eighty minutes *without a single thought.* Considering the demands of human life on Earth today this would be rather impractical. But you see, this is what it would require if you feel that you do not require the assistance of Angels, or that you do not need Ascended Masters in your life, now that you have found your Presence.

Your Presence still must release the higher power that lifts you from the human creation of this world—it must release the Sacred Fire into you. And the Sacred Fire is the Consuming Flame of Divine Love that is the Heart of God. And your Presence cannot release this Sacred Fire through you sufficiently without a hundred and eighty minutes of concentration on your part, if you do not include us.

This is why you have been asked, when you turn your attention to your Presence that you will also turn your attention to any of the Ascended Host and include us. We, then, can respond immediately *with* your Presence. And as your Presence begins to send forth the answer to your calls, then we can maintain the space-energy-frequency that is necessary for those calls to come into your life *tangible and fulfilled*. We love to do that for you and this is why we offer our service to you.

Call forth our Cosmic Purity, Power, Love and Victory into yourselves, to force the purification, so that your body can be a beautiful temple—so that your body can restore its youth, beauty and perfection. Call it forth so that you can have a power that brings balance and divine order into everything in your lives—that your lives can be exquisite manifestations of love, of beauty and victory.

Without the mystical Sacred Fire there is no Light, there is no Earth, there are no Elements, and there are no Kingdoms...there is nothing!

The world needs victory. The sinister force has had its victory longer than you care to know, and now the sinister force in your world is moving into a place of less and less and less as the light is taking its toll. But the light, My Dear Hearts, is the manifestation of the Sacred Fire. Without the mystical Sacred Fire there is no light, there is no Earth, there are no elements and there are no Kingdoms. There is nothing!

If it was not for the Mighty Saint Germain who opened the door for the rest of us to reach out to you—if it was not for the light inside you that gave many of you the ability to accept the reality of your own Presence and Ascended and Angelic Host—there would be no life on this Planet today. So as much as we need *you* to carry this light to the Earth and humanity, do you need *us* if you are to be free!

We have watched the Earth for ten million years. And I assure you that the condition the human race has fallen into in the past has been a thousand times worse than

322

any condition of evil and hatred that the human race experienced in the two Armageddon's of the last century that were your World Wars. It is for this reason that those who own this System of Worlds—the Great Cosmic Beings who oversee this system—have seen fit to afford human beings *the veil*. The veil in which you are not demanded or required to *remember* the misery, the tragedy, the hatred and the evil that human beings have fallen into in past life.

Today most of humanity do not have the knowledge you are receiving, but they are at least constructive to life. They are peace loving, and they are moving towards the higher activity and constructive use of life. The greater number of humanity do not have this knowledge but have some acceptance of God and try to live good and rightful lives. However, there was a time on your Earth when the majority of human beings on Earth were completely selfish and destructive, who lived by the lower nature! Can you imagine!

And that, My Dear Heart, is why you have deserts. Because you have made your own Planet rise up and take her toll and shake her mountains and raise her waters— to cleanse this Earth. And yet it is over, the Age of Planetary Cataclysm is over. The great Karmic Beings, the Lords of Karma, have decreed—no more continental cataclysms for the people of Earth; enough people are turning towards the light.

If you let your nations take you into a Third World War, your own Kingdoms will rise up

Yet I say, my Dear Hearts, we are not out of the hot water yet, because there is a cleansing and a purging coming if you let your nations take humanity into another Armageddon; if you let your nations take you into a Third World War, your own Earth Kingdoms will rise up. The

Powers of Nature and the Forces of the Elements will rise up and remove the destructive portion of humankind from the Earth. And those who are of Pan—that Precious Kingdom where all the elementals, the fairies, the little ones lived; that first kingdom that was destroyed by human beings long ago—they will come back. If that is the purging and the cleansing that human beings demand, then Pan shall rise. And Pan will save those who love the light!

I have decreed—and I joined with the Mighty Saint Germain—that if necessary, if America does not arise into the light, the jewel that is her destiny, I will cause, under the Authority of the Great Central Sun's Presence, a light equal to one thousand physical suns to hit the atmosphere of Earth! And I do not feel that those who are discordant could survive that much light. And that, My Dear Heart, is the purging and the cleansing that is to come, if human beings insist on taking your world and your Planet into a Third World War. Those who are of the light, who love the light, would survive.

Young people demonstrate and try to stop World Organizations and World Trade, because behind all of this is some of the last of the old archetype energies

Wonderful is your soul! Wonderful are the young people who are starting to look for something that is beyond what the world teaches them! Some of your universities are poison to the people of Earth. No wonder the young people today are demonstrating and looking for something real; for their hearts know there is something *greater*, there is something lost in this world. No wonder young people demonstrate and try to stop world organizations and world trade, because behind all of this—which has a divine plan to it—there are some of those who represent the last *of the old archetype energies* that must and will fall, my Dear Hearts!

You are moving into a great time for the people of Earth. But, my Dear Heart, it is this group here and all the beautiful people who love the light and who love freedom, it is *you* who is going to make the difference as to whether you allow the mass of humankind to be convinced as to whether they should be drawn into another world war! And how can you do that, my Dear Hearts? You can call upon the whole Family of Venus, the whole Kumara Family! We are the Royal Family of Venus. We have loved God from the beginning and we have gained our freedom, and we offer it to the people of Earth. We have anchored into the structure of the Earth the Cosmic Love, the Cosmic Purity, the Cosmic Power and the Cosmic Victory of our Sacred Fire of Venus that loves to remove that which is the sinister force. This is how we freed our Planet long ago!

You can help to stop an impending disaster if you will call to us on Venus

Call upon the Goddess of Venus, my cousin the Mighty Sanat Kumara, or myself, Victory, and my brothers, the Lords of the Flames from Venus, and *demand* the Sacred Fire from Venus, because we placed it in the structure of your Earth. It is already here. It is not that we have to *deliver* it to your Planet. We placed it here when the door opened for us, and all you have to do is to call The Sacred Fire Love of Venus forth into your lives. You see we had the permission to bring it here, but we did not have the permission to make it a Commanding Presence to all human life, because you are enjoying—or not enjoying—

325

the last few years of free will in which human beings' free will can be used in a destructive manner.

You can help to stop an impending disaster if you will call to those in Venus to release our Sacred Fire Love and Power into your nation and release the Sacred Fire of our Power and Victory around all those who are war-mongers, all those who stand for the sinister force. If you will demand rivers of our Sacred Fire from Venus to enter into every level of government, corporations, the banking institutions and the insurance companies and command our Sacred Fire purging, *we* have the authority to stop all selfishness in its tracks! We have this kind of authority when you call upon us to release the Sacred Fire, Dear Hearts!

The Consciousness of Pan will rise

Do you understand what I am saying? If human beings are hypnotized into believing it is necessary to have a Third World War, your Planet, your kingdoms and the elements will say, "Whoa! Stop!" The Ascended Host decree there shall never be war again on this Planet. It is too much of a toll—it takes *hundreds of years* to heal humanity and the Earth from a world war and it takes the intervention of Cosmic powers to clean the hatred and the tragedy of life that is lost to war. It only takes *seconds* to cleanse and restore the souls of those who have been lost when the oceans rise and there is a cleansing and purging when a portion of the human race is commanded to leave this Planet because they are willing to take it back into war!

Understand my words!—we decree, there will not be a Third World War! Your Planet has issued the decree. She has asked for Cosmic assistance and we have answered her. But if human beings want it and put this Planet on a perilous path again, then we will join her in giving power to her kingdoms to remove the destructive elements within the human race!

The consciousness of Pan will rise! Pan, while the destruction of the forces of the elements move, Pan will rise. And those who love the light—those who have lived a good life, those who love God in *any* understanding— will be saved during that great cleansing, as *The Light of a Thousand Suns* passes through the Earth's atmosphere. This is not the divine plan, Beloved of the Heart, this is an *emergency* plan! This is the last plan if humankind willingly come into the belief that war is necessary again.

Rise up! You have a voice!

There are many activities that are going on in your Earth. Strange things are taking place. Those who you *believe* are warmongers—presidents and prime ministers, be careful, my Dear Hearts—if you have a belief that maybe these are in support of war, and if you are mistaken, that is a Karmic debt you will have to pay.

It is better to think that there are 'some people' who want to take you to war and there are those who stand for the God Government and God Freedom of all the peoples and all the lands of this Earth. And pray that all of those who stand for war be removed from any authority by our Sacred Fire Love to the people of Earth. This we can do. We say to you, "All of those who are under the radiation of the Great God 'I AM' Presence—those who are under the radiation of Akasha & Asun, the Mighty Saint Germain, Jesus the Christ, and other Ascended Masters—rise up! You have a voice!" Because when you call to us in your prayer calls, our Ascended Master Victory is complete and all we need is your permission and will. Your world is still under your free will. We cannot release our power to save humankind unless you *ask* us to.

327

If the great *Student Body*—those who love God and are awakening on some Spiritual Path that is growing here and around the Earth at this time—if you love your freedom that your nations have attained, if you can come to love justice, as is the nation Canada's destiny—to be the Crown of Justice to the Three Americas, I, Mighty Victory, beg you to use my name in the following decree:

"In the name of Mighty Victory, I demand the Sacred Fire of Victory into the Earth to take its toll in the sinister force; and to stop in their tracks those who have planned destruction and those who want to take the good people back into another world war.

"Great Sacred Fire of Venus, Mighty Kumara's, Goddess of Venus, Jesus the Christ, Mighty Legions of Angels, Archangel Michael, great Forces of Light, descend into the lower atmosphere of Earth and release your Cosmic purity and power. Release your Cosmic victory and love that is your Sacred Fire Supreme, into that which is the hatred, the selfishness, the sinister force and the evil. Surround those who stand for the dark side and seize them and stop them in their tracks. Take that sinister force out of this Planet so that it cannot exist anywhere in the universe again, we thank you!"

If you could see the energy in your atmosphere...you would climb inside yourselves, look up to your God Presence quicker than anything else you would do

If you could see what is in your atmosphere, if you could see the energy, you would climb inside yourselves and look up to your God Presence and us quicker than anything else you would do. It is yet a good God-Glorious thing that your sight has not been raised *as* quickly as your beautiful hearts have been opened. Because, if you could see the shadows that your own Earth Angels cleanse in your cities, if you could see the shadows of human beings' selfishness and discord filling the lower atmosphere of Earth, you would prostrate yourselves and praise God that your Heavenly Mother and Father have sent Beings of Light to you; and Legions of Angels who are purifying some of the discord in your cities and your atmospheres.

We are at a perilous time in the history of the Earth. I will bid you just a momentary and victorious greeting. God bless you, Beloved of the Light. 'I AM' Victory and I offer you the Garden of My Heart inside your consciousness as that Victory which will certainly want nothing but perfect manifestation in your life. God bless you! God bless you! God bless you! The light of God never fails! I trust you will integrate now the meaning of my words to you.

CHAPTER *T*HIRTEEN

I, Victory, greet each of you out of the Garden of My Heart that I freely offer to you. Again, there is joy in our hearts that a small portion of Earth people have come to understand what has been the hidden knowledge of the Great 'I AM' Presence.

One day your eyes shall be opened—and you shall *see* that Mighty Presence!

The greatest of all knowledge in every world, all throughout the universe, is the knowledge that every individualized thinking Flame of Life—which each of you blessed ones are—has a mighty Great God Presence that is the individualization of the Infinite Mighty 'I AM' Presence Creator in the Great Central Sun. This is *The Greatest Power in the Universe.* This is the greatest knowledge, it is the end of all mysteries—it is the great riveting, unraveling truth, 'I AM That I AM'. It is the recognition of your glorious God Life, and one day you shall rise up and your eyes shall be opened—and you shall see that mighty Presence!

I dare say that some of you have already seen that Presence in lifetimes past, thinking it was your Guardian Angel that stood above you, not knowing it was the glory of your own Ascended Self—that Being that has given you life, that Being that loves you and is Life's Deliverer Come; that Being that has waited for centuries of time while you have journeyed in the experience of duality on your Earth journey.

Long has been the sleep of human beings, and long has the Cosmic Law permitted the *free will* of humanity to forget one's own divinity and being. So I join with the Mighty Saint Germain and I join with your Beloved Akasha in encouraging you, Beloved, that this is the Great Deliverer of your Life—your own Beloved Presence, 'I AM'.

God loves you so much that even your own great Ascended Self will respect any feeling you are having

Akasha spoke recently—and it is a great truth—that when you may not *seem* to have results to your prayers and your calls to your Presence, there are reasons that results do not come. And often most, the reason that you do not get results to your prayers, your calls, is that you are holding the vibration of that which is exactly the opposite of what you are calling forth. The Presence never fails, Beloved of the Light. It never fails! But often what you called for is set aside in a sphere of light and waits and waits, due to the emotion in your feeling body that opposes that which you have called forth.

There are many of you who have great assistance and vast amounts of money and supply waiting for you. This fully-qualified energy—delivered from the great God 'I AM' of your Being—is waiting to come into your life. But you did not stand *behind* your decree; you did not reach up to the glory of your God Being and *demand* the release of your full financial freedom. You did not stand behind that command to life, but rather re-entered into a place of worry and fear about money. Which means the energy your glorious 'I AM' Presence released that would have answered your call and manifest itself as the money and the supply, or the healing in the physical body, is just off to the left side of you. It is just off to the left of the receptive side of you, waiting for manifestation. Because God loves you so much that even your own great ascended self will respect any feeling that you are having. This is your will!

Free will is a vibration, the will, the quality that you hold within your Feeling Side of Life

Forget not that free will is not just the ability to be the architect and to design life—free will is a *vibration, the will*, the *quality* that you hold within your feeling side of life. And not I, Victory, or the Beloved Archangel to your world, Beloved Michael, could ever interfere with this. And it is often the feeling that you hold in your feeling body that is the interference to the very thing you are calling forth.

God cannot answer your prayer when you have a feeling of being poor. God cannot answer your prayer when you have a feeling that a life-threatening disease will take your physical body—God must honour your feelings! I must honour your feelings. Michael, Blessed Mary and Jesus, who have given more miracles to the mankind of this Earth in the last two thousand years than any Ascended Being, must honour your feelings!

And that is why Akasha, my Dear Hearts, has mentored you wonderfully. She reminds you that when you go to your Great God Presence and you command the release of that which sets you free—you demand that your *Presence* orchestrate the expansion, comprehension and understanding of your higher purpose in your daily life. But you have to make the command that if there is anything in your feeling side of life that could interfere with your calls, that it be taken out. "God 'I AM' of my Being, if there is anything in my feeling side of life that could interfere with you manifesting the results of what I call forth, release your Mighty Hand through me, release your Cosmic Flame of

Divine Love through me and take that feeling out of me. And give me the feeling of what I am calling forth!"

You must have the *feeling* of what you desire in life. And if you will do this, and if you will call to me, I will help you and fill you with *My victory*. Longer than your sojourn unto the Earth I have known Victory, my Dear Hearts—Victory I have known for millions upon millions of years. And like your own Earth Ascended Host, I stand ready to give you everything you could possibly desire that will help you to express the love, the beauty and the perfection of your own Great God Manifest in your daily life, my Dear Hearts.

Your Presence wants you to come in joy, not just when you are in trouble

Your world is hungry for peace. Your world is hungry for the Splendour of Light. Your world is starving for that which says *yes* to life and restores life. Children are starving in your world. There are tragedies taking place in your world because the criminal side of free will has not yet been erased from mankind; for there is not yet enough desire to reach up and change this.

We watch through the All-Seeing Eye of the Mighty Elohim Cyclopea. We watch and see that too many humankind reach up to God *only* when the suffering is at a deep level and you want to reach up to something that would correct the tragic condition or event. Your Presence wants you to come in joy, not just when you are in trouble! Your Presence wants you to come in the victory of your light and joyful being of love. And yet with this momentum of the human limitations that are still within your feelings, there is a momentum of the divine powers of life, the divine quality of life that is growing. And that is why, my Dear Hearts, you are bold; you are courageous to awaken to the full God Glory of your Earthly Beings!

We honour your sovereignty; and you are bold and you are courageous individuals to know there are those individuals who have sojourned the way before you; individuals who have gained their victory over every human limitation, including *the change called death*, and they all stand ready to answer your prayers and your calls. But none of us can over-light you—none of us can stand with you and be the strength and pour our light to you—if you allow fear and doubt. We cannot allow our Light to *amplify* fear and doubt. We must withdraw for a while as we have done hundreds and thousands of times. We must withdraw and wait for another day.

You are more than a physical structure, an atomic body...

Akasha has done you a wonderful service in begging you, almost, to command your Presence to take all fear and doubt out of you, and strengthen you with a force of light. So then, as you carry the Sacred Fire of Purity and Harmony, we can make you a Pillar of Light and we can help you once again become the Ray of Light that you were a long time before you were physical human beings.

Is your memory, my Dear Hearts, so *frozen* in human limited experience that you are yet prey to the belief that you are not more than a physical structure, an atomic body? Are you yet prey to forgetting that your magnificent forms are an absolute orchestration of the forces of the elements that composed themselves together as your physical body; elements—Earth, Air, Water, Fire—that loved you so much that the very elements of your body are willing to be the vibration of everything that you think and everything that you feel?

Eternality and immortality is your Gift of Life

Your Beloved Asun, we love him. We love his humor; we love his brave Heart; and we love when He says to you "Stop it! Stop holding the vibration of fear and doubt. Stop holding the vibration of judgment against yourself and others. Stop holding the vibration of unforgiveness of self and others. Stop believing in 'appearances'. Believe that you are the Eternal God Being that you were created to be!"

Eternality and immortality is your gift of life, and it is your responsibility to give immortality to your physical body through the Eternal Flame of Victory that resides within you; it is your responsibility to do this, instead of destroying physical embodiment, one after the other. For ten million years we have watched human beings come into embodiment—destroy their embodiment—and come back again, hundreds of times over.

Human beings enter into some hypotheses and some brilliant intellectualizing as to whether reincarnation takes place. What ludicrous use of one's time! You have lived and you have never stopped living. You have never experienced death, instead only set aside broken earthly garments. There is only what seems to be gaps in memory, and thank your merciful God that there are gaps, because it is those gaps, those veils, that allow you to not remember the fall and the deprivation that humankind fell into in the past.

But it is a new time now, my Dear Hearts. You are now in the Seventh Golden Age of Earth. And nothing—nothing and no one—can turn back the light as it takes its toll upon the Planet. Nothing can stop the resurrection that is now taking place under the authority of Jesus the Christ!

Many places on your Earth are going through a significant increasing of Light

Nothing can stop this resurrection; for the light must come and take its dominion in human life. You will see the light expand throughout the Planet. Soon, you will see physical manifestations of the Sacred Fire Light above your cities, manifestations of Rings of Heavenly Light—violet and pink for the cleansing and purging of discord and destruction. And so, much will be given to humankind as an offering of cosmic assistance so that humans, of their own free will, will come to love God and wish nothing of war in their lives.

Many places on your Earth are going through a significant increasing of light. There are Sacred Sites that hold the original Divine Spark of Life; in which former Mighty Threefold Flames of God have been held in Sacred Temples, before the people turned away from the light, will once again be lit. America must rise; Peru must rise; Babylon must rise; Arabia must rise, all back into the light and Freedom's Flame.

Be very careful with your opinions, as Akasha & Asun have mentored you—you do not yet know all things that are going on in the Middle East. We, where the Cosmic Law permits, send forth rivers of our Sacred Fire Purity there to assist. However there is so much hatred amongst the peoples in certain areas of the world; there is so much misunderstanding. It is very difficult for a portion of humanity to live under that which is not democracy and to watch you blessed Canadians, Americans and individuals in other nations of this world who live in lands of liberty and justice and democracy. It is not necessarily easy for those who live in other lands, especially the lands of Arabia, the Orient and Africa and to live where there is no democracy!

The activation of the Threefold Flame—Peace to the people of the Middle East

There are reasons why these people rise up. There are reasons why many of them find themselves pawns of that which is the sinister force and hatred. These were great and mighty lands, the lands of ancient Arabia and Babylon, called Iraq today. *She* must rise and become again a centre of new freedoms in the Middle East. There is a great Temple in the Etheric Records of Babylon. If the Threefold Flame in that Etheric Record can be activated, then this will help greatly to bring peace to the people of the Middle East!

This will bring a peace that nothing else will bring, because there is too much destructive free will for everything that is going on in the Middle East today. And there will never be an agreement that anyone will keep *until* your own Earth Ascended Masters can activate the Threefold Flame of God and Etheric Records of the atmosphere where a Mighty Temple of Light existed in the centre of Babylon long ago. *Human beings* cannot do these things—*Angels and Ascended Beings* can do these things. And we know that if we can ignite that divine spark turned off so long ago, that blessing, will bring the people of the Middle East together!

All races in the World are of the Golden Race

I say to you, Blessed ones of the Golden Heart, you are on a great journey home, a journey back to life, freedom and perfection. You are of the Golden Race. All races in the world are of the Golden Race, and you are on your great journey of awakening. There is no difference between the blood of a Jew and an Arab; yet the hatred that is spawned there is so tragic. I, Victory, looked into the records where that hatred comes from, and it is not within the Arabs, and it is not within the Jews—it comes from a source of evil created by human beings *long ago* that waits for pawns —weakend humans, to act itself out. Therefore, I say, "O humanity, arise! Realize that you are the One Race! You are the Golden Seed of God's Heart! The future is yours!"

God is always greater than its individualizations. This is the Miracle of Life.

The reality is, that life can move into a place of such grace and happiness that there doesn't have to be difficult times for this human race! You who have come to realize that the very life you are is God's life—you who have come to realize that there are Realms of Light beyond, stop turning your attention *downwards*. Turn your attention *up to God and the Great Master Presence that dwells within your heart.* Turn your attention within and above and realize that the whole Host of Ascended Beings, Angelics, and the Cosmic Light, are ready to stand forth and direct all the Cosmic Light through you and out into the world.

You can be such a force of light that the hordes of darkness dare not even look in your direction! Every one of you can do this, but you have got to turn your attention back to God. Love God, because it is the truth of your beings and command that God Presence to come forth in you, as you, and through you and fulfill the destiny—I AM Race that is your destiny on this Earth. Love life! You are the lovers of life! You are the fulfillment of your Jesus Christ's ministry to the Earth.

Long has been the Divine Plan for the *Students*—those individuals around the world in various spiritual groups who are awakening at this time. A plan that each of you would move into the hierarchy and the sovereignty of your God Being and the Ascended Masters of Light—invisible for as long as the Cosmic Law demands it—would stand behind you. Each of you, forces of light in human forms, would move out into the world. And there, My Dear Hearts, you would send your light, and weave your light into all life on this Earth, and love this world free.

But you cannot do it alone; you need to reach up to the *greater*. No one—no human being, can even gain the ascension back into the Ascended Self that they left in Realms of Light fourteen million years ago—you left the greater part of you there when you drew part of your life into a physical body. I know that you use the term *Higher Self*, but, I, Victory, feel that it does not do your Presence justice to refer to this great Presence as your Higher Self—for your Presence is the Individualized Presence of God, *The Greatest Power in the Universe*, the 'I AM', the Glory that loves to fulfill itself through an individualized thinking being that is each of you. Just as I, Victory, have the Glory of *my* own Mighty 'I AM' Presence that stands above me, you will always have the greater, because God is always greater than its individualizations. This is the Miracle of Life.

Speak to the Elements of your physical body; they have placed themselves under *your* command

I want you to understand and accept the power that is at your fingertips, to reach up and command your Presence into action, to create such love and perfection in your life! Offer your body as God's Temple. Command your Presence to stop the aging of your physical body. Speak to the cells of your body; they are *your* cells! Speak to the elements which have come together as your physical body; they have placed themselves under *your* command! It is because of discord, poor diet and your accepted belief in aging, that the very elements of your body are giving you challenges in your physical body. Speak to these elements, sometimes loving, adoring—other times commanding "Stop! Stop your action against my light! Stop all aging now!"

Aging is not of the light. It is a human creation. It is the belief in polarity, duality, and good and evil and discord. Ah, Dear Hearts, if only you could think of living in beautiful bodies that have no appearance of age beyond twenty-two. If you think you could accept that, then I invite you to command the Sacred Fire of Mighty Victory to come to you.

"I command Mighty Victory's Sacred Fire of Eternal Divine Balance, Perfection and Youth, come forth and take its toll within my physical body!"

Your own God Presence can produce its Perfection in you, when you maintain harmony in your Life...and in the face of all appearances!

We need you as much as you need the Ascended Host to assist you to become strong. Whether it is peace and harmony or purity, love these qualities! And whether it is the Sacred Fire from our world—or from any of your own Ascended Masters—call upon us to fill you with our Sacred Fire Purity, Sacred Fire Harmony and Sacred Fire Peace. For the great, great premise upon which your own God Presence can produce its perfection in you, and out into your world, is your ability to maintain harmony in your life and in the face of all appearances!

Once again, my Aunt, the Darling Goddess of Venus, offers you Her Cosmic Love Supreme. I offer you my Cosmic Purity, Cosmic Power, Cosmic Love and Cosmic Victory that is the Sacred Fire of our Home Planet; it has absolutely perfected our world. There is no imperfection; there is no hatred; there is no death and decay in our world.

All kingdoms thrive in excellence, in beauty, in joy and in unity and in perfection. There is no death. Our Planet has not experienced death longer than you have been in the experience of duality.

Long will we be your Guardians. We will be your Guardians until the sinister force is removed from the Earth. And the only way we can make the sinister force retreat from your Planet is if you give us permission to do so. Call to us, in your prayers "I call forth for the absolute saturation of the Sacred Fire from Venus into all life on Earth; that forces the purification of life on Earth from all discord that has been imposed upon it!"

Make that call for your world; for your nations; make the call for yourself; make these calls three times a day and you shall see what the Sacred Fire of Venus can do! It will liberate you and fill your lives with so much love, happiness and joy and it will bring you into the most dynamic and intimate relationship with the mighty God 'I AM' of your Being!

I, Victory, offer you the Garden of My Heart; and within that Garden are all the activities of our Sacred Fire Love Supreme. God bless you! God bless you! God bless you!

I AM Victory!

CHAPTER *Fourteen*

I Am Asun and I enfold you in the Diamond Heart of my Love. Well, my Dear Hearts, there are just a few things that I wish to speak about here. The great raising of the Earth and her kingdoms into a Higher Light Vibration has begun, and unlike all other Cosmic Cycles that have allowed an emergence of light to come forth from different sources, this new emerging Cosmic light is a constant. It is like having the sunlight of your physical sun turned on at all times, except these Light Rays you cannot see; this light is Electronic Light Force from Godsource and the human eye cannot register it. Yet this light is coming in and is constant now.

The Light of the Resurrection Cycle

This new cycle is the transition of the Christian Dispensation into the Resurrection Dispensation—in Cosmic terms—the Christian Dispensation authorized the light from beyond to be given freely to *all*. In the year 2003, for three days the Cosmic light withdrew from the Earth and the Earth was sustained only by the love that is *the sun of even pressure*, or that which you call your sunlight of your physical sun. And after three days the Cosmic light returned in greater measure; however, this Great light—and the light that is coming in this Resurrection

Cycle—will only enfold those who love the light, love God and seek to live a constructive life.

Many changes are coming forth. But let us just say, my Dear Hearts, you have got to remind yourself, even if you have to put a little band around your wrist, to mind your thoughts, to mind your feelings, and your spoken words! Even though you may have some misery or limitation— some 'human moments'—it is not a good reason to *stay* in those moments. If you get yourself into some despondent place, get yourself out of it as quickly as possible. Remember, Dear Heart, whatever you feel now is going to be amplified into manifestation much more quickly; for our Heavenly Mother gave you feelings and heart so that you could manifest what you think into physical form reality.

You cannot manifest in a physical Universe without the Feminine aspect of God

You cannot exist in a physical universe without the Feminine, the will, the feeling side of life. There are beings, Dear Hearts, who are *visiting* your system of worlds, like our friend, the Mighty Lazarus. He has been visiting your system for some time; and he comes from a Universe of Light, that is not like the physical manifestation of your system of worlds, as a beautiful Being of Light. But you, Dear Hearts, belong to a *physical* universe; and you cannot manifest in a physical universe without the Feminine aspect of God.

It was the Divine Mother who gave you feelings and heart, because it is *feeling* that clothes your thoughts with the first level of energy and substance. Then your heart becomes just like a radiator—your heart radiates the vibration, the vibration goes into that which is termed the outer atmosphere and it marries with the universal particles of your atmosphere to produce experience and manifestation. Not too difficult to understand, Dear Hearts. But more difficult is it to get the old patterns of thought cleared, to get those out, yes? Keep reminding yourself that you are a *Creator Being*, remind yourself "My thoughts, my feelings, my words and actions, are manifesting my reality!"

You know, Dear Hearts, we have said it before, that 'I AM' is the name of God; 'I AM' is the name of your Divine Self. 'I AM' is the most powerful word in the vocabulary of humankind, and 'I AM' is the means that you use to qualify your intent, purpose and direction, each and every moment. So now that you know this—and you are increasing in your understanding of the laws of metaphysics—do you think that it is wise to continue to use the words "I am sick, I am tired, I am broke, I am in chaos." Do you think that that is a wise thing to do? Absolutely not! It is a better thing to realize, "Well, yes, there *seems to be an appearance* that my body is not so well today. There seems to be an appearance of sniffles." Rather than use the words 'I am'; realize the words 'I AM' is a Declaration of Life! Did you know that the words 'I AM' keep you visible?—that's what keeps you here in this world. God has given you the use of the words 'I AM', so that you don't blink out invisible! Asun is having some fun here with you, Dear Hearts!

Energy is being amped up on Earth at this time

And now the energy of Earth is going to be amped up greatly. It is just like the Ascended Host is bringing in a rather large super battery and is plugging you in. Now watch your thoughts and feelings manifest more quickly! And Dear Hearts, it is wonderful, wonderful, your evolution! Happy Violet Soul's birthday! Many of you who are awakening on the Earth are evolving into the Violet Soul now. The Violet Soul—what does this mean for you?

It means greater self expression, greater creativity; feelings that there is something else that wants to express through you, those feelings emerging, those feelings pushing through, pushing through dreams, up to the surface. Creativity! The Violet Soul loves to express; and it allows a greater piece of you to come into expression.

Being a Violet Soul means that you want to express more of you, and you want to do it in this body. Life is no respecter of *age* in the body. For those of you who are seventy or more, and think that you're out of here soon, phew, lucky! No, Dear Hearts, Life knows no boundary except the boundary that *you* impose according to what you are believing or accepting.

"I am here; I am here as my God 'I AM' to fulfill the Divine Plan of this life. And I love God. I love the Ascended Masters. I love the Angels. And I love the fact that this world is going to evolve now, it's ascending into a higher vibration of light and love and out of the tragedy that has almost destroyed human life! And I'm not going anywhere, thank you very much!" Now, that's attitude!

The Resurrection is the lifting back up into your Whole Divine Mind and Being, your Christed Self

You see, you have a *Higher Intelligence* above you, and it exists between yourself and your 'I AM' Presence. It has been given many names—it has been called the Holy Spirit, It has been called your Higher Intelligence, It has been called your Higher Mental Body. *We* love to call it your Christed Self, because that is what you called it before it left you at the end of the Second Golden Age twelve million years ago when you all decided that you were going to have this *duality experience*—the experience of what God is *not*—down here on Earth.

Your own Higher Intelligence said, "Well, I need to leave because if you are choosing to have a duality experience here I can't hang around. I am your Higher Intelligence and I know everything, so if I hang around then you're not going to have the experience of mastery through a sojourn in duality." So guess what your Higher Intelligence did? It went bye-bye, and ascended up out of the human brain and has remained up in your life stream above you! It is your Christ Self. It is that pure mind, that Omniscient Mind that contains no impure thing. And what is the resurrection? The resurrection is the lifting back up into your Infinite Mind, your Christ Self. This is the whole process that is ahead of you.

If you keep talking about the chaos that you seem to be in sometimes, you are just furthering it

With all that is coming forth, Dear Hearts, if you have human moments, limiting moments, you do not want to empower those human moments. Yes, maybe you do have some chaos going on in your life, and you may think, "Well, I'll look at this, I'll process this..." And yes, there is some time for process. But, you see, when Akasha and I came to all of you, and you came to us, we kind of figured out that you had done the processing part, you see? But sometimes, perhaps, you have still the desire to go and find someone, a counsellor or friend, and get it off your chest—speak what's going on; get it all out; process it; look at it. And that's fine.

In fact, if you have your knickers in a knot about something and you are really going through a human, limiting, condition—you are really going through some chaos in your life—better then to speak that out to someone who crosses your path, it is better to find one person you trust and say, "Let's talk." That way you get it out; get it done. But, Dear Hearts, the raising activity is going to be so fast now that you are going to find that if you keep talking about the chaos that you seem to be in sometimes, you are just furthering it; you are just making sure that not only tomorrow but seven weeks from now, this chaos is going to be fully present in your life.

The three Phases on the Path of Mastery

Eventually the *undoing* is the *unspeaking* of it, and being willing to know that you have come through into a very magical time. You are Violet Souls now. You have awakened as Diamond Heart Souls, advanced as Indigo Souls and now are in your higher evolution as Violet Souls. And another thing that has happened is that you have moved into a Third Phase that we talked about; three Phases, that human beings made a choice to experience on the Path of Mastery:

First Phase—Pain and suffering, denial of self, unity and life. Separation, absence of Life, Love, Light.

Second Phase—All my relationships, all my experiences, are a teaching device, but I won't know it until I've had enough of them and realized it!

Third Phase—a phase in which everything in your life can be seen and understood as an outer reflection with absolute ease, a conscious reflection of everything that is going on inside you.

And you are all moving forward into the Third Phase of the Path of Mastery now. Isn't this wonderful? And in this Third Phase there is nothing that we can teach you about it; in fact, you cannot teach yourself about it! And that is good because you would probably get in your own way if you could! We encourage you to be aware of what is reflecting back to you in your life for they are signs. Will you choose to see the signs!

The mind is vast beyond anything that science dares to speculate

The thing about this Third Phase is that you are going to discover it for yourself. You are going to find it happening in your daily life. In the Third Phase, there cannot be struggle; there cannot be chaos in the mind. You do not have a seamless mind yet, but you have more moments in which there is greater clarity in the mind. And it is in those moments when you can be reflective and contemplative and you can be taking a walk or whatever and just be with yourself in the garden and all of a sudden you *know* a thing.

You are in a nice receptive place there; you are not attacking yourself; you are not down on yourself; you are not there judging someone *else*; you are in a good gentle place with yourself. When that happens and you find yourself thinking about something in your life, or thinking about someone in your life and all of a sudden, there is a knowingness about that, and you understand everything about what you were contemplating. It is like your attention just drifts to something in your life, a condition—no intense thought taking—your attention just goes there. You are kind of looking at it. And then all of a sudden you realize you know everything that is behind that. You see all the pieces that brought it into manifestation. You see the cause; you see the effect; no thought taking was necessary.

This is what we mean, in the Third Phase everything in the outer experience of life is a *conscious reflection*—it consciously reflects back and shows you its source and its cause; it shows you what created it. This leads us to mastery and a more purposeful use of the mind. And it doesn't require the calculating intellect, as the mind is vast beyond anything that science dares to speculate.

It is the Light of the awakening Heart that frees and raises the mind into a higher frequency of consciousness

The only way the mind is illumined enough to experience its vastness is when the light of the Sacred Heart Flame, because you love It, you commune and call upon It to expand—expands up into the brain and the mind. It is the light that illumines the mind and raises the mind into a higher consciousness and energy frequency. And it is in this way that you start seeing what is behind everything. This becomes a natural experience. And then once you have the experience you will be able to talk with each other and share about it; you will have the perfect words to describe this new phase that you are in.

For you, it is to help you to realize your power of thought and feeling, and to see what is behind it all, "What thought, what belief way back, what concept, what perception, what feeling that I held onto, created this condition?" You will be able to see back, and going into it, you will have the power to change the energy in your experiences and manifestations. You will have the ability to adjust probable outcomes so that you are experiencing what you truly desire. And there will be no resistance. You can teach yourself to re-qualify the energy the way you want it to be, and find that life is giving you the manifestation you desire. Isn't this wonderful?

All manifestation is a vibration of energy

These next years are keyed perfectly for all of you awakening through the Violet Soul now; they are keyed perfectly for this resurrection time and moving you into this phase in which life seeks to be a conscious reflection, giving you another step in showing you that you are the

Creator—you are the authority for your life—through the choices and the decisions that you are making.

Lots of speakers have come into this world and authored ideas for personal empowerment, Dear Heart. And yes it is true, thoughts and feelings do create reality; desire does create reality. But not too many people speak about 'vibration'. The last time you were *angry*, you had a vibration, that is, energy in you was vibrating at a certain level. The last time you were really *depressed*, energy was acting at *another* level of vibration.

When you understand that all manifestation is a vibration of energy that has been first qualified and determined by your choice to allow yourself to feel, then you will start to accept that you are a Creator Being and realize that you can change things much quicker than before. And that is why if there are yet some things to move through, you know you can move through those experiences quicker than before—you know that if you get a common cold you can get that common cold out of your body sooner than it took previously. You know that if there is an issue that comes up—life is saying you need to face this now and you can face that issue quickly and transmute it, and make a powerful choice and have your feeling body hold the *vibration* of that powerful choice. And, you can reach up to God; you can reach up to Mighty Victory and Master Jesus, and ask Them to fill you with the Sacred Fire Purity that heals the feelings of old issues that you are sometimes compelled to face.

The strangest thing to us, Dear Hearts, and Akasha and I have had a good fireside chat about this, knowing that we have joined others of the Ascended Host to introduce to you the Sacred Fire; knowing that you have this Higher Power that you can reach up to—why is it that you oftentimes do not use this knowledge? What is going on with you when you do not reach up to your Presence to say

"I am really feeling depressed, or I have a fear of success here?" Now you know that whatever you are feeling, you are creating—it is energy vibrating in you; and whatever energy is vibrating in you is going to find itself out in the world in terms of experience and manifestation. So why don't you reach up to *The Greatest Power in the Universe*, your own Beloved Great God Presence that is both within and above you, and the Ascended Host and call in the assistance when you require it?

Or maybe you try it and you say it doesn't work. Interesting! What kind of value do you have in saying that you are more powerful than God is? So, here you are, saying that you are more powerful—that God cannot take your depression from you; that God cannot take your fear. So you say:

"I have cancer in this body and I have reached up to my Great God Presence and I have commanded it to release its Mighty Healing Currents of energy into every cell of my body. I have commanded it to release its Sacred Fire Love, Purity and Power.

"I have even reached out to the Angels of Healing and the Ascended Jesus Christ, and I have called upon Him to release His Sacred Fire Healing into every cell of my body and take that nonsense out and it doesn't work!"

Well, Beloved, I would say that your *altered* ego is in charge here, because you think *you* have more power than God's Presence. There *is* no greater power than your Great God Presence. There is no greater power than an Ascended Master. There is no greater power than the Sacred Fire. And if you can look at me and say it doesn't work, Dear Heart, you are coming from an altered state of ego; or you are giving the outer self more power than it deserves to have. Too long have human beings usurped the power of

God. Are *you* going to? So stop it! That is all. That is what you have to do to transcend any appearance! Or, perhaps your will is driving your fear which is creating an obstacle to receive your perfect healing.

Where are you in your consciousness? What do you believe?

So, Dear Heart, if you wish to engage in process, I will give you a process to work with. To all that is a limiting appearance in your life—whatever is going on—your process can be, "I do not believe in you any longer! I do not believe in you! I do not believe in lack; I do not believe in disease; I do not believe that I have to walk this path alone." Whatever it is, withdraw your energy, power and attention from it. Whatever appearances are showing up, say with feeling "I do not believe in you! I believe only in God, life and love. And I believe 'I AM that I AM'. I believe that I can reach up. I can be the Prodigal Son!—the story that Master Jesus told! I can live a life of havoc and discord; I can go out and do all those things, but, at any moment, I too, can be like the Prodigal Son. I can knock on God's door and I can reach up for that deliverer. I can lose everything in my life and reach up to my Great God Presence—knowing that it is the true infinite storehouse of everything that I could ever desire in this life—and have everything replaced, when I turn back to the light!"

Where are you in your consciousness, Dear Hearts? What do you believe? Are you down on yourselves or are you allowing magic to happen in your life? Your responsibility is to choose it, see it, feel it and speak it— that's your responsibility! *You* choose it, and then you let *God* in you do it!

You literally have got to forget everything you don't want, Dear Hearts; you have got to be willing to forget it and focus on the results you desire in your life!

The future Christ Beings will fulfill Their Higher Purpose in all walks of life

You see, what you forgot was what you were not supposed to forget, and what you remembered was what you were supposed to forget. So now, you have got to forget that disease seems to be a human power. It only has a human power as long as you give it energy. You are preparing to be raised into your Christ Consciousness on Earth. And Dear Hearts, just relax, because it doesn't mean you are going to walk around in sandals and long robes and burning incense and sitting on camels with big lovely leaves fanning you. That is not what the future Christ looks like, my Dear Hearts. The future Christ has it all!

The future Christ is in beautiful clothes, fine suits, garments and beautiful fabrics. The future Christ Being has all the health and wealth they should ever require in the world. The future Christ can be in any place, show up anywhere in the world and see individuals in trouble and say, "Here, let me help you!" They will just send a ray of light and it is done! The future Christ Beings are Light Ray Projectors, Dear Hearts. They are inventors, scientists, musicians, business people and mechanics. I daresay there may even be a few future Christ Conscious Beings out there that are lawyers! Indeed.

The future Beings of Christ Consciousness are going to come into every aspect of life. Remember, Dear Heart, we also stated that humanity entered another cycle, and it is a second Renaissance period. Life has granted that there shall be a second Renaissance on Earth. Now, you remember the great Renaissance, the great music that came forth;

the great architecture; the art; the literature, the music and the inventions. There is another one coming. And it has begun now.

You do not have to learn anything, rather discover everything!

Now, when there is a Renaissance period, the Great Beings who own this system of worlds have to be obedient to the Cosmic Law. When we ask you to be obedient to love and harmony, we cannot do things outside of what the Cosmic Law allows. And the Cosmic Law is allowing a great Renaissance—another three hundred year period— Dear Heart. And that means that Beings of Light can over-light you directly, and transmit down the life stream of an individual that which the world calls genius; that which the world calls an expression of creativity and open the door to your soul. It is the soul that orchestrates genius into creative self expression.

What I am going to share with you, in human terms, is really, really mind stretching, because it is going to poke a hole in your reality. *You do not have to learn anything, rather discover everything!* And there are those who have come into this world and proven it. Do you think that Mozart, as a child, was learning? Who could teach Mozart? All that was put in front of him in terms of an understanding of musical notes was simply a path of association so that the genius that was going to come through him could express itself. And that is all you need, a path of association, an understanding of the language of words, symbols, notes, and the natural laws of the universe, that is the mechanics, the structure!

In fact you are using paths of association in your mind and thinking every day. And everything that you know in your consciousness as *the world*, every time you wake up, you drag the world back into your reality again—you keep imprinting it; when at any moment, new things could start to blink into your world, if you released the walls and veils that imprison the human mind. Contemplate this, that you have *everything to discover rather than anything to learn.*

It is very interesting your ideas about being born into a masculine body or a feminine body

"...If only life wasn't so hard, if only I wasn't so hard and frozen, I can't change..." I daresay, you might not like to hear this, but there are a few light-workers among you whose concepts and ideas are more frozen than the ice fields in northern Canada! How are you going to allow the wonder back into your life? How are you going to allow the magic in? You can have fun, Dear Hearts and enjoy your lives immensely!

So, here you realize, "Right, I really do get to choose; for right choosing I must have my masculine—the mind—and my feminine, the feeling/desire." It is very interesting what you have done here with this thing called boys and girls —this thing about embodying into a *masculine body*, or a *feminine body*. You come down here to Earth and you play all these silly little roles out and you will say "*You* are *masculine*, *you* are *feminine*; and *you* cannot be masculine and *you* cannot be feminine." When the thing is, you are basically seventy/thirty. When you are born into a male body, thirty percent of your being is feminine; and if you are born into a female body, thirty percent of you is masculine. Lighten up! You are a living, thinking Flame of Life. Push back the limiting boundaries of your thinking! "Be as an empty cup" the Master Jesus said. Be as a little child. Forget all the things you know, all these race beliefs, become more magical and more natural in your life!

You are here to create your highest truth, not search for it!

Let God do the detailing

Ask yourself, "What is it that I really want to remember? What is it that *my Presence* wants me to remember? What do I believe in? What are my desires?" And then you talk to your Presence each day about your desires for your Life. You call it forth. You want results! But oftentimes it seems that the results you want are not showing up in your Life; you are doing all the right things; you meditate; you do your calls, but where are the manifestations you called for?

So, Dear Hearts, *before* you talk to your Presence, you have got to tell yourself the truth—even though it may not be your presonal experience. You have got to tell yourself the truth if you want results, "The Presence never fails to fulfill the call. Even though I may not yet seem to have results, the Presence never fails—*God Never Fails*. It is just that the answer for what I have called forth has not arrived yet. The mail is late, but God is on the job!" And what we say, Dear Hearts is—Let God do the detailing! Remember, your Presence is the Individualization of God, *The Greatest Power in the Universe.*

"Let God do the detailing" that is, if you understand that you are an aspect of God in this outer self expression you call *human being.* And then there is that aspect of you that is called *God* that is your *Ascended Divine Higher Self 'I AM'—God the human, God the 'I AM' Presence.* So in this role as a spiritual human being, in this experience of yourself, your responsibility as a living thinking Flame of Life was to use masculine (mind) and feminine (feeling/desire), and bring the two of them together to give direction to your life, through the power of choice and the use of your attention faculty and the presence of passion. That aspect of you that is your Divine Ascended Self 'I AM' Presence, Its job was to provide the *energy* that fulfills what you think, feel, see and speak. Not too difficult metaphysics. The difficulty is in remembering it. It is all right. I love a good laugh myself. Humor goes a long way, indeed it does.

I believe...

It is just that the old world loves to roll over you. There is so much pressure out there in the world, and it wants to take your attention. The world is made up of duality, of old belief systems. So it is not *just* the sinister force, which is nothing more than the worst of human beings' thoughtforms accumulated that is a constant pressure on humanity. And it is not that we are speaking of some monstrosity that came from another system of worlds, although there are a group of speakers and philosophers out there who are still into blame, and blaming mankind's trials and woes and tribulations on the Pleiedians, or the Syrians or whomever else!

I assure you that mankind's woes were created by mankind and none other than mankind. And that which is termed the sinister force is nothing but a human manifestation. That is how powerful human beings are. Who do you think created the dark beasts of old legends? Humans did. It is all right, it is all nonsense anyhow.

The thing is, stop believing in it. Don't believe in it and remind yourself "I don't believe in age. I don't believe in disease. I only believe in God. I believe in love, life and liberty. I believe in 'I AM'. I believe 'I AM' an open door into the Light. I believe 'I AM' awake. I believe that tomorrow I will be one day younger, not one day older." Change what you believe. "I believe in infinity. I believe I am an Immortal Being now. And I do believe that my body will eventually catch on and respond accordingly." Understand, my Dear

Hearts? This is not done overnight, rather is an attitude that is lived which ultimately brings you the desired results. And remember, act accordingly!

Call in the Cosmic Troops from above. And just say, "I am going to lay here for ten minutes, and all I want is God's Perfect Healing!"

The light does not take you, that is, your life will not take you out of your body if you are committed to growing, to awakening; if you are committed to making a difference in this world and place yourself in service to the light. There are many people who have so much pain in the body; and Dear Hearts, your Higher Self, your Great God Presence 'I AM', and the Angels, will just take all the pain out of the body, if you *will* it to be, and get the help that you require. But my goodness, getting the lot of you sometimes to lie down on your bed and get a good old-fashioned *healing* from any of the lot of us is like pulling teeth.

Most of you are well with your prayers and calls, but surrendering to receive healing is not yet in place, Dear Hearts. You do yourself a great service when you lay down once a day—in mid-morning, afternoon or evening and you get yourself in very comfortable clothes and lay down—and anoint yourself with some essential oils, have some lovely music playing, and say, "God, I know you are within me and I know you are up there. Mary and Jesus, I know that you have performed billions of miracles already, but one more? Beloved Angels of Healing, Angels of Peace, Beloved Mighty Victory..."

Just call the Ascended and Angelic Troops in, Dear Heart—the Cosmic Troops. And say, "I'm going to lay here for ten minutes every day, and all I want is God's perfect healing and health in this body!" Then stop giving the ill appearances so much of your attention and go on about your day as happily as you can.

You know, Dear Hearts, sometimes it is the wrong idea or the wrong thought or it is the wrong feeling that is acting up in the emotional body that is creating a condition in the body or a condition in your outer life. And you can say, "God I am going to show up every day for ten minutes for healing. I desire that you heal my mind; heal my body and heal my feelings." God will not do anything unless your feelings are included, because that is where you get to qualify life. Or you could *desire* something "I desire my relationship with this person to be healed. I want to heal my finances." *Everything in life is a relationship.* Haven't you figured that one out already, Dear Hearts? If you have a bad relationship with yourself, look out, lots of troubles out there for you unless you heal that relationship!

The way people act towards you, is a good indicator of a limiting perception you are secretly holding about God

Everything is a relationship. You want your relationship with yourself, with your Presence, you want your relationship with God as you understood Him/Her to be, healed. You are still carrying the last of old perceptions about God. Still buying into a belief that God is this long-bearded individual, sitting up there on His Throne, who cannot wait to get His hands on you to decide what direction you are going in—believing that God abandoned you; believing that you angered God; believing God will cast judgment upon you. Its all man made nonsense.

What is acting out in your life? Do you still have something acting out in your life? What did your parents act out to you? Ask yourself, "Is there any perception that I am holding onto that is a lie, that God abandoned me, or that I do not deserve God's love, or God is angry at me?"

"How are people acting towards me?" The way people act towards you, Dear Heart, is a good indicator of a

Chapter 14

limiting perception that you are secretly holding about God. If you are being abandoned, perhaps it is because you believe God abandoned you. None of those concepts are true. Why? Because you know God is your life and you are here, reading this book in your wonderful human forms, so God is sitting in every one of these bodies. So where did God go? God didn't go anywhere! It is just that you put the phone down, a long time ago. But God has always been on the line; Beloved, God has always been on the line.

The Seven Sacred Weeks

Some other final thoughts I would like to share with you here. Well, my Dear Hearts, there is that which comes forth every year, and that is the Seven Sacred Weeks of the Ascended Masters. It has been a gift to the world ever since the Ascended Master Jesus assisted His Mother and several of His disciples to take their ascension. At the close of that part of Their ministry, They wanted to give a gift to humanity. Once the calendar was created as you know it today, They came together and decided that They wanted to give a gift; and that gift would begin on the eve of what is known as the American Thanksgiving Holiday.

If you check your calendar on that day and walk through the calendar seven weeks forward into the New Year, this is the Seven Sacred Weeks. Those are the weeks in which Master Jesus and His Mother, the Ascended Mary—and the eight of the twelve Disciples who are currently ascended under the authority of the Archangel Gabriel and certain of the other Ascended Host—enter into their great Temples of Light and project tremendous Rays of Ascended Master Light that is to be the True Christ Mass every Christmas. And so I remind you that there is this great sacred outpouring that comes from Mary and Jesus and others of the Ascended Host at this time every year.

361

With this knowledge, you can turn more of your attention to these Ascended Masters during prayer and meditation to receive the blessings they are offering humanity each year at that time.

2003, the last Christmas under the Cosmic Dispensation, the Christian Dispensation

2003 was the last Christmas, as it is celebrated by Christians and people around the world, which came under the Cosmic Dispensation—the Christian Dispensation. For once that Christian Dispensation ended on August 15, 2004, the duties of Beloved Jesus and Mary became quite different; although Mary and Jesus will still over-light the church—and what people think of as being God—to the best that the Cosmic Law allows them.

Master Jesus came to you, Dear Heart, upon the Golden Ray—the Ray of Illumination, the Ray of Comprehension. This is the Father's Ray, the Ray of the Christ Mind. This is the Ray of the Christhood and the Discipleship in Christ. And this is the Ray that Master Jesus gained His Ascension upon. And as the centuries passed—regardless of what was going on in the Earth—the Master Jesus continued in His evolution and became part of the great Ascended Masters who are trying to help humankind.

When His Teachings about the 'I AM' knowledge were covered up in the year 325AD by man, there was very little that Mary and Jesus could do, except answer the call that was in individuals' *hearts*. They could not really respond as much as they desired to as the *early church had embraced a shadow to cover up of many of His teachings*. It is for this reason that a shadow has remained within the church. I do not say this to infringe upon those who yet find peace and inspiration within the church as it exists today, for now the church and the world is held under the new great

Resurrection Cycle that is to fulfill the ministry of Jesus. All aspects of civilization are now lovingly held within this new cycle and this includes religions, science, medicine, arts, technology and individual aspirations and more.

From the Electrical Age, through the Wireless technology, and into the new Crystal Age

Perhaps something of great importance that you might like to know is this—the Master Jesus has received a big promotion, and He is not the Guardian of the Golden Ray anymore. Actually, He now represents the Thirteenth Ray. He is now Cosmic Christ to all this System of Worlds, and He is now Guardian of the Thirteenth Ray. The Thirteenth Ray is the Highest Ray known to this sector of your solar system, and it is the Luminous Crystal Ray of God's Light. It is the Ray that seemingly has no colour. It is a colour invisible to you. It is the Ray of Luminosity.

Master Jesus will intensely focus the Crystal Ray—the Thirteenth Ray, the Luminous Ray—onto the Earth during these next nine years. Because it is the Crystal Ray, my Dear Heart, that will move forward the evolution of humanity from the Electrical Age, through the Wireless Technology, and into the new Crystal Age and technology that will come in quickly. The Crystal Technology Age cannot come to the people of Earth until there is a Master projecting the Crystal Ray in which that technology is given to the people. First came the Mechanical Age, then the Electrical Age, then the Wireless, and what follows—and is the last age that moves the Earth into her ultimate ascension—is the Crystal Age. And Master Jesus, with His Mighty Seraphim, must be freed up of many of His former duties to begin projecting the Crystal Ray to the Earth.

The eight Disciples who are ascended—by the way, the other four are on the Earth in embodiment today—will come in and take up His many former duties. These eight Ascended Disciples will watch over the Christian Church as it exists on the Earth today. They will continue to minister unto the calls and prayers of the people who believe in Mary and Jesus in the way that they do.

Beloved Mary has been raised within the Spiritual Hierarchy, as the Sacred Mother, Goddess of Earth

Beloved Mary goes forth in Her journey that She has prepared for hundreds and hundreds of years. As Cosmic Angel of the Rose Pink Ray of the Heavenly Mother—who made that ultimate fateful decision to enter into a physical embodiment and take on a human life form as She did— this journey is Her destiny.

She began Her earthly journey within the House of David, and Her life streams carried the House of David all the way to the birth of her son Jesus and after which, years later, She gained Her own ascension. Now, with the completion of the Cosmic Christian Dispensation that brought Their ministry to the Earth, now Beloved Mary is free to fulfill Her destiny, for Her service is complete. Now She is raised, in Cosmic terms, within the Spiritual Hierarchy, as the Sacred Mother, the Heart of the people of Earth, the Goddess of Earth.

In Universal Systems of Worlds, there are Planets that are masculine in nature and there are Planets that are feminine in nature. Venus and Earth both belong to Divine Feminine Houses and they belong to the Daughter Universes. Both of these Planets have a future destiny where they will move out into the universe and be future suns, physical suns—stars to other worlds. The head of a Masculine Planet always has a Masculine Ascended Being oversee it. The head of a Feminine Planet is always ruled by a Feminine Ascended Being and it was Precious Mary's destiny to become the Sacred Mother of Earth. Or, what might help you is to think in terms of your royal families that you have on the Earth; however think in terms of Divine Mind, Divine Heart and Divine Order when considering the Spiritual Hierarchy.

Just as you understand that you have a Queen of England, in Systems of Worlds there is a Spiritual Governing Being to every Planet—you have a King/Emperor or you have a Queen/Empress/Goddess, never both. Not until a Planet and a Sun come together to create a Great Central Sun do you have both. Your Earth is a Feminine Planet and she is about to receive her Sacred Mother, Mary, as Spiritual Head of State, so to speak. Beloved Mary has been raised into Her Sacred Throne as Goddess of Earth. I am certain this may stretch a few minds on Earth.

You have an expression on your Earth...You ain't seen nothin' yet!

So, wonderful new activities are coming forth for Earth and humanity, and I trust that I have teased you into a place where you are yearning for more; and there is much more to come, Dear Hearts! So Akasha and I close this chapter by asking you to love your Presence, love God within you and above you. Remind yourself that the Presence always answers your call. Remind yourself that a *human appearance* is anything less than perfection and that you do not believe in human appearances any more. Remind yourself you believe only in God and your own Beloved Great God Presence 'I AM', *The Greatest Power in the Universe*. Know that through your spiritual life on Earth, through daily prayer, meditation and mastering yourself, you can come to embrace, embody, experience and express more of that Great Presence in your daily life.

We encourage you to Love, Love, Love to worship God in private and to be of service to the light. Remember you are here as peace mediators, to go out into the world and set this world free of all the tyranny and the hatred and discord. How will you do it? By saying *yes* to all your heart's passion and giving yourself permission to do what you love to do, knowing that as people cross your path in all that you are loving to do, loving to be, your life will be a blessing to others. Already we see so many times where the light of your Presence is shining forth from you and blessing your friends and families, and going ahead and protecting people and doing all sorts of wonderful things for the Earth. And that is a good thing!

Dear Hearts, you have opened the door for God to be fully realized, in you, as you, through you, and out into your world. Love beauty! Love glory! Love perfection! Get ready for a new tide of love and peace and happiness—get ready for the experience of joy and love in yourselves, your bodies and your relationships, the likes of which you have never experienced! You think you have experienced human love in your bodies? Well, you have an expression on Earth...."You ain't seen nothin' yet!"

I do not come to judge you; I come to love you free! My darling Akasha and I greet you out of the Diamond Heart of our Love for you and the Earth. God bless you.

❋

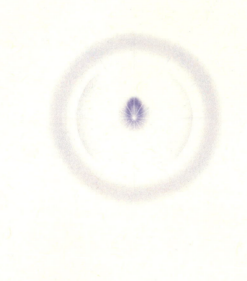

THE GREATEST POWER IN THE UNIVERSE

PRODUCTS FROM THE AKASHA MYSTERY SCHOOL

Other Books Available from Akasha & Asun

• Ancient Wisdom Revealed
• Self Realization
• Prayer Calls, Affirmations and Sacred Decrees

Meditations

The following Guided Meditations from Akasha & Asun are available to order from the Akasha Mystery School and are available in an audio CD recording format. These meditations are supported by the meditation music of world class recording artist Paul Armitage.

Please contact the School at 604-267-0985 or e-mail angels@akashaonline.com to order these meditations.

A Sacred Alchemy of Meditations, Prayers and Contemplations

Single CD's
• Cosmic Ascension Gifts, Volume 1 (1 CD) $20
• Journey to your Ascension, Volume 2 (1 CD) $20
• The Messenger; Sacred Prayers
  (Akasha & Asun and Sanat Kumara) $15
• 28 Pillars of Light Meditation (1 CD) $15

Two CD Sets
• Behold the Gifts (2 CD) $22
• Master Jesus, Gift of Faith (2 CD) $22

Four CD Sets
- Receiving the Oracles (4 CD) $49
- Awaken your Inner Power (4 CD) $49
- Alchemy of Miracles, Meditations and Contemplations (4 CD) $49
- Sacred Prayers, Invocations, Journey, and Meditation (4 CD) $49

Audio Books from Akasha & Asun

The following Audio Books from Akasha & Asun are available to order from the Akasha Mystery School and are offered in CD and audio cassette tape format. These workshop/audio books are supported by the meditation music of world class recording artist Paul Armitage.

1. Living and Walking in the Light, $79
2. Standing by your Presence, $79
3. Personality, Presence, Spirit and Soul, $79
4. Loving Life and Living Forward, $79
5. Live Now! The Life you Desire, $79
6. The Power Within, Part One, $79
7. The Power Within, Part Two, $79
8. Let the Force be with You, Part One, $79
9. Let the Force be with You, Part Two, $79

Akasha Mystery School

Web Site: www.akashaonline.com
Email: angels@akashaonline.com

❋